LETTERS FROM
THE LAND OF FEAR

Intimacy, Beauty and Death in Central Asia

MIROLAND IMPRINT 5

**Canada Council   Conseil des Arts
for the Arts   du Canada**

ONTARIO ARTS COUNCIL
CONSEIL DES ARTS DE L'ONTARIO
an Ontario government agency
un organisme du gouvernement de l'Ontario

Guernica Editions Inc. acknowledges the support of the Canada Council
for the Arts and the Ontario Arts Council. The Ontario Arts Council
is an agency of the Government of Ontario.

We acknowledge the financial support of the Government of Canada
through the Canada Book Fund (CBF) for our publishing activities.

LETTERS FROM THE LAND OF FEAR

Intimacy, Beauty and Death in Central Asia

Calvin White

MiroLand
publishers

MIROLAND (GUERNICA)
TORONTO • BUFFALO • LANCASTER (U.K.)
2015

Michael Mirolla, general editor
Connie McParland, series editor
David Moratto, cover and interior book designer
Front Cover Photo: Deena (Marcell Nimführ, used by permission)
All unattributed photos by the author
Guernica Editions Inc.
1569 Heritage Way, Oakville, ON L6M 2Z7
2250 Military Road, Tonawanda, N.Y. 14150-6000 U.S.A.

Distributors:
University of Toronto Press Distribution,
5201 Dufferin Street, Toronto (ON), Canada M3H 5T8
Gazelle Book Services, White Cross Mills, High Town, Lancaster LA1 4XS U.K.

First edition.
Printed in Canada.

Legal Deposit—First Quarter
Library of Congress Catalog Card Number: 2014950178
Library and Archives Canada Cataloguing in Publication

White, Calvin, 1950-, author
Letters from the land of fear : intimacy, beauty and death in Central
Asia / Calvin White. -- First edition.

Issued in print and electronic formats.
ISBN 978-1-77183-011-9 (pbk.).--ISBN 978-1-77183-012-6 (epub).--
ISBN 978-1-77183-013-3 (mobi)

1. White, Calvin, 1950-. 2. Doctors Without Borders (Association).
3. Mental health personnel--Uzbekistan--Karakalpakstan--Biography.
4. Mental health personnel--Canada--Biography. 5. Tuberculosis--
Uzbekistan--Karakalpakstan--Psychological aspects. 6. Mental health
services--Uzbekistan--Karakalpakstan. 7. Care of the sick. I. Title.

RA395.U93W45 2015   362.109587   C2014-906218-4   C2014-906219-2

To G.A.
No one has greater kindness, courage, and integrity.

Introduction

She's no longer in the TB ward, the cold bare walls painted a peeling yellow, the heat from one lone wood stove several rooms away. There are no other patients lounging nearby wondering what this odd foreigner has to say to them, amidst their boredom in the village sanatorium. There are no echoes in this room where the 22-year-old in the swaddled, traditional dress is not smiling and exchanging laughter as she was just two weeks before.

She doesn't have the multi-drug resistant strain of tuberculosis, only the regular TB. Only. It will kill her just as surely, but the medical regimen she needs to follow to prevent that early death, the relentless disappearance of lungs, is not so arduous. Just two drugs that are barely noticeable to her system. But every day for three or four months.

We are in her home seated on mats across from her. My translator, me and this sweet-faced girl who stares at the floor more often than she looks at me. She has stopped the medicine. Her grandfather has come to the sanatorium and taken her home. He came with another old man, and together they did their own treatment on her. *Don't take those drugs anymore. They won't work. We will cure you our way.*

What was she supposed to say? What could she do? They walked her home and had her face the wall. Then, as they spoke strange sounds, they struck her over and over on the back with a long stick. *Whump! Whump! Whump!* That's how to bring the disease out. How to chase away its cause.

She looks at me trying to smile, a quiet confidence. A quiet resignation clothed in a familial duty of hope. In this country, despite its outward modernity, its ubiquitous cell phones, and its Russian legacy, the ways of the past are still the ways when they want to be. A shaman is a shaman. The evil eye is real. And what are the Western TB drugs but other kinds of inner sticks beating from the inside? She now beats her own back three times a day.

I look at her and nod. *Your grandfather is wise. You can keep doing his cure. But he doesn't fully understand this disease. I do. You must start taking the drugs again and do both cures. If you do both cures, then you will become healed, become well enough.* I smile and nod, looking her in the eyes.

She smiles and agrees. I'm a good liar.

☙

For 11 months in 2010, I undertook a mission with the Nobel Peace Prize-winning international humanitarian organization, Médecins Sans Frontières (MSF), known in English as Doctors Without Borders. I went to Uzbekistan in central Asia to work as a mental health specialist with the MSF team there to address an epidemic of multidrug resistant tuberculosis.

Little did I know that such a nonedescript role actually meant emergency counselling. It was as though, each day, a human being was placed on a ledge ten stories high and I had to talk them out of jumping. They hadn't chosen to go there, but they were definitely thinking of jumping and it was up to me to search out some rationale, some aspect in their lives, or some convincing bit of hope that could bring them off the ledge, at least for that day. And I had only minutes to do it because there were a whole bunch of others on other ledges that I had to get to.

If I couldn't find the right words, couldn't understand clearly enough what they needed to hear, couldn't connect with them deeply enough, then they jumped. Not the quick plummet to instant death, but a slow fall of days or weeks to a death just as sure and in some ways sadder and more far reaching.

So, I became a negotiator, and each case was different. Sometimes, I could see them ease away from the edge. Other times, I'd have to leave knowing they were teetering. I'd have to close my eyes and hope fate was on their side, that my interaction had added to the life side of their ledge. Hope they would still be there the next day when I could give it another try. And just as with anyone considering or attempting suicide, preventing it once didn't mean they wouldn't try again.

Every single day there was never any certainty other than that the number of people finding themselves perched on a ledge hovering over death wasn't going to stop. We were offering the drug treatment that could save their lives, if they would stay on it. The ugly truth was that, in some cases, the drugs might not even work. The ugly truth was that the epidemic was winning.

In the 1960s the Soviet Union decided that cotton could be a major cash crop in its Central Asian Republics. That area is very arid so the need for constant irrigation was obvious but not deemed to be a problem. Two major rivers traversed the region and they could be dammed, diverted, and exploited to flood vast swaths of land for the cotton. And cotton, indeed, did grow and the area became a world player in cotton exportation. They termed it "white gold". After the Soviet Union fell, an independent Uzbekistan morphed into its current autocratic rule and the cotton production continued, the irrigation continued.

But, as is often the case, other consequences followed. The rivers, Amu Darya and Syr Darya, were the only water source for the Aral Sea. When the rivers were so drastically drained, the Aral Sea began to shrink. It has continued to shrink to this day and the whole scenario is now infamously known as the Aral Sea Disaster. It is an unprecedented global disaster because the Aral Sea was not just some innocuous body of water. It was the world's fourth largest body of inland water. For thousands of years it was the living constant for the inhabitants of the region. And then, in a generation, everything changed.

The southern half of the Aral Sea is in Uzbekistan and more precisely in Karakalpakstan, which is nominally an autonomous region in the west of that former Soviet republic. The Karakalpaks have borne the true effects of the Aral Sea's demise. When the waters shrank, an immense sea bed of salt was exposed along with pesticides and all manner of toxins deposited over the centuries. In this desert landscape, the winds carried the poison-laden dust for hundreds of kilometres in every direction. The health of the population began to deteriorate.

At the same time, all the economic and social benefits of this fishing and tourist habitat ended. The water of the Aral Sea, having become so salt concentrated, no longer sustained fish species. A poor population became even more impoverished.

In 1997, MSF came to the region in the belief that the environmental degradation had to be causing severe health problems. Indeed, it was. MSF realized that tuberculosis was prevalent in epidemic proportions. The organization began working in collaboration with the Uzbek health ministry to implement the World Health Organization recommendations for TB treatment and control. By 2001, MSF could see that the regular TB epidemic had escalated to a more alarming situation. It was clear that Karakalpakstan was in the midst of an epidemic of multi-drug resistant TB (MDR-TB). The tuberculosis bacillus was transforming. When people with regular TB don't complete their treatment or take the wrong treatment, the risk of the bacillus becoming a super bug increases. That means the normal drugs no longer work. When those already with multi-drug resistant TB prematurely stop treatment, it can lead to extreme drug resistance (XDR-TB) and the prognosis for cure is minimal.

Tuberculosis is a poor person's disease. It stopped being a concern in the developed world decades ago. Improved nutrition, education, health services, and the general material well-being of Western societies are responsible for that. But worldwide it is estimated that one third of all people are infected with the regular TB bacillus, though of these only a tiny percentage develop the active disease and need drug intervention. Active tuberculosis seems to be an immune system illness. When the immune system is compromised or at risk, the TB bacteria becomes active and symptoms develop. As an airborne disease, infection happens by being coughed, sneezed, or breathed on.

Because TB is a poor person's disease, the drugs used in its treatment are largely the same ones used in the 1950s when Western nations were also afflicted. There has not been the financial incentive for research to develop new drugs. To treat MDR-TB, patients must take more drugs and for a much longer time, and all of these drugs are of the same 1950s' vintage—and have toxic effects on the body. These side effects are the biggest obstacle to patients adhering to the full duration of treatment.

☙

So it was that, in early February of 2010, I ended up in Nukus, the capital of Karakalpakstan in western Uzbekistan to work with 450 patients suffering from MDR and XDR-TB. I knew nothing about disease, nothing about TB or MDR-TB, and nothing about Uzbekistan. Like everyone else on the planet, I had never heard of Karakalpakstan. In fact, it took me a month to be able to pronounce the word correctly—after all, it does have five syllables.

I never really lived in the space that I physically inhabited. I lived within the reality of those hundreds of Karakalpaks who fought one of the world's most terrible diseases. Very early in my time there, I realized I was each day immersed in the human heartbeat. Culture, language, gender, and age all disappeared.

MDR-TB is a killer. Though it can attack other parts of the body, most often it is lungs which are ravaged. Slowly but persistently the bacilli destroy. There is no guarantee that the massive amount of drugs will even work. But everyone starts with hope. Thus, this is a story about living and living with hope. It is a story about dying. And in both cases it is a testimony to a population which struggles each day to make the best of its breath. It is a story of intimacy. It is a story about beauty.

Salt

Imagine you are being swept along in the slow waters of a great river. Every so often a fleck of gold surfaces and catches your eye as it glints in the sunlight. Then it sinks again into the depth or floats beyond your sight. Occasionally one keeps its direction near you for some time. The wonder of all that. There and gone, but bright and textured, the brilliance there for you to see. And if each of these individual flecks had a name, you would say that name, but then forget. You would only remember those who stayed longest. But all, all would remain the gold they really were. And then you would be left to whisper: "What a river. What a great river."

It is the end of January 2010 and I'm on a plane from Kelowna to Calgary to Frankfurt to Moscow to Tashkent. Twelve hours away to the other side of the planet to Uzbekistan, one of the five stans from the former Soviet Union, now a stan on its own run by the same guy who ran it under the Soviets: Islam Karimov. Like probably every other westerner I had only heard the word Uzbekistan and knew it was over there some place. On the map, I had seen that my project was located in a city called Nukus in the west of the country. It was close to the Aral Sea. I was happy. The Aral Sea. Wow! A long way from Silver Creek where I live. I can't wait to see it. The fourth largest body of inland water in the world. Only the Caspian Sea, Lake Superior and Lake Victoria are larger. Wow!

Below us suddenly are thousands of glowing spheres. The phosphorescence of a tropical sea suddenly reborn instead as gathered eyes searching upwards from this land of central Asia.

When we land at the Tashkent airport, everyone claps. I climb down the stairs from the back of my plane and cross the tarmac to the bus. It is a frosty, still night with a full moon. And it suddenly sinks in that I am walking in the centre of Asia. Marco Polo's route.

Tashkent, January 30

It's cold but not too bad. I wear my t-shirt. I walk to the MSF office. It is afternoon already. I am 12 hours different from where I last woke up. I am walking upside down. The sidewalk feels the same. This is another big city. Small cars whiz by on the two lane street. Big trees are on its edges. A drainage ditch separates me from the road. No one pays any attention to me. Some men wear dark fur hats. I am in Central Asia. This is it.

I am badly jet-lagged, having only slept intermittently in the MSF Guest House, an immaculately appointed, warm, two story house within a groomed, locked courtyard. And now only a few hundred metres away I walk through the metal doors to the MSF headquarters.

Everyone is friendly, if not especially interested. The financial officer gives me a big wad of money. The currency is called *sum* — pronounced *soom*. A 1000 sum note equals half a dollar. I am informed that my HIV test is useless. It needed to be stamped and signed by a Canadian doctor. Unbeknownst to me. It might have been helpful to tell me in the first place exactly what documentation was needed. At any rate it should not surprise me. I just hope they get on my missing bag that never arrived on the plane with me. The guy that the job was given to says he'll check it out tomorrow. I say that I might be leaving for Nukus tomorrow. "Oh we'll check today then."

I meet Stefan, the head of mission — HOM. All of MSF is abbreviations and shortened forms. I'm MHO — mental health officer. Stefan seems like a good guy. A Norwegian who has a PhD in Sanskrit, he stays here with his wife and two young daughters. Today is his day off and he has only come in to say hello. He tells me Nukus is quite a safe place to be, likely because all fear the police and the state authority. I can't tell if his large eyes are because he is open and friendly or because he is uncertain about me. I learned earlier that I was not the first choice as new mental health officer.

Next, it's into another office for the meeting with the Medco, the MSF medical coordinator for all medical activities in the country. Jorge is the Medco. He has dreadlocks. Big guy, Spanish, tells stories about missions in Africa and India and Moldova. He seems surprised when I ask a question about TB, mentioning that I know nothing about the disease. He says, eyes big with surprise: "You don't?" And then: "What diseases have you worked with?"

I respond: "None." His eyes get even bigger.

I know this much: MDR-TB stands for multi-drug resistant tuberculosis, meaning the regular TB bacteria has mutated to become resistant to many of the basic TB fighting drugs and that the afflicted person is in shit. I know also that my job is to be the mental health expert who will lead a team of local counsellors working for MSF, trying to keep MDR-TB afflicted patients on their drug regimen. This drug regimen will save their lives. If they stop, then the bacteria might become more resistant. Each time a patient stops taking the drug regimen the epidemic worsens, the patient likely dies, and the people around the patient can become infected.

The Medco tells me the drugs are quite terrible. They are the same drugs developed in the 1950s and they cause rather awful side effects. Nausea. Headache. And worse. That, since they have to be taken every day for two years, the patients often would like to refuse the treatment. Unlike the case with cancer chemotherapy though, if the patient opts for no drugs and no terrible side effects, it means they infect others. It's my job to get them on treatment and, once on, decrease the level of defaulting. I'm replacing an American PhD who has been here two years and who set up a good system but has now finished her mission.

"So, what are your plans?" the Medco asks, his words coming across as a combination of needles, knives, plea, and *Should we start re-advertising for your position now?*

☞

February 1

The train is green. I am in car 7. To get in I show my passport to the train man. "Kahnada," he proclaims, smiles up at me. This is the start of my 28-hour ride across the country to its western end. I am on my own.

Leaving the station, the only other person in my four-bed compartment, a man named Bronya, takes an unlit cigarette from his mouth. Receding hair, maybe 45, he works at a crossword puzzle. Nice, friendly smile. We are on the way. Outside, a car passes with a bathtub strapped to its roof. We leave behind straight lines and gazing faces, move to brick walls, mud walls. Early spring cows, chickens pecking, small plots. We are still in the city. Metal roofs on squat, rough homes. Tall, thin poplars, leafless and straight. Shanty hovels low to the ground for lowly lives. Apartment blocks. Plot after plot of earth in squares. Walls reaching up to the train tracks. Then, finally, larger fields flat with brown furrows still grayed by winter.

On the tiny, jutting table between Bronya and me are four handleless china cups, and a similarly dark blue patterned teapot. Dark blue swirls with gold rimming. On the padded bench seats that face each other in our compartment are elegant, deep blue, satin covers and matching pillows. On the floor between us a strip of carpet. Very nice, indeed. But, within five minutes, an attendant comes and collects the seat and pillow covers. The show is over and the journey has begun. The carpet stays.

We are now fully out of the city and passing a straggling village. A child yells out like a stone being thrown at the locomotive. Then tin roofs. Tin. Tin. Tin. Bending people. Staring people. Long coloured dresses billow to ankles. There is a solidness here and antiquity: together they are pulling me in. I want to live in each of these houses.

Clay brick walls, craggy fruit trees gnarled yet before the greening of real spring.

Bronya pours me tea, pure Ceylon leaf tea. Premium quality. The lid falls off the pot into the cup as he pours. We drink together, steam curling about our lips. The land passes us. On the train, you only see one side, the side you look at. Momentary embracings, then gone. The start of a relationship with the way it is. The way it is.

Outside is a long gathering of shaggy haired goats, black, grey, white. Ambling in their field, scrub ground, low surrounding hills, faint patches of green tight to the soil. Goats always look happy. Alive. Independent. Trundling along, the herder on his donkey, his feet almost touching the ground, his bobbing stick a baton for what must be *Goat Symphonic Etude #4,000,002*.

After another couple of hours, two Uzbek men come in to sit. Soon, the compartment's curtain is closed and my buddy pulls out a small bottle of vodka. The blue tea cups are poured, toasts are had. They are perplexed that I don't want any. My buddy says with a smile and a bit of sign language that the *polizee* would take them away in handcuffs if he caught them drinking on the train. After several drinks they leave.

At midnight we stop for passengers. A young man in a black pea coat and round face, black cap, comes in. The attendant pulls on the compartment light for him. He gets on the upper bunk. In the weak bath of moon, the land outside squeezes us forward. Steppe land. The barrenness yields to the tracks passing us through, only the moon and misty air knowing we're there, accepting the intrusion.

And by 8 am we sit, the three of us drinking hot, Ceylon tea until the latecomer rises to get off. He shakes our hands, the Uzbek one which has a mouth and the Canadian one that is mute. He says: "Bye-bye," for the first time smiles ... a full upper row of gold-coloured teeth.

Bronya and I remain. He has a small inked tattoo on the top of his foot just above the tendons to his toes. A skull and cross-bones. He has four daughters and eight grandchildren. Or vice versa. My mastery of gestures is not what it used to be. He is a truck driver on his way to Russia, a day more of train past where I get out in Nukus.

We have stopped now for four hours. Bronya is outside smoking

Lucky Strikes in the sunlight. He looks in at me through our window, waves. The smoke from his cigarette competes with the frosty air. His slightly pushed in nose gives him the visage of an ex-boxer or mafia thug. But he has taught me to say thank you and explained that it is one letter away from saying insane. Beside him, school children walk by in their coloured toques, little dresses, smart orderly trousers.

ᗥ

February 2

Nukus arrives at dusk. Jenny, my predecessor, has come to greet me with two of her counsellors and her translator. They all speak English. We greet. The two counsellors leave for their homes, and Jenny takes me to a restaurant to have supper with her translator who, she explains, will be mine for a month until a woman is hired allowing him to become transportation manager. Supper will be with them and the other foreigners on this project, who soon arrive wearing colours of dread. The meal is uncomfortable. I am just another arriving expat. They are tired. They and Jenny don't get along. Two doctors, a nurse, a lab tech, and a logistician. We eat in silence. And then we all share the bill, even though I, unlike the others, ate no meat dishes and drank no beer.

We go back to the same expat house, called Vostachnaya for the street it's on: "eastern" in Karakalpak. This is Karakalpakstan now. It's a part of Uzbekistan but the people refer to themselves as Karakalpaks. My room is the only spare one, the guest room. It is the biggest and has a double bed. Since it is on the ground floor near the hot water radiator tank, it's also the warmest. It is very cold outside.

ᗥ

February 7

QARAQALPAQSTAN ------------------- No'kis

Three days after my arrival: Jenny is leaving today. I have followed her everywhere and I have been briefed and introduced and briefed and introduced to every MSF expat and significant National Staff. But I am lost.

"What will I actually do, each day?" I ask Jenny. "After I finish the little one week schedule of visits and meetings that you have given me?" She says not to worry, just take my time, that it will all emerge. She's on her way home. She is sad to leave. Her mind is elsewhere, not on me. The nine counsellors on our team, they've all had her for two years. Their minds are on her. Now I'm alone.

Uzbekistan is bigger than Germany, slightly smaller than Spain and has 25 million people. It is in the middle of central Asia with a tiny south-eastern border on Afghanistan and otherwise surrounded by the four other stans, Kazakhstan, Kyrgyzstan, Tajikistan, and Turkmenistan. No relation to nearby Afghanistan or Pakistan. It's where Timur was born, where Genghis Khan rode and where the Silk Road wound through the desert.

And in February it is very cold indeed in Nukus, a city of 300,000 and the capital of Karakalpakstan, a huge so-called Autonomous Republic about a third the size of Italy and with a population of just over one and a half million. A region of Karakalpaks who are divided into tribes which they must marry outside of, who speak their own language and think of themselves as separate from Uzbeks, and a people as proud as they are resigned to being beleaguered by the more powerful forces in their world. Forces such as a Uzbek majority, a secret police called National Security, and an epidemic called MDR-TB which is the much more dangerous brother of an epidemic called TB.

In February in this desert land, the trees are bare that line the narrow streets and the few wide, grand ones that move to criss-cross the city or flow past the White House, home to the president of Karakalpakstan. The trees are bare to the wind that flies relentlessly from the desert, keeping the ancient crows tucked into their beaks on the shuddering branches.

I am in Nukus with the crows.

⌒ I walked to the bazaar yesterday—about three kilometres. It was cold but not as cold as in Canada. I'd say about 6 below Celsius, dipping to 11 below when the wind rose. The bazaar is the main market place. Much is outdoors or in small shops and then one big central venue with tables set up. But no heat anywhere. I don't understand the language, either spoken or written. The alphabet is not like ours. So I couldn't tell what was what. I did manage to get cheese, bread, some cookies, walnuts and a jar of strawberry jam. I point and then hold out my wad of money for them to take what I owe. As far as I could tell, they don't try to rip you off.

Speaking of money, the highest bill is 1000 *sum* which equals half a U.S. dollar. So everyone has to carry this big wad of bills to pay. And there are no coins.

We aren't allowed to take public transport so, every time we want to go out, we get a chauffeured MSF car if available. Or we can walk. In other seasons some bikes are available. Not much traffic here so it's pleasant to get around. In the residential areas, the houses are low style, squarish, featureless and fronted by a wall. All you see are entrance doors. Then into courtyards and then the dwelling. Nothing like a country in south or southeast Asia with its constant visual stimulation.

⌒ The crows huddle in dark clumps on the bare branches. The desert cold sticks to them. Twenty below zero to a crow must seem much like it does to a human. Their beaks are hidden beneath tightly folded wings, pretending the vulnerability to freezing fingers of this wind doesn't exist.

These are the wise birds of Karakalpakstan. Aziz, my 30-year-old senior counsellor, tells me they can live to be 100. But he doesn't like them, their parallel lives unreachable, unlike the dogs with whom Karakalpaks have formed a working relationship. He knows they must be wise, the keepers of how it is, how it's been, seen it all but never sharing any advice, as they hop on the ground with less impudence than the magpies but too much self-assurance. He's seen one suddenly die, fall stiff onto the ground. Seen others with beaks cracked with age. He doesn't like how they huddle in the trees like dark winter fruit which no one would ever want to eat.

☙ I am a foreigner, another expat with MSF. Thirteen years of revolving door expats all arriving and departing, from many different countries. Manas has seen them all. He's been a guard in Nukus for 12 of those years. He sits at his 15-hour shift—6 am to 9 pm—ready to answer phones, send cars for needy expats, answer the doorbell to allow someone in. Long shifts. Good pay. Manas has eyes that burn into you. He studies expats, harbours deep cuts. He teaches aikido, urges me to join his class. Maybe I will. At least, I've actually heard of aikido, and it will take me out of my norms. Might as well go all the way in that department.

I am a foreigner. For the Karakalpaks who work for MSF, the drivers, the cooks, the logisticians, education planners, guards, assistants and translators—referred to as National Staff, we are diversions, something to add a bit of interest. Whenever a new one arrives, at their first lunch in the main MSF building when all eat together, the expat is introduced and asked to say a few words. When it's my turn, to add some levity, I give myself a female name and claim to be a former lover from a past life of the cute Kyrgyz expat doctor. Everyone laughs. I want them to see me as a bit strange. It will make my life easier if they expect non-normalcy.

Then we eat. Two long tables, plates of salad, bread wheels, peanuts in the shell, cookies, a fruit, large common dishes of rice plov, or dumplings, tea, and the contented cackle of chewing teeth. Each work day at 1 pm, Gulya, one of the cooks, will holler: "Lunch!!!" And all 53 of us expats and locals crush against each other to get to the table with the biggest bowl of fruit.

☙ Just a few years after my brother was born, my mother was diagnosed with tuberculosis. Treatment and a cure meant many weeks in a sanatorium. This was a time when it wasn't so unusual for Canadians to contract that dreaded disease. Because she was put on heavy doses of sulfa drugs, my mother believed she would never be able to have any more children. So, years later it was a big surprise when she became pregnant with me.

It is a rich irony that, just a few months before the same age my mother was when she died from cancer, here I am on the other side of the world in the forgotten country of Uzbekistan working with TB patients. Not just ordinary TB but the new age kind which resists my mother's drugs.

The team of counsellors I supervise has the job of convincing and supporting patients to stay on the treatment that can save their lives. This means two years of medication, often with serious side effects such as continual nausea, head and joint pain, and sometimes much worse: hearing loss, mood shifts, tinnitus, liver or kidney damage, disturbed thinking, or psychosis. In the end, there is no guarantee of success.

I understand now that the counselling part of the MSF project is really the crucial missing link. The doctors and nurses administer the treatment regimen, but if the patients won't accept it then everything breaks down. Reaching inside the psyches of those afflicted, educating, bolstering their resolve, and solving the riddle of why some stop are the only ways to stem the epidemic. Nurses and doctors don't do that. Counselling is not in anyone's consciousness here. It does not exist in Uzbekistan. MSF has brought it, and even the MSF people don't really understand it.

This is a country where respiratory disease contributes to almost 50% of deaths. It is epidemic. Regular TB is epidemic. MDR-TB is epidemic. And it will spread.

The Aral Sea—once the 4th largest inland body of water in the world, larger than all the Great Lakes other than Superior—was abundant with marine life. It supported a thriving fishing industry that fed hundreds of thousands, and attracted tourists to its picturesque shores.

But, by some estimates, it has dropped to 20% of its size. Every living thing died because the salt content became so high. The exposed sea bed, now a vast and barren plain, offers up millions of tons of fertilizers, pesticides, salts, and other contaminates to the winds throughout the year. There are high rates of birth abnormalities, more than triple the norm. Soon after leaving the station in the capital of Tashkent, 800 kilometres from Nukus, the train starts to cut through flat, arid land and a light skim of white appears. Since it was winter when I arrived, I thought it was skiff of snow. But it is salt.

Despite being a long way from the Aral Sea, salt covers the land. People here talk of the taste of salt in vegetables and fruit. Drinking water in Nukus, over two hundred kilometres from the old sea, has a slight tinge of salt. Being here and seeing the salt layering the earth around me indelibly drives home the depth of the environmental carnage.

I had learned of the situation before coming. But it was travelling across the land and seeing the white of the salt everywhere that drove it home. Each day, when I am driven in the Landcruiser away from town, I look out at the barren, flat land. It is all white. In town, bare lots are white. I think of it as the colour of tuberculosis.

Masks

I don't really know what to do or what I am doing. My own personal life is as comfortable as it can get. My room in Vostachnaya is warm. Each day, after helping to prepare the MSF lunch, Gulya comes to clean our whole house, do the laundry, iron our clothes, even wash our dishes. Clean towels, sheets, face and laundry soap provided. Cars will take us everywhere we want to go. Someone buys food for us at the bazaar if we request it. How could it be easier? But the reason I am here and how to fulfill it is another matter.

Twice a week, I go to the main MDR-TB hospital called TB2 which was set up through the efforts of MSF. It is 19 kilometres to the north of Nukus far off the highway in the desert. I ride in the car sitting inside my skin, yet outside my skin, alien to my self. I am swept along, to walk and talk as though I am present and real. But I am still in shock, pretending to know something that matters about a disease reality with which I've never remotely been familiar.

When our car arrives, I am swept across the paved walkway behind the main buildings through the metal door into the back of the hospital—just where patients pass in order to go to the squat toilets or take a shower. There are two wards. The first is a long concrete hallway of rooms where the new arrivals reside until the medication reduces their infectiousness. It houses up to 40 patients. These patients have a small kitchen in which to cook food before returning to eat in their own sparse rooms. That wing connects to the less infectious two-story wing which has a high ceilinged foyer area and a large lunchroom with floor-to-ceiling windows. In the foyer a tree with recurring orange blossoms grows. Up to 50 patients reside there for the weeks to months they remain infectious.

For patients in both wards, the metronome is the daily intake of drugs. Fifteen to 20 pills of varying shapes, colours, and smells. Two pouches of hated granules. And a painful injection in the hip. Most take it all in the morning. Some break it up into morning and after-noon segments.

In the first ward, patients make a dreaded procession to the nurs-es' room and, once finished, retreat to places of privacy to face the onset of the side effects. In the second ward, they gather en masse in the foyer, receive their shot in the upper rump, collect their plastic container of pills and begin the woeful gulping and swallowing. A ping-pong table serves as a centre point for holding the booklets they use to record their intake.

On Wednesday mornings, I go to TB2 with a translator to do doctors' rounds. This is the ritual set up for the Ministry of Health (MoH) doctors to usher the expat MSF doctors and nurse and Mental Health Officer—that's me—and their translators from patient to pa-tient to check on their progress. Actually, it's to walk out the relation-ship that both medical sides agree to have, to walk out accountability and competence and supervision. Of course, whenever we enter a ward, we have to wear expensive masks which go over our nose and mouth. Two elastics up over the head and behind the neck keep them snug. Press the wire top part along the bridge of the nose and out to each side to ensure a seal. Breathe in to see if the fabric moves in and out. Okay, all safe. At least 95% safe so I'm told.

When I was offered this job, my question was: "How safe is it?" There was silence on the other end of the line each time I asked. Then: "Yes, well, I guess it's pretty safe. No one has contacted the disease. Yet." When I asked Jenny on the phone before I left home, she had been more comforting. "Don't worry. You won't really be in con-tact with patients very much. It's mainly work in the office, meetings, consultations, etc. I've been here two years and I have no problems."

So, I'm keen to get the mask on right. And it's good for four hours of continual use, they say. Right. I got it. In and out.

But the masks are yellow. Like beaks. And, when all the expats and MoH personnel are together, we become a flock. The patients are ordered to be on their beds from 10 to 11 am every Wednesday in TB2 which now holds 73 patients and every Thursday in our other MDR-TB hospital in town called TB1, which has 51 patients in two wards.

In every room in both hospitals, there are normally from two to ten patients. In a new case or an especially infectious or infirm case, it's usually a lone patient. On the rounds I make it a practise to go to each patient and shake hands. I sense this makes the others in the entourage a bit uncomfortable. The expat and MoH docs talk about the patients as though they are inanimate, discussing personal details about each regardless of what is heard by other patients in the room.

After my first experience of rounds, I decided to take matters into my own hands. While the medical people talked, I'd sit with a patient, get them to look into my eyes, say words to them through my translator and, after the rounds team left the room, maybe do something with all the patients there. Conversation, jokes, anything to convey interest and warmth.

February 17

Today in TB2, I let the ducks go on by themselves. Talking their talk. Aziz, who speaks English well and acts as my translator this day, and I linger behind and decide to sit with the three women in the first room of the first ward, the more infectious and smaller of the two wards. I want to know their names, which I realize I will have to later write down and review, my ears so poor at wrestling with this strange new language.

The oldest, grandmother Shakargul, is late forties and tells us she has been on treatment in TB2 now for 11 months. The youngest, red faced Gulnas, only 26, has been in hospital for four months. The thinnest, Kizlargul, about 34, has been here only two weeks. Two weeks of two years. Her sentence before death or life. Her bones wait, her memories gather. I pull three chairs in a circle to connect with the oldest one's bed where she is sitting. She wears a multi-coloured head scarf wound in brightness around her hair. I have Aziz sit beside her on the bed next to me in my chair. The other two are in the other chairs. We form a circle. They stare at me, wondering what the hell is going to happen. I request we hold hands.

I have never stopped to talk to them before, don't remember seeing them, yet they are so easy to see. We talk. Who am I? How old am I? Am I married? How old are they? How long have they been on treatment?

I don't want to be too long away from the main flock of ducks. But before I leave, I look at the thin lady and say: "Of course, it will be hard for you, but when you need support you should turn to her because she has been here four months." Then I look at Gulnas. "And when you need help, when the suffering is too much, the nausea too hard to take, you must turn to Shakargul. She has been through it. She can help you." Then I look at Shakargul and tell her the same only that she can turn to Aziz who is experienced and has a good heart and he will help her. Thus, we are a circle, I say. But what about me? Hmmm. I don't lose a beat. I turn to face Kizlargul, her sunken cheeks, red dress. "And for me, for me, when I need help, I will turn to you and look into the beauty of your eyes." They all smile and nod.

I say that, in Canada, I embrace people that I care about and I ask if they might like a hug. The thin woman nods and we embrace. I look at Gulnas. She blushes and her eyes flicker. She backs away and laughs. I can tell she wants to but she protests: "No, no. I'm a virgin. I can't." They all laugh. Then Shakargul takes the hug. As we leave, the women continue to smile, matching those on the faces of Aziz and me.

February 18

Frail. Oxygen mask. Within it, teeth in a steady grimace. Her eyes look about. Gauging the ducks in this room of six women in TB1 Hospital. Gods. Talking about her. Small and frail and silent. Months before she had become negative—no longer infectious—and so had been discharged from hospital. But then two weeks ago she had a serious relapse and so here she is … feverish, weak. Just such a short time ago, walking about, smiling, legs pushing forward beneath a thick woollen overcoat to stop the desert's winter chill. Two weeks ago, breathing the same as me and the gods talking about her.

The other women in the room sit on their beds waiting their turn with the duck gods. Wait and watch us upright, but in truth bored, ready to answer a mobile phone, talk to friends or family.

The dreadlocked Spanish doctor, our Medco, here on a week visit from Tashkent, walks over to the frail woman. He kneels down beside her, takes her pulse. He lifts the blanket, lifts her shirt. Prods her abdomen. The side. The front. Taps it. He doesn't say a word, doesn't look at her. She winces. He sighs, stops. In a while, our MSF Kenyan doctor stoops, does the same. Gentler. She does not wince. He doesn't look at her. Doesn't say a word. To her. They move on. Flesh. She is only flesh.

When the rest leave the room, I go over to her. Place my hand on her forehead. The other on her shoulder. I sit beside her on the bed. Her eyes are alarmed. She does not know why a duck god is doing this. Wonders if I think she is dying. I look into her eyes and smile. I relax. I don't know what to do. I keep my hand on her forehead and wait. I tell my translator to say that I will come back when she gets better and have a dance with her. She speaks. Whispers through her oxygen mask. Asks why I say this just to her and not the others in the room.

I say to my translator: "Tell her: 'Because you are so beautiful'."

She answers: "Thank you."

Her name is Aizada.

☙

February 19

OPD. I am becoming familiar with the medical jargon. OPD — outpatient department where patients come once they are discharged for no longer having a positive smear of their sputum sample, maybe no longer being infectious. They come here each day to take their drugs, lower their pants for the injection, and wait for more weeks to find out if the culture from their sputum is also negative. If they are fully non-infectious. Or if it comes back positive and they are forced to return to the hospital. The smear is the first quick microscopic evaluation of their sputum, the deep lung mucous, coughed labouriously up from healthier patients and which spews like tears from sicker patients. The presence of tuberculosis bacteria is seen or not seen on the slide smear. If not seen, then maybe they are no longer infectious. Maybe not. When the smear is negative, they get sent home from hospital, but must come to OPD for their daily drugs. They aren't deemed safe enough to take their drugs at the polyclinic closest to their homes. That only comes when the sputum culture analysis comes in maybe two months later and shows no TB bacteria. Then, they can believe the drugs have worked. Then it's the rest of their two-year sentence. I am proud of my new knowledge.

How long have you been in treatment? Three months—she's only 18, she still tries to go to a polytechnic college but not every day, only in the afternoons on the days she doesn't suffer so much from the side effects. She doesn't tell anyone she has MDR-TB, for fear that in their minds she would be seen as trying to kill them. She smiles brightly as she enters the room. She was only positive and infectious for one month, only one month in hospital. Aziz beams when he sees her. She is a gem. Her aliveness ignites his aliveness.

And then the 20-year-old arrives. She is even more beautiful. Hair brushed back, smooth perfect skin of youth, perfect aliveness, dark curls down her neck. She is my daughter, eyes brighter than death, so bright death could never be dreamt of.

After awhile, the six-foot-three grandson of a mullah comes into the room in his grey turban and blue robe, dark sunken cheeks, a three-year treatment marvel who should have died or been cured long ago, but who stays here in the ward because he has no other place to go. His eyes as bright and piercing as should be for one who has refused to sicken and die, refused to whither but instead rises each day just a tiny bit closer to the sky.

I sit with them. Speak about courage, service, the struggle to stay on the drugs. Viktor Frankl said the concentration camp inmates needed something bigger than themselves to believe in, some purpose, in order to endure the relentless sadness and oppression. MDR-TB patients in Karakalpakstan need the same. They need to see their disease, their treatment as part of them, only part of them.

I ask how often they have considered stopping the drugs. Often, they reply. I say that they have chosen this journey to recovery, to health and by doing that they serve their family, their neighbourhood, their community. The disease chose them and now they sacrifice with such dignity in order to fight the disease, do their part to defeat the epidemic, protect others from the infection. Their suffering each day a testament to their worth, their service. Two long years of never knowing if they will ultimately be cured. The tall man, smiles and holds up three fingers. Aziz whispers: "He has stopped and started and he had regular TB first."

February 24

I sit with Natasha, fifty-one-year-old Korean philosopher. There are noticeable numbers of people in Nukus of Korean ancestry. I don't know why. Natasha is called a treatment failure. Not a patient anymore, but a treatment failure. She is on her bed. There are two treatment failures here on the bottom floor of TB3. It's where MSF has its palliative ward, where patients are sent to die. The rest of the building is a four-story regular TB sanatorium still operating from Soviet times and fully administered by the Ministry of Health. We are 10 kilometres out of town in the opposite direction from TB2. Outside are lanes between treed and furrowed plots. A park-like setting with outbuildings for staff, and farm sheds. Farther still, a wide, iced-over canal from the great Amu Darya. Since they took her off the drugs, Natasha has been here 11 months. She has had regular and MDR-TB for five years. But she hasn't died, hasn't deteriorated.

She wants to live to see new grandchildren. Her two daughters don't visit her often. Once a year. Apparently she is "difficult", the doctors say. I ask if she has photos of her family. She goes to the end of the bed. Unrolls the mattress and pulls out two small albums, one photo per page. One has several photos of her grandson who died at six months. He lies so tiny and real on his grandmother's legs. She says he died because his fontanel closed too soon. She says he was already talking in the days before he died.

The other photos in this album are of patients that she's been in hospitals with. Patients at parties. At the canal here in the summer, swimming. At the canal in another winter. Patients in various groups at various times. This one died. This one died. This one moved to Chimbay. This one died. This one she doesn't know about. And on it goes. Ten or 12 pages. Natasha speaks with a mixture of profanity, Russian and Uzbek proverbs, and common sense.

The other treatment failure is also human, also a real person with a mind and heart. Also been here 11 months. Also a victim of TB for many years. He's thinner than Natasha but not too thin. He's doing okay. He's not dying either. Not yet. His name is Massor, but I recognize who he really is, he's Leonard Cohen, here doing research for songs of *Life and Death*. His silver hair, elegant lines, and basso voice give him away. And the sly, confident look in his eyes.

I ask him if he can sing. Sure, he says and laughs a laugh that must come from years of touring and wooing and meditating on meaning. I ask if he will sing now. He laughs again, not as crazy as he sees I am. Massor tells me he used to box. He dropped out of school and boxed. But he never made it out of tournaments in Karakalpakstan. Welterweight, tall and slick. Then he became a driver in Russia. Then tried his hand at acting but didn't have much success. Painting was better. He married his first wife in Russia. He walks to his cupboard in this bare room in TB3, clear plastic over the window to keep out the cold, keep in the low heat that stops the water from freezing up. From out of a cloth bundle he takes the photo of his wife of 40 years before. She is with her sister and two friends in this black and white in a padded frame. She is beautiful. He is 62 now. She stayed in Russia when he returned to Karakalpakstan, not wanting to leave her home and family there. "What can you do?" he says. He had a daughter with her in Russia but has never seen them again. He knows, at least, that his wife has died now. Long before that, Massor had married again. But the girl in the photo remains the love of his life. "You never forget your first love." He touches his heart and smiles, looks down at the photo, places it back in its cloth swaddling.

Massor puts on his brown fur hat, new running shoes, and a thick overcoat over his pin-striped blazer. Leonard Cohen and I are going for a walk. Outside, the bare poplars poke into a blue sky filled with sunshine on this cold February afternoon. We walk along the lanes in the sanatorium compound. He makes a motion with his arms of a hockey player taking a shot. 1972, he says. 1972 and the Canada-Russia super series. Thumbs up. He laughs. He mentions Mikhailov. Boris Mikhailov, I say and nod. He says, Kharlamov. Valeri Kharlamov, I say. We both know the Russian hockey stars from all those years ago. He laughs. We walk in the sunshine.

☞

February 25

TB2, TB1, TB3. The names are becoming normal for me. MSF is a busy outfit. Everyone is doing something. Going here and there so time is served by shortening the language. And we are not about people, not about wholes. We are TB. That's why we came here 13 years ago. So, our hospitals don't need grander names. TB1 is the big complex right in Nukus. A wall encircles it. There is a large treed and laned outside area and then several big buildings, an administration and lab building, a block of offices and examination rooms, smelly latrines, various logistical buildings, a children's sanatorium building, an Outpatient building for potentially negative MDR-TB patients, a building for the chief doctor, and a large three-story building stretching all along one end in which the hundreds of regular TB and the increasing number of MDR-TB patients are cared for. The MDR-TB ward is divided into two floors and it is the only ward in which MSF collaborates with the Ministry of Health. The top floor is nice and modern compared to the rooms at TB2, simple but new beds, bright rooms with up to eight patients, two small, refurbished kitchens for the patients, nice bathrooms. The second floor situation is easily the best condition in this rambling TB hospital. The bottom floor is for patients who are slightly less drug resistant. Their floor is dingy, practically basement fare. I guess MSF didn't have enough money to remake both floors.

TB2 is outside town. It's all MDR-TB with some XDR patients. It's actually a pretty peaceful place. On entry through the gates, the front is roughly landscaped with trees, some shrubbery, sitting areas. Its spartan concrete halls and rooms are not so bad—bare, but clean and habitable. Each of the two wards has its own common area for the patients to watch TV and socialize.

I am at TB2 this morning, sitting on a bed with 25-year-old Saperbuy. He's only two weeks into treatment and scared. He comes from Karauziak, a village an hour plus away from Nukus. Two weeks into treatment. Only 102 to go. He has missed his pills the last few days, the twenty ovals and oblongs he will have to take these 102 weeks, six of every seven days. He's refused his injection, the needle that is to jab into his upper buttock six days out of seven for at least another year. He did take his drugs today though, and now he is nauseous. But he wants to ask me something.

He has called me into his room to sit with him on his bed. He bows his head in hesitation. Then he looks me in the eyes, looks over at my translator. He tells me he got married four months before. Now he feels like he is married to this room, its four other cots, the strangers he has been placed with. He wants to go to his wife. He is new to the hospital, his mouth and nose are covered with a surgical mask, and still doing what the doctors told him to control infection when he was first admitted. I only see his eyes. He is scared. He tells me he has night sweats. How long will it last? Is it bad? I say I don't know, that I will ask the doctors and get back to him.

Then he says what he really wants to ask. He wants to know if he can go home to see his wife or if she can come to see him. He wants to know if he can have sex with her. I tell him there is only danger if he breathes on her. I ask if his penis breathes. He doesn't get the joke and thinks I mean does it get erect or not.

His life has become not what he thought it would be four months after the day he danced with a bride in a flowing white dress, drank the long line of vodka toasts to every expression of good wishes for their future happiness.

~

February 26

> *She died*
> *the grimacing beauty*
> *She was sent home*
> *to die*

I wanted to see her again, but we had gone on a team building retreat to the mountains. I wanted to show her that the first meeting was only a first meeting. Or if I could see it was ending, I could have held her hand good-bye. But I had been too late in saying hello. And I really would have danced with her. Now she dances lighter than a single faint crystal of snow. Lighter than that.

Aizada.

~

February 27

There are ten women in this room. By coincidence it's room 10, the biggest in TB2. Being in the same room means having similar drug resistances. After a couple of months, the lab tells which drugs the patients are resistant to and what their bacteria count is which suggests the degree of infectiousness. These women are in the second ward of TB2, the two-story side, which means they are less infectious. They have told me they want to talk. I came back to see them because during doctors' rounds I had gone to each to shake hands and say *salaam alaikum* and the older one in the corner had gripped my hand firmly and looked me deeply in the eyes. Now, I have come back to know the others.

I sit on the floor against the wall beneath the windows and look out at them as they sit on their beds staring back at me. They are smiling. The foreigner has come back to see them. To talk with them. They want to know why no one else ever does that. I say I don't know. They ask what I am? I say, a human being. They say, of course we know that but what are you? Are you a doctor? I say, I am a human being. They laugh. Then they want to know about my country, its climate, my family, my age, my salary, the length of my stay in Nukus.

We talk and then I ask about them. I say that I'd like to know something of their lives, their family, when they got MDR-TB. A young woman, who has been lying on her bed in obvious discomfort, says she will start. She has her usual splitting headache after taking the drugs. She is nauseous and her whole body aches, but she sits up to tell me her story. Her face is ivory, eyes almost blue, muted orangey-brown cloth bandana wrapped around her head, traditional housecoat. She speaks slowly, pausing to let the truth of each revelation sit in the hollow air of this room 10, with the foreigner who wants to know what too many here want to forget.

"My name is Gulshat. I am 26 and I have two daughters, two and five." Pause. "I got MDR-TB five months ago and came to TB2 in November." Pause. "My mother died from MDR-TB in 2007. It was difficult. I attended to her every day, wishing her to gain strength. Wishing for the coughing to end. Her face to fatten. Her laugh to return." Pause. "My father died from it in 2008. He never recovered from my mother's death. His heart was broken. His lungs became broken." Pause. "Two of my sisters died from it in 2009. We tried everything we knew to save them. They were younger then me. I loved them so much." Pause. "So, there is lots of sadness in my life." Pause. "I want to be cured for my children's sake."

I stop her there. One of the other women is crying. The room is silent. The spoken words have shattered the nausea, shattered the illusion of being safe in solidarity in this routinized hospital room. I am astounded. I cannot imagine Gulshat's loss. I say that I don't want to continue talking as though her great tragedy is just another anecdote, that we need to sit with it a while, honour her truth. Sit in some silence and just be. Later, I say I need to leave, that I will come again on another day and hear other stories.

How many will be like this?

❦

I am learning. There are cockroaches in this house called Vostachnaya. Longish, brownish, lots of legs. I think they are cockroaches. They seem to have lots of legs. They like the bathroom and kitchen the best. In the morning, I'll find one trapped in the bathtub, its steep, inclined walls with their slippery enamel. I'll stick in a plastic container for the cockroach to skitter onto and transport him to a more liberating environment. He or she gets out of the light and exposure as quickly as he or she detects a hiding place. I don't know why people dislike cockroaches. What did they ever do to us?

We have a project team meeting each Monday at 4 pm. PT meeting, it's called. All the MSF expats gather to exchange their news, plans, and requests. I have learned to measure what I say, how I say it. Better not too much information or else a need for explanation. Or worse, justification. I can't explain. I don't like to justify. I've just come here to do. I have been working directly with the patients. Nine to six each day, talking with them, knowing their reality, holding them sometimes. I call it giving energy. Sick people often perk up if someone says they have energy to give. Whatever that really means. I'm not going to tell the other expats that I hold patients. Hold them for a full one to two minutes. Letting our realities communicate without words, letting our breathing move together, our hearts beat together. Allowing culture to disappear, age, gender, language transform to being. Being together. My counsellors, the nine left by my predecessor, think I'm odd. Say that their people don't touch like that. Men don't hold women. Even a husband and wife if they haven't seen each other for a week and meet on the street won't touch like that.

I'll just mention starting a weekly newsletter, say: "I'm learning. All is well. Is there a way of getting a heater put into the counselling room in Chimbay? And, we have no room to counsel in, no privacy, in Polyclinics 6 and 7. Kuanish, the counsellor there, is using the sputum room in one and the hollow beneath the stairs in the other. Counselling doesn't work without a space to have some privacy." They'll nod, reply that there will be renovations sometime in the next few months, and then move on to the next topic. I like it that way. I get to listen. But I have to get Kuanish a room.

☞

February 27

Senior counsellor Altinay comes with me to Chimbay, a city of 70,000 an hour's drive north of Nukus, to introduce me to some patients. Aside from Nukus, Chimbay is the only other place in the whole country where MSF operates. Altinay is 45 and has been with MSF for 10 years. She's the eldest of our team. But she doesn't like me much. She's a seasoned counsellor who cried when my predecessor left, thanked her for making her a human being. She isn't keen on me.

We march into one of Chimbay's polyclinics. Some patients come into an examination room to meet with us. A young woman of 29 —prominent mole above her lip to the side of her left nostril, dark, curly hair and nervous eyes—tells us she always feels frightened. She says the last weeks have seen her fretting, worrying, unable to sleep easily. A man with grey hair and long grey overcoat speaks. He says he struggles with anger, always feels irritable. They look at me.

In the west, counsellors see clients who need help dealing with various issues in their lives. They come to an office and unburden themselves, receive active listening, empathy, attention, feedback, maybe some coaching, maybe some exercises to try. Therapy has many forms. Some more adventurous, some more conservative, but always on the premise that the issue was there before the person came and that the issue can be resolved or addressed to make it less of an issue over time. The premise that the person will keep living after the visit and keep functioning, that there is a milieu which allows all of us to live relatively productive or at least manageable lives and have as many issues as we do. But here in Karakalpakstan, it's different. The issues must be addressed so as to keep the person alive. It's life and death. Issues stop patients from taking their drugs. When they do that, they die. When they do that, others become infected. So, there is not time for lots of future appointments. It's all now. Do something. Do anything. But do it now. Get them back on their drugs or prevent them from quitting, but do it now. Give some kind of help.

Altinay looks at me. Waits. The three others in the room wait and watch. I speak. I have only been here a month. But I came with an advantage. I realized that I didn't know anything. I realized I would need to learn from the patients, and I have figured out that living and dying has only one therapeutic response: go to truth, stick with truth. The patients are truth. Their sickness and its deadly swath have done two things here. One, it has created great stigma. No one wants it to be found out. No one wants gossip, to be treated as a pariah. No one likes to accept it. TB has long been a scourge. The second thing is that, because MDR-TB is especially lethal and requires such arduous treatment, patients often become more open, more alive, more aware of life. When an MDR-TB patient looks at someone, they really look. So, I soon concluded that I better not pretend, better not hide behind jargon or title, but match them in their openness. And I knew that the foundation truth that I had to offer was my self, my humanness. My experience and training, for what it might be worth, was clearly second.

I already learned from Gulshat how terrible MDR-TB is when a family lives it. So I looked at the woman with the mole, and I told her the truth. "Yes, of course, you are frightened and nervous. This disease is frightening. It is trying to kill you. It is an epidemic here. And the drugs you take every day are terrible. They are fighting a war inside you with the bacilli. The side effects are so bad. And one of the side effects is this nervousness. So you should be frightened. It means you are aware and that the drugs are working. You are a warrior. Each day that you take the drugs, you are a warrior. And each day if you feel frightened, that makes perfect sense. You should be frightened. You have been on treatment now for many months. You can go through the fear. Just breathe it in and breathe it out." I speak slowly, looking as deeply into her eyes as she allows. Then I ask if I can hold her, give her some energy. She nods. We embrace for over a minute, breathing into each other.

Next, I address the grey-haired man with polished shoes. He looks as dapper as a self-made man out for a trip to the theatre, pressed trousers, elegant cut to each of his mannerisms. He wears a grey flat cap, one of those hats from an earlier era when the streamlined look of a man with a vision, a man with purpose, was a style accessory that defined one's sense of belonging. He looks at me expectantly. "Of course, you are angry. You are fed up fighting this disease, going every day kilometres on foot to this clinic just to feel sick on your way home, wait through the hours of sickness from the drugs just to do it all over again the next day, and then the next, and the next. You have a right to be angry. Maybe you should find rocks to throw. Maybe you should smash your fists into a pillow tonight. If anyone tells you not to be angry, answer back that the anger helps you to know who you are." We talk a little longer. He mentions what happens when he gets angry, how frustrated he feels, how helpless. When we finish, I ask if he would like me to hold him also. He nods. I move toward him. We embrace. He is shorter than me. We hold for a long time. This must be a lifetime first for him, to be held so long by another human.

Then, as we part and he moves back to his place, he is looking only downward and I see that his eyes are watering. I don't speak, keep watching him, waiting to catch his gaze. He rubs at his eyes and looks around, looks back toward me. I fix my eyes into his and nod. I walk over to him and shake his hand. We embrace with a hug, a quicker one, and I tell him how proud I am of him.

Altinay has been translating. When we leave, she says nothing. She must not know what to think.

When we drove to Chimbay from Nukus, the wall outside of town, which was built in order to stop President Karimov from seeing the bareness of the homes dotting the desert, stretched a few kilometres before empty desert took over to either side. After thirty kilometres we had to slow down for a herd of camels that had begun crossing the road. Casually grazing on the sparse winter scrub, they were in no hurry to get to the other side. Humped and shaggy and huffing in the morning's frosty air, some ambled down the centre of the highway as though it was their traditional pathway. The vehicles slowed, veered to the side, stopped and waited. Camels are big.

But our day in Chimbay finishes by driving along another road, one filled with deep ruts and holes that make the Toyota Landcruiser jump about like a rodeo horse. Along each side is desert and silence. We arrive at the home of another grey-haired man, older than the one at the clinic. He sits on his cot while his obese wife in her frock and bandana tries to clean up for these unexpected guests. Obese, but limber enough despite her age to flicker her fingers over the carpet plucking loose strings and doubled down to flat hand the fabric as though she was a gymnast. This grey-haired man has been out of hospital for several months and now, because of disabilities, takes the drugs at home each day when a nurse brings them out. His side effects are not so debilitating, but his legs ache greatly — from his knees to shins to ankles and toes. And he has diabetes.

They have a 25-year-old son and he has two children, but they live elsewhere. This home is mud and straw over timbers, ceilinged by straw and beams and more mud. The brown-grey mud of the desert. The home is bare but warm. A good home, its two rooms are easily enough. His cot is mainly springs. He sits before us and coughs gently. I ask him to show me where his legs hurt, place my hands where he points. My hands are still cold from the outside, and I feel the warmth of his knee and down his brown skin. I rub his limb. He says his relative comes sometimes and caresses his legs the same way.

He tells me that he would prefer to go to the clinic each day in order to take his medicine even though it is freezing outside, even though the clinic has been freezing inside. He'd rather go along the bumpy road each day on foot and walk the kilometre to the main road to catch a *marshrutka* and go to the clinic if he was more able to walk. He would like to share the company of the others who come to the clinic, spend some time talking, swapping news and stories. He laughs.

I ask if I can come again. Of course, he replies. We leave. On the way out, we pass the community doctor. She has come to tell him that he has lung cancer.

The Boy With The Beautiful Eyes

March 2

Today is the first day of work for my new translator and assistant. Her name is Aynur. She is 29 and has dimples when she smiles. Before I arrived, Jenny had hired her for the future because she thought it would work better for me as a male to have a female translator. Her previous assistant was scheduled to become solely the transportation manager. But our Project Coordinator had been on holidays so the official job start couldn't take place until today. They had wanted me to meet her first anyway, make sure we fit. Someone mentioned they had heard that Aynur's husband was National Security, Uzbekistan's secret police. They wondered if maybe she was being sent as an informer.

When we first met, I could see that her English was very good. She looked right at me. And when I told her how we'd be doing therapy, doing whatever it took to help patients, she nodded. Then I spoke about counselling patients who had been raped or suffered sexual abuse. Her eyes became emotional, but she still nodded. The advertisement had said the job was mainly office work with lots of written translation. Unexpectedly, I was telling her we'd be going into a fire each day.

I have just told her that up to now I had been using Jenny's previous translator, Aziz, Altinay, and my young English-speaking counsellor, Deelya, for translators and that they had allowed me to get to know some patients, become familiar with hospitals, clinics and routines.

But I am ready to take on patients as my own, counsel them, discover what was possible, go through all aspects of adherence counselling from pre-admission to final outcomes. In Karakalpakstan there is no such thing as counselling. Aynur had never heard of it before other than what she deduced from television.

Now, we are sitting in an isolation room in the first ward of TB2. We are with a boy with beautiful eyes whom I had met a week before when he was in the second ward. His name is Islam, and he has become more infectious. He seems thinner, and he is unhappy. Unhappy to be alone in this room. Says he would eat better if he was in a room with others. He was in hospital months before and had become non-infectious, went home and took his drugs from the polyclinic. But he converted to positive so he stopped taking the drugs. After another few months his condition worsened and he came back to hospital. He's been in TB2 since the start of January. As he recounts this, his head is bent down to hide in his hands. He admits it upsets him to recall it all. Aynur has to lean close to hear him speak. I tell him I will try to arrange him getting into a room with another patient.

Then it's on to the room with my three women, my first friends, the ones I held hands with. They are all flat on their beds, hooked up to IV's. Infusions they are called, and the patients love them, believe they rejuvenate and cleanse. The MSF doctors laugh about the infusions, say they are the same as regular electrolyte drinks, but that the patients believe in them and so they work for all matter of concerns. This time they are supposed to be helping them deal with the nausea. We stay to talk and our smiles continue the bond.

Aynur and I go outside to talk to 25-year-old Guldana. She is another "old" friend. On one of my first visits to TB2, she called me into her room and convened a meeting with me and a bunch of other patients all totally fascinated to have the foreigner at their relaxed disposal. She and I sat on the floor like two old buddies resuming a relationship, her eyes curiously inspecting every inflection. As a group we talked about Canada, about how often I would be talking with my family at home, about what I might be able to do to get the food in the hospital improved. "We can't eat it," they insisted. They told me about how terrible the side effects were, asked if once they were cured would they still suffer from the side effects, would there be aftereffects that lasted, and how each day when they awoke in the morning they began to brace themselves for the coming of the drugs, how it made it difficult to enjoy any breakfast, how their whole bodies repulsed at the sight of the pills, the smell.

Now, we walk with Guldana to sit on a bench away from the building, under some still bare trees, the warm sun pushing away the reluctant cold of this start to March. She is troubled today, her brows knit together in consternation. The anti-nausea medication once worked to abate some of the nausea. Now it doesn't. The doctor tells her it is in her head. She feels distressed, can't stop thinking about her illness. Her eyes move side to side. She is talking to me, but she is not fully with me. She doesn't know if she deserves to be cured. She feels she will die. She looks at me, brown eyes probing: "Will I be cured?"

She wants me to say yes, but she won't believe me. I say: "Yes, of course. Absolutely. If you take your drugs every day, you will be cured. Hundreds are cured." And, of course, I'm lying. What do I know? I do know the drugs sometimes don't seem to work, but I'm not going to tell her that. She's obsessing and there is no point in saying, in effect, yes, go ahead worry as much as you want. So, I lie.

Guldana asks: "How do you know?" I say, I just do, I just do.

I tell her to focus on what's around her, not on what is going around in her head. Look about you, let that reality come in, let it take your focus. I thank her for welcoming me two weeks earlier, for being so friendly to me each time we meet. I say, notice the beauty that is always here to be seen. "Yes, you are sick, but look around for beauty each day. Within your sadness, you can find joy. You have to look for it." I point to the irrigation pipe some twenty metres away. It is leaking water out onto the ground. I ask her to go there and touch that water when we finish our visit, let the water touch her. One day, after her cure, I tell her: "You will have babies."

She smiles. She likes that. "But, how do you know?" she says.

March 5

Twenty-three of us sit cross-legged or with knees folded at the low table, carpet multi-coloured and soft beneath us: Kenyans two, UK Tajik one, American one, Canadian one, Spanish one, Austrian one, Bangladeshi one, Russians two, Ukrainian one, Kyrgyz one, Karakalpaks eight, Uzbeks two. No drivers, cooks, guards, counsellors, or other lower echelon National Staff. The long low table plump with sumptuous dishes. Vodka, wine, beer, juice, cola. Expensive chocolates from the West. Mounds of rice whiter and hotter than it has the right to be. Chunks of beef simmering, pumpkin soup thick in history, chicken roasted just like that. And finally filament layered cake laboured to cream by expat Dr. Firoza and expat nurse Helena, then a plate of crepes, warm raspberry jam.

The house warming party at 3 o'clock for Expat House number three. Two floors of carpet, columns, polished mahogany china cases of glass and red sheen from floor to ceiling, pale wooden doors keyed like an Alps guest house. This is Nukus in the middle of the desert. The white Aral Sea salt all around flaking the soil like never melting snow. Corpses of MDR-TB all around. Not far away, TB1 and its two floors of MDR lungs. Silent on their cozy beds bought by international aid and good intentions. Waiting for names. The outside toilets for the other patients of the hospital. Their putrid holes amongst rubble from the broken thoughts and lives of money and power, those who call the shots while the sick of their communities shit amongst shit in the holes that are left for them. But here in this house, we are warming with good cheer and toast after toast to health, happiness, and the future.

⌁

March 6

Manas phones me at 10 to be sure I will come to the bazaar with him to buy what he calls a kimono. I need a kimono. He says it will only cost $10. At the black market rate. Aikido means kimonos. He has told me how his own Nukus sensei was a liar so he had to go to Tashkent to take classes from real masters. Now he teaches two hours thrice a week. And he's been a guard for MSF for 10 years.

He wants more. He craves the chance to become a leader or a counsellor. His eyes burn into me, wanting to have me for himself, for his uncertain English, for the chance to say he's made some headway at least after 10 years of yearning.

We walk into a sporting goods shop. There are clear plastic bags of kimonos. I need a big kimono. The best size has *KARATE* written in black across the back. Manas is perplexed that it says karate. He picks at the letters seeing if they might scrape. He muses on how to get rid of them. We talk about blackening them in with felt pen. Making them six black smudges. We buy the outfit.

Later we stand at the base of the steps leading up to the footbridge which crosses the wide canal that flows beside the bazaar. Someone carries his bicycle up the steps. There is a distinct smell of urine still on the steps. Not as overpowering as along the canal walkway where scores of vendors sit cross-legged by their sheets of wares, the pieces of used clothing, faucets, hats, used DVDs, underwear that ask for buyers to care.

Several women stand in a clump holding plastic bags of bread for sale. Golden brown bread, flat and in the shape of Frisbees. In this land, bread is sacred. It is life. Never to be carelessly treated or discarded. Crumbs on the lap are carefully swept into palms and placed back on a plate. Leftovers are left where they sit for a server to gather and either take home, offer to the poor, or leave on the street for dogs. Bread to be handled and broken by many hands and moved mouth to mouth.

⌐ I see him from across the wide avenue. Cars zipping by, throngs of people coming and going. He's beneath the large video monitor that advertises the bazaar, just as we agreed three days before. I see him looking side to side, wondering if I'll show. It's still 20 minutes early, but I recognize his uneasiness. Scanning the sidewalks, not wanting to miss me. I cross over, stop to take his picture before he sees me. But before I snap it, he looks my way and waves. Leonard Cohen on this bright Sunday noon, as warm as early March should be.

We meet. I reach for his hand, he moves to embrace. We choose both in this order. His smile of few teeth, wrinkled eyes glowing with joy. Leonard, you never looked so fine. Our two curved backs turn to stroll the bazaar. The silent music between us oversounding the lack of language. We walk hand in hand. And stop for tea. Tea and cakes. His black flat cap beside him on the table, grey hair smooth against his head, and those eyes that knew his young bride in Russia so long ago.

He has choices. A daughter somewhere back along the Yenisei where he drove the loads of logs, fished through the ice, and laughed and laughed all those years before. A sister near to here. But he lives alone in TB 3, this treatment failure. The hoarseness in his throat more melodic than not, the taper of his blazer just a clearer drop of song. Dignity. Demeanour. Slight gestures of slow hands removing barriers to the breeze. We drink our tea together. Treatment failure and Canadian friend both free from cages for the day. What need for language.

March 7

It is a holiday Monday. I am walking today. I need to be in the desert. I first have to leave the hubbub of town. It will take 45 minutes at a brisk clip to get out of town and longer to get close to the sand part where I can just wander, find a place to think. I want to ground myself in this time. I know I am no longer a part of home or Canada. That does not exist. An epidemic and the lives of so many who need will do that quite easily, quite effectively, create a world you either enter or run from. I have entered. But I am not settled. I don't yet know who I am here. I am filled with uncertainty. I don't mind the uncertainty, but I want to feel in touch with my self. I say "my self" instead of "myself" because it's the self that is in me which I want to feel close to. So, I'm heading out to the emptiness. I've felt it calling me for two weeks now. I have never been in a desert before, visited yes but only for an hour or two, gazing about like a tourist, like an observer. I have never lived with a desert before. So, maybe it has accepted me now and calls me out to consummate the relationship.

I walk from my expat house, from Vostachnaya—I can finally pronounce it right—down to the main road out of town. The cars here are entities on their own right. They follow the rules. Go in the direction of the traffic. Obey traffic lights. Small cars—Daewoo Matiz, Daewoo Lexias, Chev Lacettis, and old Ladas. Marshrutkas, the mini-mini buses with seven passengers at 20 cents a ride along the fixed route, swarm the area. They zip about, thin crafts of thin metal that break easily on impact, light on the road to gain maximum fuel production. And, of course, bigger buses often oozing their way to outlying places, packed so full with passengers that breathing is reduced. But it is the cars which rule. And their rule is "WATCH OUT!" It seems to me the drivers like to come as close as they can to pedestrians who like to offer themselves at every opportunity as they cross helter-skelter at main intersections. As close as they can with no thud.

I think maybe it's the protest of the bad times. If you're rich enough to own a car or lucky enough to get a driving job, it's your time for power. This is a land of enslavement in silence. No place for anger except impersonally on the road. *Swoosh* an inch from collision. The opportunity to kill many times a day. What a way to get anger out. To peek at control and still get to go home at night. Unless a mistake is made.

I walk out past the war memorial park with its wide clean tiles of space, its great hulking mournful mother statue, its small continuous flame, its plots of earth later to be green and its gazebos for lovers to sit in. This is the former Soviet Union and every town in the Soviet Union understands the meaning of war, of the blood that was lost.

I walk past the airport, which we are not allowed to use because an MSF honcho decided the planes from Nukus were not safe enough.

I walk past the cemetery. This is the same road to TB2, 19 kilometres out of town, the last five along a bumpy road across desert. The same road that a counsellor travels each day to minister to the patients there and, when passing the cemetery, pays respects. The walls hide all but the tops of some of the domes and low spires for family plots, but the cemetery goes on and on. I asked what it means when Aziz goes silent, puts the palms of his hands to his face and then sweeps them over to the side and down to the shoulders, similar to what polite Karakalpaks do when they finish eating and are about to leave the lunch table. He said: "I am asking that my blessings touch you who have died. Let my support go to you as food in your world. Let peace come to you and may you be blessed by God. And let my blessings reach each of you individually so that you won't all have to take from the same plate and thus someone not get enough, someone be left out and go hungry."

I walk past the bus station and the small bazaar beside it, the taxi stop, the junction toward another part of town. It is cold because of the wind and I wear my woollen toque. The sun is out. Then I have gone farther. I pass a restaurant. Some homes, low grey boxes with bare plots of earth around them. I pass a flock of goats crossing the road to the scrub on the other side. I follow them. We are on the land next to the walls that surround the airport runway. There is a turret up ahead on the corner in which a soldier stands with a rifle. Maybe he's a policeman. He watches me, watches the goats. Their long shaggy hair in mottled colours.

I decide to walk farther on this patch of desert by the airport and cross over to a neighbourhood, go through that neighbourhood to get to the farther part of the highway that leads past other subdivisions and out through the pure desert to Chimbay. I want to go to the pure desert. The neighbourhood is nice. Nothing there but the square grey homes of mud bricks, but lanes and roads criss-crossing, and nice. A nice energy. Few people are out. No one pays attention to me. I feel free.

Then I go around a corner and approach a car with hood opened beside a low walled house. I am almost past when a white dog comes out. He is barking and snarling. I angle out farther away on the lane, watch apprehensively. He's a medium height dog, barking intensely and telling me he doesn't know who the hell I am but I better keep going. I am happy to comply. He moves just a little closer, still barking angrily. I turn away to show him I am no threat, that I'm going else-where. And then ... then the little fucker bites me in the back of my leg. I pull away and yell. He lets go and backs up only a couple of metres challenging me to show my anger and try him out. I am furious. I scream at him to get away and I search around for a rock. He just keeps on barking. I don't want to move lest he come at me again. I want to get a rock and smash his head in. My leg hurts. Mercifully, the owner comes out and pulls the dog back into the house compound.

I walk on and find two rocks to be ready for another attack. My leg is bleeding just above the back of my ankle but the pant material is not ripped at all, so I conclude I am safe from rabies. Plus, this was just a dog protecting his turf. An asshole dog, not a rabid dog. I like dogs. I wanted to kill that fucker. Up ahead I see two other dogs coming in the distance. I clutch my rocks. The bastards. Word has already gotten around and now they'll all come after me. I like dogs, but they know I don't belong here. I'll be ready this time. But, hold it, there's a small footbridge going over the large drainage ditch. I can cross over and then, when I do pass those bastards, they will be separated by the wide ditch. No problem. But I don't want to let them force me to change my path out of fear.

I cross the footbridge. I'd rather be afraid than bitten. My rocks are not as accurate as teeth. Two sets of teeth.

Finally, I'm on the highway far out of town. I can leave it and walk out into the desert. I only need a couple of kilometres off the road to find what I'm looking for. Twenty minutes later and I'm lying on the sand making a sand angel. I never realized before how silent the desert is. I understand now why I needed to come here. This is a land ocean. It is more than us, has always and will always be more than us. I see small holes here and there where rodents live. I have seen a bug picking its way on the sand, but now when I am here all is still, all silent. Just me and the hardly noticeable breeze. The blue sky and the dropping sun as the afternoon fades. I am alone. I sit and let myself be. I am on the other side of the planet. This is my life. I am sand, moving ever so slightly each day, not able to stay nor fully decide where I'll be. I am millions of tiny pieces, memories, moments all loose together within the cells and molecules and spaces of my body. Sand within sand. Air, space, sand. All beneath the dropping sun. The patients, the counsellors and me. For now.

Then after half an hour I'm ready to walk back to the highway. It's been a two-hour walk, I'm tired, and my bitten leg hurts. As I near the highway, I phone for the MSF car to come to pick me up. I never had a cell phone until I got here, but it's obvious they have their use. I can go to the desert, stop in the middle of nowhere and call for a car. Nice. I formulate in my mind how to explain where I am. The guard and the driver will be impressed at how far out I have walked by myself. I bet other expats don't do that kind of hoofing. I phone. The guard answers. "Salaam alaikum. This is Calvin. Can I have a car pick me up?"

"Ah, Calvin, how are you? But, I'm sorry. Didn't Asker tell you on Friday that there are no cars available on Monday?"

Arrghh!

I'm glad it is not any later in the day, any darker or colder. I stand on the road and do what I've seen locals do. I wave my arm to try to get someone to stop. There are not so many cars now, fewer marshrutkas. *Whizz! Whizz!* Each one is going like a bat out of hell and each is full to the hilt. Geez, it's going to be harder than I thought. It wasn't my idea to walk the two hours back. I'm an expat.

Twenty minutes later and the breeze has picked up. Must not be many foreigners to have ever stood out here almost in the middle of nowhere trying to be a local where the locals wouldn't be standing. Maybe I should start walking. Hold it, an old red Lada is chugging to a halt. The seats are leaning back. I'm in. *Rachmit! Rachmit!* The only Karakalpak word I really know how to say properly. Maybe the most important word in every language.

Three kilometres later he's turning and I'm getting out. But this is where another road joins in and where marshrutkas from town go to. I'm soon in one and off to the bazaar, from where I can easily find my way home. I pass my 1000 sum note to the passenger in front of me, she passes it up to the driver. In a minute the change comes back same route. I feel pretty happy. Breaking MSF rules wasn't so bad.

☙

March 14

Islam is 24 and all he knows is death. And sickness. He lives on TB Street. Out here on the desert at the edge of town. The sand blowing anytime it wants, colouring all the colour of sand. Grains in numbers too high to measure. This boy has watched his sister die slowly, his mother die slowly. Both from MDR-TB. His father die slowly. From kidney failure. He's watched one younger brother make it through treatment to be cured. He now has another younger brother just starting with the disease. He is the boy from TB2 with beautiful eyes, and he's gotten fed up with being alone in his hospital room, fed up with the drugs and the side effects. He has stopped and come home to die. No more.

It is after work and Aziz has taken me here to see Islam. We are in his empty bedroom, only the cot he lies on, in his aunt's home. And a guitar propped against the wall. And a jar at the foot of the bed which he reaches for every so often to disgorge sputum into. He is but a long street waif in size now. Limp and waiting.

But he has beautiful, deep eyes. They are so the opposite of death. Bright eyes that would make you look twice when you see him, make you utter: "Who's that guy?" Deep, bright eyes that make you smile.

And now, Aziz and I speak to those eyes. We want them to speak to his body, tell it to go back on the drugs, tell it to live. We talk about death, about the losses he has suffered, about what we see in him. Aziz totally understands, and his translation mimics my tone, volume, spacing. My energy. Aziz adds his own words before we leave. Islam just lies there and maybe listens. Maybe not.

His fingers are long. Music fingers. He hated being alone in the room with no one to relate to, distract him from his memories. Hated eating alone. So he didn't eat. Maybe he will eat at home.

Afterwards we walk outside back down TB street and the other houses where patients live, our TB masks off. Darker evening air. I put my arm around Aziz. We both feel tired. We both know the boy's life is hanging. We don't know which way he'll go. Don't know if he comes back to treatment whether it will work anyway. He's so thin. Beautiful eyes. Green/brown, so bright, so sensitive.

March 16

Small fires have been lit in the desert. Spring fires, their flames cutting sky, flicking over the sand, dusk just starting. All as old as time.

Even before humans or animals walked. Fires burning. Dusk. Aynur has gone home and I am with Aziz again. We are in the darkening bedroom of Islam. The window still casts a dim light. His mattress has been moved to the floor, carpet all around, the empty cot where it was. The guitar still propped. The sputum jar beside him, near to the teapot brought in two hours before by his aunt.

He seems to be dying in front of us as his mother did in front of him. Breathing in short rasps like an engine. Face darkened, his bright beautiful eyes closed, looking inward, maybe seeking his parents, his sister. Will he be the first I have been close to that will die in this land of fear? I sit against the white wall near him. I've brought three bananas. He's not eating. His voice comes out almost in grunts. His death voice. His life voice. He doesn't want to live, doesn't care if he dies. He's so angry, so hurt but unable to release it. So he lies there as nature takes its course.

Aziz and I speak about being born to have life until life itself decides to leave us, not when we decide to leave. We say he can live. He needs to go back to the hospital. His other family members have died and filled him with grief and hopelessness but that does not mean he should die. We ask him to fight. We stroke his hair.

The minutes pass, the three of us in one-sided communion. Aziz and I take turns trying to sense into his psyche, trying to intuit the right words that will flick magic, trigger something in him to rebound. Anything to change what seems to be unfolding. Islam listens, his eyes mainly closed but every so often looking into ours. Finally, we are out of ideas, out of intuition. Our words have finished. We ready to rise and leave.

Islam looks over at me leaning against the wall. He cautions me that the white of the paint will leave powder on my dark winter coat.

⟋

March 17

I am in TB1 on the first floor. As soon as Aynur and I entered the room, Death moved ever so slightly. Three empty beds and a single patient named Oleg. Hours before he had begged Deelya, his counsellor, to help him die by smothering him with the pillow, his ashen skull wanting to have some say in what is befalling him. That's why I'm here. Deelya was upset. She likes Oleg, says he is kind and speaks beautiful Russian. But the way he looks he could be time teleported from Auschwitz. That's what TB does. Oleg, 40, pasted into the dull bed sheets. Skull, skin, bones. White hands reaching out to mine. Already dead.

We'd run, but there is no where to go. He wants to die. He has no one. He cries. Golden teeth arrayed in a skull grimace. I tell him it's not up to him. Tell him that death comes when it chooses and right now it's not here, that life is, so live. I have to leave, but I say I'll come back in the morning.

In the evening, the visiting Spanish doctor tells me that she met him earlier that day. She was shocked. "He is starving to death. He needs someone to care about him, to feed him." She is angry. I tell her that Oleg wanted Deelya to kill him.

&

March 18

I am back to see Oleg. His eyes are brighter. He tells me how his father died not long ago, how his half-brother arrived for the funeral. The half-brother is a drunk and a criminal and was never in the picture until the father died. He stole things before he returned to his own town. Oleg says he has no one. His eyes are blue. But his hands are as white as a corpse's. I ask if the food is too salty. He nods, says he only drinks juice but it is too sweet. Can I bring him any food from the bazaar? No, it's no use, he says. He doesn't want anything. We talk about Deelya, about how he thinks she needs a husband. He laughs. He says maybe I can bring him some apricot jam.

I tell him I will later in the afternoon. He speaks weakly now, face flat on his pillow. Gazes off into nowhere, tells about a girl he loved in Russia. He planted watermelons and fixed cars when he lived in Russia. Not far from Lake Baikal. He was an expert mechanic. The girl would not return here with him. He never married. I ask if I can bring him melon from the bazaar on Saturday. He doesn't think there will be melon, far too early in the season. But, yes, it would be nice.

At the end of the day I come again with apricot jam. He leans up on an elbow. Golden smile. Tastes the fruit. Death moves again.

March 19

I'm not sure I completely fit in with MSF. I do the job I'm here for, doing it as fully and best as I can, but I think I'm a bit of a misfit in that I can't not be personal with all the patients. I can't be detached. When I am in the hospitals I avoid being with any of the doctors either Ministry of Health or MSF. I stay away from them. I go to the patients.

I've set up my counsellors to be stationed in specific sites. Some at polyclinics, and Aziz, Murat, Altinay and me the residential counsellors at TB2. Kairat at TB1. I ask the counsellors to start each morning at the hospital by going from room to room and shaking hands with each patient, to look them in the eyes and say good morning. I ask them to stay away from the ducks when they do their rounds. My counsellors have gone through real hesitation about me because I wasn't the PhD with whom they had bonded and because my style is so intimate. They felt safer with Jenny because she was organized, systematic, had a more "professional" approach. They used a written Plan of Care for each patient to sign. There was lots of paperwork with Jenny and it worked nicely for the team. It gave them all a sense of accomplishment. I rant about spending more time with the patients and less with the pen. I insist on riding in the back of the Landcruiser and the back of the cars rather than automatically take the more comfortable front seat assumed to be for the expat, the boss. I'm not a good boss.

I tell the counsellors that the counsellor is the counselling. That psychotherapy is human to human. That we give our warmth, our openness, our acceptance to be with the patient. We walk with them.

When some patients ask Aynur if I am a doctor or psychiatrist or what, I still tell her to say that I am a human. Sometimes, I tell the patients that I am unable to speak Karakalpak or Uzbek or Russian but I can speak with my eyes and touch and I can sense them through their eyes and tones and body language. Some patients I only shake hands with and make eye contact. The ones in whom I can sense more receptivity or need, I touch more, hug, hold.

And I say to the counsellors that they can give that openness, that warmth, that humanity also. The doctors and nurses don't and can't. We can. The patients will be more likely to stay on the arduous treatment and its side effects for the two years if they know they are valued, wanted, respected, seen as human beings, as individuals. Then the actual counselling words and interactions come later and work better.

From the start, I have had to let go of all preconceptions and answers. The counsellors want more skills and are afraid they don't have enough answers. I tell them there are no answers. It is so clear when working with so many who are suffering from this terrible disease and its treatment side effects that the only answer is truth, is being as deeply connected to the patients as possible so as to give them the steel they need to stay on the treatment and thus live and, at least for their part, stem the epidemic. And only by going into oneself, one's own being, can a counsellor go into the patient's being and connect on a deep enough level to forge a bond.

I think they are slowly realizing that I don't want them to forget anything they learned, just add this new direction, this new understanding. And of course, their previous direction had finished what it could do. It wasn't going to go further to improve the patients' treatment adherence rate. With translation it is so hard to convey precision in the concepts that I'm trying to have the counsellors internalize. The depth of what it means to live the concepts, to understand what it means to *be* with the patient, what it really means to pay attention, listen, and respond to the truth of the patient and not only follow the "manual" they have been given. They can hear the words in translation, but they often stay words. I'm not so sure it wouldn't be just as difficult to communicate the same with professionals from the English speaking world.

Each day here I feel vulnerable. Each day I meet with patients or the counsellors I feel fear. I know I don't know anything. I'm just going forward, facing what's in front of me, thinking, feeling, extending. The safety I have is that I can immediately recognize two things: one, no one else knows what to do; and two, so many beautiful people are suffering. The medical interactions by the Ministry of Health personnel can be hit and miss from region to region in terms of obtaining lab specimens, administering drugs, advising patients, and even supplying all the drugs. Plus, there are hundreds of children in wards who are without any supportive counselling. We—me and my crew—only reach a tiny minority of those who suffer in the province, and they are almost all adult, occasionally late teens. There may be no hope here. Only the hope we give those we can give hope to. Thus, we only do the best we can.

The patients tell us how they can't eat the hospital food. The hospitals provide either no food or substandard food. MSF was subsidizing it for several years but are pulling out now and hoping the Ministry of Health will take over. In Karakalpakstan, it doesn't work that way. There will be no reliable standard of food care or otherwise. In too many ways it's a broken, unresponsive system from the top down. Everyone scared of saying the truth, taking risks. The patients all survive as best they can. Or not.

I think a lot about Oleg, Deelya's suicidal patient. He has a full upper set of golden-coloured teeth—people here often have that, not real gold but golden-coloured metal coating. In his eyes I still see strength. He said he wanted to die that first meeting. And when we talked a bit, he began crying. It was this sad, painful grimace of tears. I told him that he was going to die, but that it would come on its own time and that his job like all of ours was to live until it came, to learn, that there was a reason for him to still be living. Later when I brought him some pieces of sweet melon, his face was filled with life. Filled with openness and gratitude. He said thank you. I thanked him. I could see that he had allowed me to be part of this basic human exchange, this deep intimacy of spirit. His humanity and my humanity were touching. This simple, straightforward exchange of hearts. Fully equal. No giver and taker. Just two hearts. In time, Oleg might recover after all. I will try to see that he gets nutritious food. Or he may be dead by Monday. It is the way it will be.

March 21

I just smelled my face with my hand. I could smell MDR-TB on my skin—the smell from when I am with patients.

March 22

I was trying to figure out how come it is so easy for me to have this deep bonding and mutual appreciation with patients. I think I know why. I look at the people on the streets and feel no connection or resonance. But then I realize that no one is looking at each other except in passing, quickly, and absorbed in their own realities. When I go into the hospital MDR wards, I go looking as deeply as I can into their eyes. I am totally open, wanting them to see me, know my soul. I can't speak and can't be part of their culture or change anything in their condition other than be myself. So I offer this and my hand. They in turn are so cut off, so alone with their illness and the side effects, so bored in these bare rooms that, when I come in, they too are really looking, really looking to see. And thus we meet. We truly meet, and this strange but beautiful connectedness occurs that transcends personality, culture, language, past or future. Just all now.

I sit on the floor of room 10 with the women, of varying ages in this room of open eyes. I lead them in my *om mani padmi hum* chant, adapted from a Tibetan Buddhism university course that I took many years back. The idea is to stretch out the sounds and fix one's focus only on the sound and the breathing. I want to add something to their day, something to take their minds off the boredom and waiting. Something to compete with the side effects. The chant, because it is sustained sound, creates its own entity. This draws everyone away from their usual consciousness. It calms and brings peace for the minutes it lasts. And it is outrageous in this context.

The counsellors said it couldn't work because the patients' lungs are so harmed. That they couldn't sustain the breathing for each sound. But I decide to do it anyway. Try it, see what works and what can't. We sit in a rough circle. Roza, 21, is next to me. Beautiful, olive skin, long brown curls, shining eyes, she has only been in TB2 for a month. She was made to get an abortion when the MDR was diagnosed. Her husband understands how serious the treatment is but his family pesters her to come home, to be there doing her duties. Eyes closed, the women and I chant. *OHHHHHHHHHMMMMMMM* ....

I hear Roza sounding this alien, never-heard-before sound as though she'd always done it. On the other side is a little woman, her voice also resonating and travelling out to the middle of the circle. We chant for ten minutes and then stop. Everyone opens their eyes. They seem shocked at where they've just been. Shocked in a good way. They smile. So then, I ask them to get together in pairs, to sit back to back for some touching exercises. This time a visualization while they hold each other's hands and feel each other's backs and breathing. When this is over, we talk. They really dig it. All of it.

I was afraid to try these exercises. Afraid of seeming crazy. Afraid no one would participate. Or they would just stare and laugh. That might have been just as good.

🙽 There is that big cemetery on the way out of town, going toward the north, on the highway to Chimbay and its freezing outpatient ward for the MDR-TB patients who cough their way there every day for the plastic cups of pills, injection, chaser fluids, its four-story hospital with no running water except for the thin pipe flowing from one outside corner to which all the patients bow with their plastic Coke bottles for a partial day's supply to cook with wash with drink with, its outside hole in the ground toilets mounded with detritus and remnants of excrement. Chimbay hospital where the sick go to receive treatment.

The big cemetery is really big. Walled for kilometres. Within are domes and castles and hives of intricate brickwork, tombs for the series of dead down through the decades. If it wasn't for the entrance requirement it would be a great place to reside.

But it is another, much smaller cemetery that draws more of my real attention. I have come here this late afternoon in search of a shorter route to my house. A furrowed roadway fronts the layered graves—some fenced, others not, ornate tombstones or not, dried, rusted, withered trellises and weeds and sticks protecting the plots, delineating these final homes. There are faces etched in photographic detail, start dates, expiry dates, stone chiselled in form, sadness carved to memory to lives lived. Love. It all begins and ends with love. But in this cemetery, another death has taken over. These graves are forgotten. They have become the earth. Like an empty landscape of old car wrecks or abandoned scrap metal or unwanted thrustings of huge broken pieces of concrete. Yet they are graves. People within that earth. Bodies, bone, hair, clothing in boxes, maybe now only dust, but dwelling there nonetheless, the molecules, the smidgeons of those who laughed, groaned, wept, waited, dreamed.

It is past mid-March. The winter has passed, and there was snow in the desert. There was a thin carpet of snow, and it was cold. Minus 25 some mornings. And we all shivered and spoke of it, how it bit us when the wind blew. How the drains froze, and water stopped. But the winter has gone, and days now are bright with blue. Ravens no longer slump and turn their grey beaks into their necks as they hunch for warmth on the stark, bare branches. They banter instead with the magpies, annoyed with their more stately strut, charming set of tails. And every one of us is lighter, pleased with ourselves and the day.

But, in this neglected cemetery whispers truth. Not just the end we all will face. And it does not nor never will detract from joy or thrill or expectation. No, the end here is told by the salt. The graves, the road, the slumping mounds of earth, the intent to honour, all shrouded in white salt, caked like a fungus. Everywhere. Creeping. Oozing. Ugly, waiting, growing, swarming salt.

March 23

I have brought out all nine of my counsellors to TB2 hospital. I've been here many times already building the relationship with the patients. Now I want to try something bigger, and I've arranged for the patients to gather in the central area so I can talk to them all at once with my counsellors there to hear and be seen. Just over 60 of the 80 patients have gathered. I begin my oration. Aynur has a bit of an idea of what I am going to say. This is a strange diversion for everyone. Sick people cajoled to stand or sit collectively, more infectious from ward 1 over to the left, farther from the ones from ward 2. And what for?

The nutty foreign counsellor wants to talk? I bellow out how over the centuries people have fought invasions of foreign armies, fought for their lands and people. Vietnam, Afghanistan, etc. And I say now they here in Karakalpakstan are fighting an invasion — namely the epidemic. I say how those other fighters withstood great hardships, having to hide in mountains and jungles and suffer for years, how they did that to serve their nation, people, communities, families. And so, I say: "You, too, are doing the same and for the same reasons. This epidemic is as great a threat as an invasion."

I said how heroic, how honourable their journey — two years of terrible side effects and terrible illness — how great that fight is. I tell them that I and the counsellors are with them on that fight. That we will be with them and understand them for the full two years. And I say that they are more than the illness, the side effects, that they are not just patients but that they are individuals. Full individuals with full lives much greater than this time of sickness. Then I ask Aziz to speak.

He explains that we will start small classes in Russian, English, and art so that they can have activities to take their minds off the drug side effects. Afterwards we give each a large notebook and a pen and pencil and ask them to start writing their stories, writing about their lives, and bring these stories to their counsellors.

They have patiently listened. At our finish, they clap and conversations start humming. It seems they basically get the drift. Then something unexpected happens. A guy, maybe 40, asks if he can sing a song. Everyone goes silent and the guy opens up into this great voice. A song that echoes and rises and goes on and on as he strides around as though on a large stage. Hands out and singing with joy. During the song, people clap rhythmically. One woman dances. It finishes without words, just sound undulating and holding the note, letting it flow throughout the halls.

They aren't patients. They are human beings.

The odd thing is that, as I and all the counsellors were on our way into the hospital, one of the main Ministry of Health doctors, Ayeesha, started screaming at us that we had no right to just walk in without first going to the office and informing the chief doctor that we were there. She was going ballistic from across the garden. We all stopped dumfounded. Swearing and screeching, Doctor Ayeesha went into the office chalet. I followed to explain and calm her down while the counsellors nervously waited outside.

She continued screaming in the building. I kept trying to intercede with her fury. I had to yell equally loud to get her attention. When I yelled to compete with her tirade, Aynur yelled to mimic my voice. The doctor ranted and swore and shook her head. I held my hands out and implored her to give me a chance to speak, countering that she did not understand. Aynur followed me about the room with her hands out and yelling the translation just as loudly trying to get the doctor to listen. It was a real movie.

The misguided Ayeesha had been away when it was discussed the day earlier with the chief doctor but no one had informed her. Eventually I got her a bit calmer. I don't think I've heard the last of that doctor.

∅

March 24

Islam has gone back to the hospital. I am astonished. We have been to his home six of the past 10 evenings for long and short visits. He is very thin, very weak and we had to push the TB2 doctor to re-admit him. She agreed to put him in acute care in a bed by himself, but she insisted it would be better for him to die at home than in the hospital. We don't believe he has to die. He had decided to come back because his sister came home from Kazakhstan and pleaded with him and because he knew we would be there with him.

Before coming out to see him, I had Aziz ask him over the phone—as sick as anyone gets, the cell phone is a constant—if I could bring him some food. He told us what he'd like. So we arrived to see him shortly after he got re-admitted. His frail body is stretched onto the bed in the Intensive Care Unit and they are prepping an ECG or something to determine what condition he is in to decide what drug regimen he can tolerate.

On our way, I told Aziz we'd know when we saw Islam what to do. In the past few visits he'd gone from looking close to death to robust to close to death again. Aside from the progression of the disease, what factored in was his sadness, and readiness to quit, to die. I alerted Aziz that if his eyes looked finished I'd tell him so and I'd say we would be with him to the end but if, as opposed to the doc's pronouncement, I could see life in his eyes, I'd tell him that and say he will live, that I want him to live.

When we get closer to his bed, I look in his eyes. Weak, tired, but … the sharp brightness, the beautiful depth that has compelled me and Aziz from the start. Soon, he is eating some of the food we have brought. I stroke his head and tell him I want him to eat, sleep, take the drugs and get strong. That he should live. That I believe in him.

Is any of this the right thing to do with Islam? Who could ever say what is right or wrong. I, though, can say with absolute certainty, that it is necessary to do something. Why not begin with love?

𝒪 Each day is so varied in terms of mind shifts. My poor translator, Aynur, who only started three weeks ago—a 29-year-old mom of a two-year-old son who has had no prior experience with hospitals, TB, patients or counselling—feels like she's been inside a whirlwind emotionally. I've also started doing the first personal counselling sessions with all my non-English speaking counsellors. A way to push my counsellors to open up to me—open up their own pain/fear lives—so that they can open to their patients and have a greater reach to bond with, understand what they hear and see. Not exactly something MSF would advise. And Aynur, having known them for this short time, has to hear and translate all their inner lives, then relate to them the rest of the time as though nothing was shared. The emotional nakedness is just a bit strange for her.

The first counsellor I counsel is Kuanish, 30, a big guy, quiet, slow to smile. I have already seen his fear in other instances and seen him willing to show it, though he is a terse talker. Instead of letting him lead, I shoot straight in and, surprisingly, he goes with it. He tells me of being little and hearing his father beat his mother, of how his father always rejected him, never supported, never acknowledged, and how deeply that had hurt him. He lets his tears emerge, wipes at them as though they are a betrayal. Showing vulnerability was his choice, but now it frightens him. I put my hand to the side of his face to touch him gently. What a man.

Then comes Kairat, another 30-year-old male counsellor. He starts by telling how happy his life has been. He's a counsellor I quite like, but he hates me asking him questions. He just wants to be told, wants answers, wants to stay inside the lines. So I go along with him and we begin talking about how his grandparents raised him and how much he loved them and they him, and how his grandpa died three years ago and how devastated he was and how he cared for him as he was dying in the hospital. I tear up as he speaks, as he tells me how deeply he loved. This vulnerability might be the start to the rest that will come.

I keep learning more directly how fear competes with salt to scourge this place. For 70 years or so, Uzbekistan was run by the Soviets. One counsellor's grandfather was executed under Stalin's rule. Everyone knew the power of the gulag, the bullet. Everyone knew what not to say. That informers were the rule, and one could not be sure who was the enemy. So it was best not to speak, better yet, not to think. The whole society lived with one eye closed, one part of the brain turned off. If the authorities said something was a reality then it was. If the authorities said something was not true then it wasn't. If they said that the people are happy and well off then that was true. My counsellors comment that it is a norm that, when the boss laughs at something, everyone laughs.

When the Soviet Union finally collapsed, the internalized fear remained. And when President Karimov took over in Uzbekistan, the

KGB became National Security. Everyone understands that they are not safe unless they follow the rules, stay away from controversy.

In Karakalpakstan there is virtually no literature or writing of any kind being written and none being read. It costs money to publish and everything must be first vetted by the security offices. With television so prevalent, reading for pleasure, stimulation, or learning is not necessary. In Soviet times, there was access to and interaction with Russian literature and Russian writing. During the past twenty years of the post-Soviet era, the use of Russian has diminished drastically. There are no book stores in Karakalpakstan. At the used bazaar, a few stalls sell piles of old books. Tabloid "newspapers" are fluff. Yet, the large statue erected in the centre of the expanse of greenery and fountains that front the President of Karakalpakstan's huge palace is of Berdakh, the 19th century Karakalpak poet. And everyone speaks fondly and respectfully of Berdakh.

Many Karakalpaks believe they have historically been discriminated against by the Uzbek authorities. It is said that a much higher ratio of Karakalpaks than Uzbeks were sent into the Second World War. How favouritism started in the east of the country and never reached the west. The Aral Sea disaster has piggy-backed on the fear. Everyone understands how their health and the health of their children has been impacted. No one is surprised to develop a disease.

So Many Flowers in a Desert

Gulnara — flower of pomegranate
Gulistan — flower garden
Gulsara — selected flowers
Gulbahar — the flower of spring
Guljan — favourite flower
Gulimkhan — flower-king
Gulayim — lady-flower (queen)
Gulbasara — Sunday flower
Gulbadan — flower wind
Guldana — clever flower
Guljawhar — flower pearl
Gulnaz — tender flower
Gulmira — flower of love
Gulzada — noble flower
Gulsanem — beautiful flower
Guljihra — radiant flower: a flower that shines like a sunbeam
Gulshad — flower of joy
Gulsima — flower-look, in appearance
Gulziyra — flower ziyra (ziyra is seasoning that Uzbeks put into plov)
Amangul — healthy flower
Almagul — apple flower
Irisgul — wealthy flower
Perdegul — curtain flower
Kizlargul — lady's flower
Sapargul — journey flower

Arzigul—dream flower

Marjangul—pearl flower

Bazargul—a Sunday flower

Jumagul—a Friday flower

Aygul—moon flower

Ayimgul—a lady flower (queen)

Xayitgul—a holiday flower (xayit is a Muslim holiday)

Qalligul—a flower is birthmarks/mole (parents give this name to girls
    who are born with lots of birthmarks or moles on their faces, in
    the hope that, given this name, they will disappear)

Tazagul—a clean flower

Shakhargul—a city flower

Nazigul—tender flower

Sarigul—yellow flower

Bibigul—a lady flower (Mrs. Flower)

Danagul—wise flower

Ziybagul—a beautiful flower

Altingul—a golden flower

Kurbangul—sacrifice flower

March 25

I'm on a home visit with Aynur and Kairat. We do that when a patient
needs to be convinced to enter treatment or when, once started, a patient has run away from treatment either in the hospital phase or in the
ambulatory polyclinic phase. This one, Kairat's patient, is 14 and already
had been eight months in treatment. Her name is Altingul. Altingul
means golden flower. I'll call her young Altingul, young gold here in the
desert. She's sitting on a bed facing us. This is her home. Her 10-year-old
brother has gone into the other room to do his school work. Altingul
does not look at us, her folded arms tight to her body, eyes far away.
Our words like distant natterings. We are adults, two men and one
woman. All against her. Against her and her dead mother, her broken
lungs, her fragile grip on these small moments. Against her decision.

She wants there to be no disease in her. No treatment. No more to be taken from her. Wants to forget about how her mom died from MDR only a year ago. She has folded her arms and willed it to stop. She just wants to be 14. I tell her I work with teenagers like her in Canada. I tell her I'll come again.

Then at TB1.

Death was made to watch Oleg peel the chunk of smoked sausage. Now it watches further as Oleg reaches for the full cup of semi-sweet red wine I have smuggled in to him. There is a deep focus in his eyes when he sees the forbidden wine. In his large white hand, the white cup rises to his lips, golden teeth. Tilting back in one long, sighing, defiant thrust, he swallows, swallows, swallows. The cup goes back to the shelf. He lowers back to the bed. Death watches Oleg lying back on his pillow, a straight red trickle on his chin.

TB2.

At TB2 now that the warmer days are here, all the patients break their days up by going outside, sitting in the sun, visiting with each other, bracing themselves to endure the side effects, and just waiting for time to pass. Then they go back inside, lie on their beds, watch the one TV in the common area, visit, and wait for time to pass. The patients in ward two have it better because they can gather in the large lunch room and together enjoy the meals they concoct. Whenever our MSF car drives through the gate and into the grounds, everyone outside watches. A car. Something to break the monotony. Different faces. Maybe some new person. Just the newness of the sound, matter and motion that wasn't there the rest of the day.

I have started bringing my camera so I can take photos of whoever wants one. Later I bring them the prints. Everyone wants a photo. Arms cradling each other as though life before never was. The brash, unaware smiles for my camera. These brief respites from the boredom and the nausea. They stand in the sun in the free air. Farther away around the corner, some are playing with the new ball I have brought, bouncing it and flinging at the basket. It has been a long time since there was a ball at the hospital. The doctors are convinced it is too dangerous, that should it hit a chest there could be haemorrhaging.

Inside, down the dim hallway in the more infectious ward, three women dance to a tune on a DVD. Earlier in the morning after the drug intake, they were outside on their haunches in small packs. Together but alone. Alone with the ordeal inside them. Magpies bounced on the furrows only a few metres away. Young sparrows flew freely away from the leafless poplars into the spring blue. The women waited with their pulsating nausea to find out whether it would force them to vomit up their pills, force them to return to swallow twenty more.

Another home visit.

Aynur and I are in their living room again with Nazigul, their regular counsellor. This patient has refused treatment for the past six weeks and will be declared a defaulter soon, formally thrown out of the program. Be forgotten about. She in her purple nightgown, husband without a shirt, they had no idea we were coming. Here, it's normal to just arrive, knock on a door and then walk in. *Salaam alaikum.* Homes are meant to be visited.

The 11-year-old daughter from her first marriage stands beaming at the three of us in our duck masks. We are so large and straight and filled with this power to just arrive and expect to be welcomed, make them scurry to place mats on the floor for us to sit. Us and them. Us, who want to change the mother's life. Make her sick each day, make her shake with fear over the daily drug misery. Husband, trapped with their twin five-year-olds and death whispering from every dark corner in the flat, the three children not an iota of awareness that their lives are being determined. And her. Her eyes roll. She is being told that those around her could die if she doesn't capitulate and resume treatment. She quakes at the idea of seeing the drugs again. I guarantee we can help. I say Nazigul will train her, ground her inside herself, that she will then access inner strength. She shakes her head. They just want us to leave but don't want to be impolite.

Next, a pre-admission in the regular TB ward of TB1. I want to be experienced in all the duties my counsellors perform. Preadmission is the delightful task of meeting with a patient whose test results have finally come in. Finally come in to show that, instead of regular TB and its short, doable treatment program, they have MDR-TB and that their life has just changed.

Her sister walks her into us, frail, the brittle breathing of bird bones, a rasp in and out. Into the room to meet us so we can deliver the sentence. Two years of the worst yet to come. It's not TB it's MDR-TB. She can only walk with help now. She is hard of hearing. Her chest hurts. Her throat hurts from a goitre. Any eyes would say she hasn't long to live. But I tell her she can do it. I lie. She is scared. Her eyes show a tear in each corner. She wipes at them and smiles: "I will just have to be strong."

Her sister asks if their mother can live in the hospital with her, to help her. This patient's name is Kurbangul. She is 26 and she likes to sing, to watch movies, to laugh. So many *guls* here. So many flowers, all bearing colourful petals.

We walk her back to her room. Her hand grips mine as tightly as her memories of the times she was unafraid of the next day. I tell her I will bring her chocolates at TB2. Kurbangul. I ask Aynur to repeat the name to me several times so, when she arrives at TB2, I can greet her as though I know her.

⌀

March 26

Young Altingul sends him out of the room. She doesn't like him talking about her, to her, for her. Her father talks a lot. She is silent. He leaves. Ahhh, we all relax, including him. My cell phone rings. I instantly give it to her. She speaks to Aziz who is shocked to hear a young Karakalpak voice when he has phoned me. We are all part of the moment, the joke. We laugh. Ahhh. I take her hand and squeeze it. I loosen the grip just a little. This is how we can ease the side effects. Just a little. Her headaches, nausea, pain in the legs. Her fear. Eight months she did the treatment. All the while looking for her dead mother. Alone. She doesn't want to start again. I like this young Altingul, her anger, her hard-headedness.

Later, back in the ground floor of TB1, I visit Oleg before calling it a day. Death wasn't sure what to do in the room today as Oleg sat upright. He got into his pants, faded blue jeans. A pale purple windbreaker jacket with wide lapels and green at the sash, and a grey toque. Tilted on his head as though a fashion photographer was ready to shoot. The stubble on his cheeks so ready and waiting to breathe, the gauntness almost hidden. I do take his photo but only of my head and his, no bodies in this photo. I ask if I can bring anything tomorrow, something from the bazaar. He shakes his head. Then he reconsiders. He points up at the light fixture on the ceiling. "You can bring me a light bulb. That one is burnt out." I ask if the hospital doesn't supply them. He laughs full and shakes his head: "Noooooo! Noooooo! Of course not."

Today, he is Oleg. Death could only stare. Blinking. I imagine Oleg in his dark room once the dusk faded and night arrived. Hoping I bring a bulb.

Later in Chaynaya, a teahouse cafe, I drink black tea with Aziz. We are winding down the long week. He says he was supposed to go with TB1 counsellor Kairat and another guy from the MSF office to a restaurant. They have gone to eat dog meat. He has chosen this time to visit with me instead. He has a dog that he pets when he walks over the hard earth alongside the grey walls of the new family home he has built with his father, the patriarch of the family, a doctor. They all live together: father, mother, daughter, the two sons and their wives. Plus the children. Aziz has two now and one on the way. He worries about his sister's little three-year-old daughter. His sister is troubled. They have helped her to separate from her exploitive husband, but she is unhappy. The child even more so.

Aziz loves cartoons. He wants to bring art supplies out to TB2 and big sheets of paper, spread them out on the cement floor and have the patients draw cartoons. Aziz says that, when he and his friends eat dog meat, they sometimes joke about the dog. *This piece is from a dog that had the mange. This one is from a dog that had only three legs.*

☞ On Saturday, at the bazaar there is an old man sitting on the floor inside the main building. He is right at the corner near the entrance. He is sitting alone in his long, grey overcoat, his tiny wisp of white beard, grey fedora large on his head. Before him on a cloth are eight or nine bundles of tied green onions. The aisles everywhere else are laden with walnuts, raisins, dried apricots, honey, chocolate bars, cartons and cartons and cartons. All decked out in symmetric arrays and stacks. There he is with his green onions quiet on the floor. Waiting.

We walk over to him and I ask Deelya to thank him for being there. Looking up at us, he in turn thanks us for the kind words. And suddenly he is holding out his hands, palms to the air. Deelya says we should hold out our hands as well, the same palms up way, in order to receive the blessing he is giving. Sometimes the old do this, she says. His mouth has no teeth, but his quiet words are like music, his eyes alive with earnest joy. He asks for us to have kindness and safety during this day. His skin is smooth and tanned.

I buy a bundle of his green onions. As we walk away, Deelya says his face is like a baby's.

☞ On Sunday we visit Gulishan. She is my pregnant counsellor, who once suffered from meningitis but has healed nicely. She is also a trained doctor but has never practised because she got sick and then took the better paying job of MSF counsellor. She is seven months pregnant and her baby swells her belly, pushing the bright blue pant suit into a sky. She walks inside the sky, carrying it with her each step. I have seen her touch patients with such deep compassion it is as though she was a holy person. Only 30, her deep eyes glow with understanding. She is divorced. It had been a mistake to marry her husband and enter into that extended family. Not a mistake to get pregnant. She is happy.

I ask what it is like to be about to have a baby with no husband. She stops smiling. Her eyes water. Cheeks shudder. She cries.

"My son will have no father. A boy should have a father." She goes on to explain that she had no hesitation to leave her husband. There is shame in divorce in Karakalpakstan. And family and neighbours gossip. The lash of gossip cuts especially deep in this culture. But Gulishan did not care. She knew after a few months that her character and expectations would never match with her husband's or her husband's family. They saw her as a servant—how most Karakalpak families see the daughter-in-law. They saw her as someone to stay silent when problems arose. They saw her as someone to receive daily criticisms and beratings. Her husband sided with his mother, joined in with the berating.

How could a baby be raised in such an environment? So, Gulishan packed her things and went back to her own parents' home in Hodjeli.

How are things with your ex-husband now? I ask. As the birth nears, what involvement does he offer? She shakes her head and says he sends her text messages. He sends one a week threatening to come after her and beat her, to come once the baby is born and kill him. "Are you scared?" I ask. "You must be stressed by that!"

She laughs, eyes twinkle a bit. "No, not at all. I know him. He is a coward. He can only talk, never do. But I am worried about my baby's future health. Yesterday, I visited a patient, she's a treatment failure now. Her body is wasting. All of her is dying, becoming nothing. I had forgotten what it looks like."

 The people who get TB and MDR-TB are seldom the rich or the educated. They are usually from the lower economic classes. Less commitment to infection control, poorer nutrition, more familiar with losing, more prone to unaddressed illnesses which sap strength, weaken immunity, and more likely to know death intimately. They are also more inclined to open up to foreigners, believe they have superior tools to help them or intercede on their behalf. More inclined to smile and appreciate.

When the car brings us out to TB2, it is a sign for the patients. A sign that they exist, are not forgotten about. A sign of hope. At TB1, the far bigger complex within the city, it's the same only they can't see the car coming.

The car takes us everywhere. TB1, TB2, TB3 for philosopher Natasha and Leonard Cohen Massor, nine polyclinics where the MDR patients go to their separate treatment corner while all the other people in need from that section of the city spend hours and bribes in queue for x-rays, blood tests, eye exams, prescriptions, examinations, pregnancy check-ups and on and on. The car takes us out to Chimbay and along the bumpy back roads to outlying clinics and pop-in health huts. But this is only a part of Karakalpakstan. Only if someone lives in these places can they get treatment for MDR-TB. These are the lucky parts of this region.

Being in that car means having to have something to offer.

April 2

Venyera. When I first saw her she was on the bed in TB2 wailing as her mother tried to comfort her. She seemed all shoulders and sobs. Dark hair coming down over her forehead and partly covering one side over her eyes. I tried to see into them but she was wailing and moving about. I couldn't reach her. The next day she was in her wheelchair and complaining about not having any music to listen to, nobody her own age—17—to visit with her. I brought her my iPod, some music from my part of the world and various other places. Later, she told me the iPod battery had died. She hadn't much liked the music anyway.

On another day, I talked with her outside. The trees were beginning to green and it was sunny and warmer. She was in her wheelchair, her mother nearby, and with two of the other girls at TB2. Her eyes were deep and aware. She was no longer being difficult. She asked about the meaning of life and spoke with maturity and depth about impermanence. She said she wished she was strong enough to walk. Her mother and I took one side each and lifted her. The stick legs shaking, but determined. No point in wondering and hoping. Give it a shot. She stood. But only for a few seconds. We brought her back down to the seat of the chair. A white, plastic lawn chair on wheels.

Later, on a Saturday afternoon, I came out to TB2 to visit the patients without a translator. I brought along a new expat to meet them, see our hospital. We entered her room. She was crying. I went to her, but she started screaming. "Kamila! Kamila! Kamila!" over and over. Her friend didn't come but her mother did. She was scared, eyes large, wondering if we had done something to her daughter. We backed out the door. The screaming had unsettled us.

Then, a week or more later, after the National Day celebrations and the small prizes she won for her needlework, I took photos. Her and a friend. Her and Aziz. Her and me. When I got them made into prints, I was surprised at how sad her eyes looked. I hadn't noticed. Tired eyes yes, but I didn't see the sadness. Bright young girl, the kind of energy the young have despite themselves, despite whatever affliction haunts them. It was always easier to see just that. Want just that.

Three days ago when I said good-bye to her outside with her sun visor on, the other girls nearby, she looked sad again. Yet, Kamila told me today that they had only yesterday been outside together having fun. There had been several of the younger girls chatting in the afternoon, the drugs having worn off, their bodies and moods coming normal again. They laughed. Venyera had told them she wished she could walk. They all talked about visiting each other's homes when they eventually got discharged from the hospital. Then early this morning, when Kamila had finished washing her hair, someone told her Venyera had died in the night. Now, just before lunch I have found out. Just like that. Gone.

Her mother had been living in her car outside the hospital the past month while she was in hospital. Was with her every day. Mom and daughter. Frail daughter. Now, just mom. Far away from the hospital. The last photos with her sad eyes.

Venyera, her name was Venyera.

⌀

April 2

This is the sixth time we've come to young Altingul's house trying to get her to go back on treatment. Aynur is no longer afraid of the withered mother dog outside, teats all stretched and her puppies yipping beneath the porch. They will soon call Altingul a defaulter, forget about her if she doesn't start the drugs again. But she's 14 and she does not want to go to hospital, does not want the injections anymore. Her lungs have become worse, we've been told. She sits on the bed as usual staring straight ahead, away from me. When I asked her before if she wants me to stop coming, she would never answer. I'd try to engage her in conversation. Sometimes we'd talk. Then I'd come around to asking if she was ready yet. Instantly, a click of the teeth. Not as impolite as if a westerner did it, merely a Karakalpak way of saying no without giving any energy to actual words. *Click!*

Today, I am more persistent. We don't want her to die. To infect her 10-year-old brother. I try all the cadences I can. Go over past arguments. Push, back off, change subject, cajole, plead, reason, threaten to carry her off. She laughs, says this is exactly how she goes about getting her little brother to do something she wants. Ahhh, finally, she gets it. "So, we'll bring a car tomorrow for you, okay?" *Click!*

Later, a driver and I drink tea in the cafe after work. He tells me he loves his wife spiritually and physically. He is hers. But. But he will have sex with other women if he feels the urge, has the chance. Seldom. But it happens. Whenever there is a party or a gathering, individuals often come to it without their partners or families. His wife complains. He says, it's only the body, his urge. Not him. He is hers, he tells her. If she did the same, while he was away in another country for months say, if she did the same, how would he feel, I ask. He says it scares him to think of that.

April 3

Venyera has been dead a day now. The first day of her afterlife. Her death. The hollow of her death is nestled inside my own lungs as I walk into Sergei's wedding.

Two hundred people in the hall. We are grouped around tables according to affiliations. His relatives on his father's side. His relatives on his mother's side. His wife's relatives on her father's side. Lots and lots of relatives. And the MSFers whom he works with every day in his job of delivering TB educational materials to schools.

Salads, snacks, bread, fruit, tea, pop, wine, beer, vodka, juice crowd the tables. Decorations. Everyone dressed up. The bride and groom's table at the front facing the rest of us. And the never-ending yelling into the microphone by the MC who seems to be announcing the names of every relative whoever existed. Their lineages. All acknowledged and presented to the new couple, the bride especially. She in her flowing white dress, creped and sequined, a veil dipping just slightly over her forehead to the top of her eyes. At least 500 names with such percussion from these amps that my ears aren't sure they are still ears. I find it hard to tell whether there is another utterance in the hall other than the continuous blare of names with the same continuous exuberance as though Abraham himself was the original sire. Then the music begins. Even louder. I have to get out of here.

I'm outside and Murat has come out to see me. He's the best man. And he's another of the counselling leaders. He says that he thinks his cheeks are black. His throat is very sore. He has vomited repeatedly since 4 am from the vodka. In his fine suit and splendid white bouton-niere he looks as superb as a 30-year-old can look.

Inside, the groom and bride stare passively at the festivities. Small clusters are dancing. A paid dancer moves from table to table flashing her eyes, flicking her hands, gyrating in satin. Aziz has finished sev-eral shots of vodka. This morning, another of his patients died. He feels the hollow in his chest. Then the music stops and speeches start again. Aziz leans to me and muses how nothing was nearly so grand for Sergei's first wedding.

☞ What is a victory? Whatever feels great after having felt bad. An upturn. The upturns are what fill us. Islam and his beautiful eyes walking out of ICU at TB2 because he promised Aziz he would. Get-ting a hair cut from another patient. Sitting on the hard steps outside ICU looking across the foyer. Beside a young woman patient and enjoying the company. Sitting and looking outward. Not curled up in his ICU bed alone and waiting to cough up the next load of sputum, cold tea in a chipped cup by his bed, broken pieces of bread.

Or Oleg. Oleg from Auschwitz pulling on a blue checkered shirt with green-tinged white hands, long fingers stretched out as though there were no palms. Pulling on the unwashed fabric over an un-washed chest and standing up. And walking slowly, carefully step by step over the tiles, over the door jamb, down the six stairs. Walking beside Death, out through the wooden entrance way, through the doors and onto the broken flatstones of the walkway. Past the men playing their board game, the others squatting in concentration. Past their unease at seeing him. Oleg, gone outside to sit in the sun, bones on the slats of a bench for 10 minutes for the first time in two months. Oleg with the gold teeth and blue eyes. Still alive. Death moving aside for some sun. Victory.

Or Altingul. Sitting stiff on her bed, staring straight ahead, eyes narrow, the TV going, father sitting away from her watching his program intently, her x-ray showing the damage has moved from left to right across the top of her lungs, her 10-year-old brother striding across the room, and us wondering if we will watch her worsen. Watch her waste to skin and bones, become merely a cough rather than the dark-eyed beauty who only dreams about a future lover coming to her on his knees. We sit beneath her as usual and go through our litany of pleas, my list of insights, of truths I have sought for this visit. *I love you. I won't leave you. I want you to live. Your mother would want you to live.* And then she's gone to lock herself in her room. This low house with its mud brick walls, the hard earth courtyard, the mother dog outside growling to defend her emaciated puppies. Altingul with a father watching TV and waiting to run off to Kazakhstan to find a new wife. Altingul coughing but still angry, still snarling from behind the bedroom door that she will not ... will not ... will not go back to treatment. Then silent behind the locked door, locked window. Aunt arrived and pleading. Then uncle. Ten-year-old brother pleading.

Then, hours after we have left, oldest uncle coming to the house and saying he knows someone who went to the hospital and was cured, saying she has to go. And us arriving back later as Altingul waits for a taxi with her cousin to go to the bazaar and buy slippers for the hospital. And an hour later placing her things by a hospital bed at TB2. This is all victory. For one day, anyway.

☙

April 5

Achmed, a 40-year-old patient, says he has wanted to talk to me for days. We are in the counselling room in TB2. A long, narrow room in which the nurses take patients to weigh them and measure their height and which we have been allotted to use for individual and group sessions. I ask the counsellors to have at least one 40-minute session each week with each person on their case load, and a group session as well if possible.

At the polyclinics it's pretty tough sometimes to achieve that. The patients like to come in the mornings and don't want to stick around after taking the drugs. They know there is only a small time gap before the side effects come, and they want to be on their way home. Home to a routine or a bed to brace against the pain.

I have given up on my fancy idea to hand out appointment slips. "Schedule your patients. Get them on an appointment schedule. Give them these slips so they remember. That's how it's done elsewhere. It works." Yeah, right.

It's now become: "Find a way to see them. If you miss them in the morning then go to their homes in the afternoon. Okay? Don't worry about no car to take you. Just get a taxi and bring in the receipt. If we don't see everybody regularly we can't be there when they need us. We won't have the relationship we need to intervene when they want to quit treatment. Okay? Do your best." And in the hospitals it is easier because they are a captive audience. The women don't have to go home to serve their husband's families.

But in the hospital they are still new to the drugs. Still new to the devastation of the side effects. After drugs they want to lie motionless on their beds. Before drugs they want to psyche themselves up, eat a morsel of breakfast, wash themselves. After the side effects wear off in the afternoon, they want to finally eat a full meal, prepare the food for that. Then the day starts to disappear and it's time for the counsellor to go home. So, more often than not for the patient, visiting with a counsellor on any kind of a regular basis is an imposition on their simple struggle to make it through the day. But when they really know us and know we care, then they can access us when they really need us.

Achmed says he is struggling. Coming from a different district, he paid a $75 bribe to a doctor to falsify his residence address in order to get admitted, and now he hasn't been able to take the drugs for three days. He vomits them up right away. He's been here two months and frets over how his family is, two children 16 and 12. How he misses them. He begins to weep. Head down, the tears drip to the floor between the fingers hiding his face.

"I am weak," he says with resigned certainty. I put my hand on the side of his head. I counter that it is good to cry. When someone is sad, they should cry. We are built to cry. Facing truth means facing what we feel. I tell him that I respect him. He looks up. Looks me deeply in the eyes. He wants to see if I am just bullshitting, just trying to make him feel better. I let him look. It scares me. I breathe.

He tells me that his brothers went to college but he failed the entrance exams. That left him to stay at home to attend to his parents' needs as they aged. He says he has had to do black work most of his life. Black work is what Karakalpaks call manual labour. Low pay, long hours. Now, because he is sick, he can't work. Now he can't stay home and look after his own family. Another indication that he is a failure. His disability pension has not yet been given. As small as that is, it would feed his family. His wife criticizes him.

"I'm a loser," he quietly asserts. It is strange to hear such a familiar idea and comment from the other side of the world. *A loser.* A failure. Not good enough. And now his drugs have gotten the better of him and he can't even take them, is allowing his disease to win. So, what to do?

I tell him the truth. You are a warrior. You have come here to fight for your life. There are many defaulters. It's because the drugs are so hard. They will save your life. Each day, when you wake up think to yourself yes, I want to feel the nausea, I want to feel the aching and the headache. I want to revolt when I see those pills. Open up to all of it. Ask for it. When you resist then it chases you. When you invite it, some of its power goes. The fear drops. Ask to be afraid, and you will feel less afraid. You are wise enough to know the truth. You know that you are a warrior. You know the drugs are terrible. You know that your family depends on you to be cured. You know that when you are cured you will provide for them. You know the drugs will work. You are taking care of your family by being here on treatment. Your wife doesn't understand, but you do. You are a warrior.

Then we talk about intelligence, about his childhood. We do a guided visualization. Achmed goes back out to take his drugs. I see him later rubbing at his hip. There are two images of MDR-TB patients that are universal. One is being hunched over in anticipation of having to vomit. The other is walking gingerly on one side, a hand rubbing up and down below the hip where the needle has gone in. At some polyclinics the patients will bring gifts to the nurse every so often just to ensure she gives the injection gently rather than stabbing into them to show who has the power and who does not.

Later I'm with Alisher and Saperbuy in their room. Saperbuy, the young husband worried about having sex with his wife, is drawing a large pair of lungs on a piece of white sketch paper. One lung is pink and healthy, the other with spots on it and dying. He tells me his wife is pregnant. Smiles. He says the drugs are hard to take. On the other bed Alisher sits, fear in his eyes. He is only 18, tanned boyish face, light brown hair sticking fashionably up. On the street in my home town he'd turn the heads of all the girls. I've seen him smile. What a guy.

Today he's upset. He says it's the drugs. I know it's not really. I know he's just suffering. I ask about his mother who died less than two years ago. I know his father has never been in the picture. Alisher starts crying. Head down and crying. I place my hand on his back. This is men's day.

In the afternoon, I walk with Daniyar and Aynur out into the field outside the TB2 compound fence. We find a clump of weeds to sit on in the middle of this desert field. It is warm enough to sit comfortably now. Daniyar is special. When Aynur and I first talked to him a week ago, we were blown away. This 19-year-old boy with the handsome, sultry looks of a movie actor told us his story.

When he was two, his mother died. Like Alisher, he never met nor knew his father. His grandmother raised him. A few years ago his grandmother died. A month after he had one of his kidneys surgically removed. A year ago he got TB and afterwards it became MDR-TB. He came to TB2 in January. Daniyar has an open, full smile, eyes that look so mirthfully into you that you are forced to smile. We asked how he has managed the pain of such losses. He smiled and said, what life brings is what life asks to be managed. He told us that no one is special. All are human. All are changing. There is purpose. What matters is to go into life as fully as one can. To walk into it and fight when it's necessary to fight, accept when it's appropriate to accept. Discover who you are.

We asked where he got these ideas. He blushed, looked sheepish and said he just thinks them himself.

He came by later that day to give me a DVD disc of some songs he had recorded. I watched it that evening at my house. It was professionally done. The first one was about his mother, about missing her, wanting her now. Even though it was all in Karakalpak, the emotions shone through. One scene was Daniyar at a tombstone on his knees, his fingers trailing down over the etched writing on the stone, tears streaming down his cheeks.

Out in the field, Daniyar talks to us about what he wants to do when he is cured. He wants to work weddings. He wants to be the guy who announces all the names! It's called opening the bride's face. He explains it's all about introducing the bride to her new family and them to her. It involves poems, blessings, good words, the lists of names and, depending on the guy doing it, singing as well. He will sing. He knows the kind of poems that he wants the bride to hear. Poems on how to love, how to manage in marriage and life.

And he wants to do concerts.

I ask where he got the finances to make the DVD disc, and I tell him how impressive it was. He says he recorded the songs when he was 17. He sold his cell phone to pay for it.

I ask him to tell me more about the deaths in his life. He says his grandmother died in 2006. He was lying in bed with her two hours before she died. She spoke to him despite her weakness, told him he could do whatever he needed to in the future, that he would have the strength he needed. He says how her sons, his uncles, have rejected him. That they have never recognized his accomplishments. They did not like how their mother had taken him so close to her, raised him as though he was her son too. Daniyar says when she died it was like an earthquake. He puts his head in his hands and cries. Then he continues to speak about the rejection from his uncles.

This is men's day.

And Daniyar is wrong. He is special.

April 7

ICU is the intensive care unit in TB2. It's where there are three separate cubicles to hold up to three patients whose physical condition is extreme. I am with one of these patients. She has a headache that has spread all over her upper body. Her head is warm with fever and her eyes wander. She is scared of the pain. When the fan starts she is frightened. Thin. Her beautiful little hands. Thirty-three years old and sick on and off with TB for 13 years. No husband, no children. She carries the family pain and its sickness. No one else has been sick. She smiles when I say she is an expert on pain. The first time I saw her was in early February on doctors' rounds. She was in an oxygen mask in this same bed in TB2. Her shirt was red. She looked frantic. I thought she was pretty weak and dying. I didn't know anything yet about MDR. When the doctors left her cubicle, I stayed and asked her to look me in the eyes. I smiled and told her to breathe and relax. And then I never came back to talk, just looked in through the doorway and said *salaam alaikum*. This is the first time I stop in to visit.

She tells me her name. Gulbasara. So many names. I swim in names I find hard to pronounce. Names that I forget unless I see them again and again until they become family. But I remember the stories.

Is Gulbasara afraid of dying? Yes. Eyes sad.

"When will you die?" I ask. She shakes her head. I ask again. She says she doesn't know. I say, I do. She says when? I say, at the same time I do. When life decides to end. I stroke her hair, the sides of her face. Her hands. Her forehead. Over and over. She doesn't want to lose her sight. She is in pain. I am glad I came in to visit. To take the time to know her. I say that I will find out about her left eye, why it has become dim. When I leave I promise to return later in the week.

And now in the main part of TB2, second ward, I have woken up 25-year-old-Guldana — Clever Flower. She has been sleeping because she has a headache. It's too soon after her drugs, but I want to talk with her. I haven't seen her in a week and it's time to deepen our relationship, to find out more about her. There have been intimations from the doctors that they'll soon call her a treatment failure. She's been here too long. Eleven months and still no negative smear, still infectious. World Health Organization guidelines say the patient should convert to negative after four months of drug treatment, six months at most, and if they don't they should have the drug treatment stopped, be considered a failure. The doctors wait longer here. They know enough to wait. Some patients are so stressed their bodies' immune systems don't work right. Some struggle with the drugs, miss too many days, make it hard for the war against the bacilli to proceed properly. Guldana has been here too long.

I have to try to get inside. She feels dizzy. We go into the counselling room. I turn the ventilation fan on. She says the noise bothers her. No one likes the sound of the fans. MSF has put them in the rooms. MSF says it's how to minimize infection. The patients don't like the sound. I turn it off. I take her hands in mine.

When I do actual one on one counselling sessions, I have Aynur, or whoever is translating, sit behind the person. That way, the person I am counselling has to look only at me, be with me, and not at the translator. When I can see in the person's eyes, I can see who they are, what they feel. And they can see me, see if I'm real or not, know intuitively what's inside of me. Guldana and I look at each other, knees almost touching. This small, dark-faced woman with the turmoil of her whole life churning inside her. We talk about her past.

"How much hurt do you have in your life?" I ask. She shakes her head. None. I ask again, because her darkness comes from more than the present.

After a pause: "I don't remember." Then, she adds: "I was married at 19. I was stolen. I didn't love him. He divorced me when I got sick. He has another wife now and he's gone to Kazakhstan." We talk about this for a while.

"How was the sexual part of your marriage?" She shakes her head. Looks at the floor.

"I didn't like it. I had a boyfriend before my husband. I loved him. We used to touch each other. We kissed. But I got kidnapped. My mother died when I was 11. My sisters support me."

I hold her hands, examine each one, touching the skin on her palms, each finger, the backs of her hands, her wrists. I ask her to do the same to mine. I want her to connect with me. To feel some control. I hold my hand up, ask her to slap it. I grab her hand, ask her to pull it away from my grip. Simple touch exercises intended to connect us as equals.

Before I leave, I ask her to spend her days imagining her future husband, a man who will respect her, know her, love her. Imagine him and plan for it. This practise of kidnapping, I have heard about it. They say that nowadays it is not what it used to be when men could just abduct whoever they fancied. Getting a wife was easy. See someone you want and make a plan and get your friends together to snatch her, take her to your parents' home and she's yours. A real wedding meant considerable expense for the groom in money and gifts to the woman's family, plus costs of the ceremony. And, of course, this has never been a culture where dating and intimacy were smoothly accepted, openly encouraged. Hence, kidnapping.

They say that usually now the girl knows the man and is told that the kidnapping will occur, it being just a stage in the relationship which allows for cohabitation and full sexuality, that the woman is ready and agreeable. I'm not so sure.

Finally, I come back to get Kurbangul who is also in ICU. She has been here in TB2 for over ten days now since I did the pre-admission session with her. I've been in to see her a few times. Each time she reaches out to hold me as though we've known each other for years. Today I want to wheel her outside into the sunshine. I've never helped patients into chairs before. I'm afraid of breaking her. But I help her into the plastic lawn chair on wheels. She is bundled in a black shag coat and a coloured kerchief.

We sit outside on the stone stepway in the sun, her hand wrapped around mine, her other fingers stroking my hand like a lover would or a mother or someone ensuring they are still alive. And she is 26 and I am 59.

And then I lift her and the chair down to the roadway. I wheel her along the paved area in front of TB2 hospital and we go over to the first ward to where there is this small tree with a scattering of small white blooms. She stops me and points at this awakening. I go to the tree and pluck one of the tiny blossoms just emerging. I bring it to her and she smells it and says this is an apricot blossom. "I've never seen an apricot tree in first bloom before." And she cradles the blossom, for her now a jewel.

Then we're farther along and looking at the water filling the plots on the hospital grounds like they were rice paddies. The water spraying forcefully out of the pipes so loudly that, even with her deafness, Kurbangul can hear what she sees. And I ask her if she likes that sound and she nods heartily and wonders if the water is clean.

Kurbangul points over to a green area almost like lawn off the trail. She says she'd like to go there. I say it's too bumpy for the chair. But next time, I say, next time I'll bring out a blanket and I'll carry you over there and we'll sit and drink apricot juice. And she smiles.

I push her back towards the entrance steps. I run a bit just to let her feel the breeze, feel the speed. She inhales. And then, then she's back inside and the nurse is depositing her onto her bed in ICU alone again. But still holding the little blossom.

And I tell Aynur that we've just been taught. Taught what life is about, how to live, how to let our eyes and minds walk when our legs can't, how to notice all that can be noticed, how to hold onto small flowers as though we belonged to them.

⟳ We are all afraid of getting MDR. Aziz goes through periods of anxiety. He becomes frantic, dreams of being sick, losing his family for two years of suffering. He goes for an early x-ray. He says if he got MDR-TB he would not take the drugs, that it's too awful. Murat says the same. Deelya says the same. They've watched the retching, the pale, far away gazes of the after-drugs internal war. We're all afraid. The patients ask if there is this terrible disease in my country. No, I say, there is some tuberculosis but not much. I don't know really if there is any at all. They nod and look at me disappointed as though to say that only in this land are they doomed to die this way. I offer that we have other killers in my country — cancer, heart disease. They nod. Maybe it makes them feel not so cursed. It makes me feel better.

We always press our masks on snugly, breathe in and out to watch that the fabric sucks in as well. Make sure the seam is tight. These masks that are supposed to be 95% effective. These masks which we are supposed to dispose of in special containers. I have taken to carrying mine folded in half in my back pocket between visits to the different venues or after leaving for lunch. It's a no-no. There are germs in the fabric of the mask. I ask why there aren't germs in my hair then or in the fabric of my sweater. The doctors shrug their shoulders.

I ask Samuel our head expat doctor again if it's safe for me to hug, to hold patients. He says yes, no problem, the bacilli is airborne not contact based. I am not so convinced. Maybe that's why I always close my eyes when I'm holding someone. Like I did when that fucking dog snuck up and bit me in the back of my leg. I ask myself if I am prepared to later get sick. I think, yes. Yes, these people need what I can give. They are alone. They are human. But is it worth it? Is the risk worth it? I ask myself what I will feel in the future if I get MDR or some other ailment from my time here. Will I feel then that it was worth it—being here, all the photos and hugs? The trust and intimacy?

Funny, before I wrote the words above, I would have answered that the patients are so open and beautiful that they make it worth it, that the truth of their struggle and me being a part of that, learning from it makes it all worth it. But I always felt that this was just an opinion, what I happen to feel in the thrust of the present, the energy of them and of the moment. That I might think differently in the future. But just now I realize without a doubt that it is worth it no matter the result. It is worth it because trust and intimacy are always worth it. That is the law of humanity.

Humanity, when it is deep and full, is about intimacy. There is no debate about that. The secret of life, the meaning of life, is to fall into intimacy, to choose intimacy—with others, with self, with environment, with the moment. So whenever we know that we are doing that, going in that direction, then we know we are safe. Safe in assuming that all is just the way it is to be. No second guesses. No doubts. And it is the intimacy I have each day with the lives of the patients—the men, women, teenagers who are patients—that strips me away from me, leaves the exchange as me. No me. Only us. Us humans. Being inside the heart of human existence. And unlike if I had gone to a war zone like Darfur with its overt trauma and threat, here in Karakalpakstan there is nothing to interfere with, to mask or override, the simple beat of the heart.

I thought I was coming to Uzbekistan to contribute. I know now that I never understood the essence of that, of what it could or would be. It was just a concept. Now here and daily counselling my own caseload of patients, I am learning about openness and letting go. I don't know what to do or say until I'm about to do or say it. I just fit in, respond. Everywhere around this epidemic there is nuttiness, inconsistencies, brokenness, mistakes. It is all a blunder. Nothing I can do to change anything. I am here like a feather in wind. All I contribute is my own smiling, willing intimacy. And I receive the same back. Who would have thought? Not me.

I tell MSF that the counsellors are afraid for their health, that being with patients all day long, day in and day out, makes them afraid. They have families. No one wants to be stationed in the hospitals for more than three days, three days being around infectiousness. Kairat is at TB1 five days a week. But he doesn't speak English, and I don't ask him how he feels about it. I'm afraid he'll tell me he doesn't want to be there. Kairat with his immaculate crew cut, smart blazer, pressed slacks, who does his job so professionally, probably feels the same trepidation. But if I ask and he tells then I'll feel I have to have someone else there two days a week in order to share the risk. And I don't want to do that. So, for once I hide behind language.

The counsellors at TB2—Aziz, Altinay, Murat—all speak English. I have split their time equally to spare them. They have not told about their fears before but they tell me and I tell my bosses. MSF says too bad, it's the job.

No one else in MSF spends such concentrated time with patients. Only the counsellors. Coal miners old style. Or canaries.

April 8

I'm nearing two and a half months here now. Here, in that this is where I am, though regardless of where one is geographically, in terms of time one can always say "I am here". And this is actually how it feels for me in the most lived sense. I know I am on the other side of the world, I know I am in Karakalpakstan in the western part of Uzbekistan and I know I am in Nukus. But I don't fully live that. My body walks the hard earth streets here and along the wide paved streets with cars whizzing by, taxis and tiny mini-buses plying like steady ants up and down, and people crossing where they will and when they will. I see the green shoots coming from the turned furrows everywhere that fill with water as the city turns on the irrigation pipes, the furrows that became furrows from the compelled labour of students and workers ordered to get out and do the digging by government decree.

I see the new leaves on the poplars lined everywhere in this desert semi-oasis, the new blossoms on the apricot trees. And I see the miles and miles of white earth, the unbelievable salt and chemical coating winded here and everywhere from the empty Aral Sea. My body is here and my eyes. I feel my own breathing, sometimes a bit laboured, a cough easily finding its way up my throat many times a day as my body laughs that it is too human, too vulnerable, that it is MDR-TB's for the taking any time it decides.

So, I know I am in Nukus. In Uzbekistan, 12 time zones away from home. But I can't say at all that I am really in Nukus as meaning I live this physical place, feel that reality, know this place where my body actually inhabits in these seconds I breathe. All my life I've been a traveller and each place I've been to I absorbed the texture, the space, the hum of the landscape, revelled in it, and hold it still inside myself like patches of my being. Not this time. This time I've come only to be inside these people. Inside their needs. All that is true, for a fact, is that I am here in the sense of here as in time. This moment.

And here in this human geography. I have been transported via some mystical or some transcendental canal deeper into the heart of humanness. I live inside heartbeats. I hold, every day, hearts in my hands and every day, hands hold my heart. I had no idea. No intention to come here. No awareness. Somehow the ticket got into my hand.

I walk across the busy thoroughfare this dusk with Murat, my affably wise counsellor. We stop and start to avoid getting whacked by the cars. There are not so many and no real danger as long as attention is paid. We are coming from the bazaar. I have bought sunflower seeds from the ladies who cart them there in wheelbarrows, mounded white and overflowing, 500 sum a half jarful. Black market 25 cents. And three bananas, a special treat. I bought them to bring to patients the next day. I call them patients begrudgingly. It's an easy euphemism for the people in the MDR-TB hospital. Technically they are patients, but truthfully they are Assan, Sarbinaz, Firoza, Kuanish, Aiyeesha, Guldana, Kamila, Achmed ... I have made myself learn the names. I want them to know that I know them.

Murat and I look at each other as we cross. I say: "It's really wonderful to be sharing this adventure with you." He smiles and says: "Yes, I was just thinking the same thing." Murat is 30 and has a wife and son. I asked him a week ago if he loved his wife and he replied: "Do you want what I am supposed to say? Or the real answer?" Murat and I had just spent an hour on the carpeted floor of a big room in a big house, carpets stretched out to also cover the walls, and the lady of the house, a woman of 35 ... 40 ... sitting beside us. We wore the yellow, duck-beak masks. The lady had been diagnosed with MDR-TB and was reluctant to enter the TB2 hospital. She was afraid of the side effects from the cocktail of drugs she would need to take every day for the next two years, her body being punched from the inside, and who knows what kind of possible liver damage, hearing loss, dizziness, fevers, even psychosis.

She was afraid. Did not want to go. She had already been in the regular TB ward for three months where she had paid doctors to administer varying assemblages of medications which not only did not cure her but led to the development of the more resistant, much more resistant strain. Now she was freaked. And I was with Murat for a second negotiation of what he had given the day before to no avail, a second dose of: "You must go into hospital and face the fucking treatment or else you will wither into sticks and skin and slow, violent coughing, and slow emaciated, wretchedly helpless death on a bare bed that will give not an iota of comfort."

For an hour, I told her stories of death and life. Of emaciation and vibrancy. I told her she was being silly. I told her that her head scarf was beautiful. I told her that she was physically strong and that I could tell by looking at her that she would be cured, though I also said there was no guarantee and that 10% didn't make it. I told her we'd be there for her. I held her hand and did a two-minute meditation to show her how we could help her attain peace in order to take the 20 pills and hip injection every day. We closed our eyes, but after 40 seconds she laughed.

I told her, she needed to go right away. That the others at the hospital were beautiful, but it was true that the food was bad. She said she needed to wait a week to sell some items she had made so she could have enough money to buy nutritious food to take. She said she was still scared. That she might run away once she went there. I said: "Do you want to die?"

She said she was a virgin. She wanted to marry and have a family. If she took the drugs would it make her infertile? She cried. I put my arm around her and told her that an MSF worker was a cured patient and had now had a child. When we left, we said we'd phone in a week. We'll know then whether she will live or die.

We hold that in our hands every day. Living and dying held in our hands. Mostly living. Much mostly, but painfully mostly, courageously mostly, paying a cost mostly, fearfully mostly, hunched over in clumps outside mostly. Much mostly living with bright eyes, open eyes, eyes looking for truth, for heartbeats. Eyes looking beneath culture, beneath language, evaluating energy. Eyes looking at me.

And a very few dying. Dying painfully, courageously, fearfully but with open eyes, eyes straining through the searing to detect truth. Eyes filled with aliveness.

Maybe like Gulbasara in ICU, her black hair not the way she wants it for a photo. Pain wriggling its little fingers all over her head and down her neck, down her sides, the fever making her eyes flutter out of focus just often enough to ensure she knows she has nothing. She hasn't walked in many weeks. Her body as thin as thin. But her small hands as beautiful yet as beauty. Her worries about how her father and other relatives will fare if she dies. She talked about wanting to walk, about wanting the fucking pain to stop, how the paracetamol didn't help for more than a half an hour. How she gets scared very easily, a sound in the night, the fan coming on, how she cries out and the boy in the next room shouts at her to shut up and how it doesn't scare or hurt her when he shouts at her because she knows he is as sick as she but if it was someone healthy how she'd be angry and hurt that they could deny her this voice, this one option she has.

Gulbasara who lives in this narrow, concrete cubicle on her narrow bed in ICU, unable to summon a nurse, only able to speak to another person when and if one decides to enter her room which has a closed door that opens to a small lane of a hall which has another door which opens to a bigger anteroom where the nurse has a table set up for drugs which has no nurse except at drug time. When the doors are all closed Gulbasara does not exist except to the two in the adjacent cells whom she does not see and can only hear if they yell.

She mentioned how she first saw me on doctors' rounds, that first time when I held her hand after the four doctors left, when I asked through my translator if she would look into my eyes because I wanted her to know I was also a human and that I knew she was human and that we both were with name and character and spirit, when she looked into my eyes and our gaze connected and for that moment we were beating with the same heart. If only in my own imagination.

She mentioned that there were four doctors with me and one was an African. "I was afraid when I saw that nigger. I had seen them on television before and I never felt afraid, but when I saw him with the others and he was looking at me, I was really afraid. I wanted to get out of the bed and run away. I looked behind the bed and wished I could crawl out the window. But later, the next week when he came again on the rounds I wasn't so scared. I was used to him. I never saw a nigger before."

When she had said "nigger" in the innocent, matter of fact, no idea that it could be offensive way that she did, both Aynur and I laughed. I live with Jonathan, a Kenyan lab expert, and I think even he would have laughed. Maybe not. Whenever we go through the bazaar together, Jonathan and I, everyone stares and smiles. Hardly any tourists ever come to Nukus and never any black people. Samuel, the Kenyan doctor gets bugged all the time to stop to pose with people who want to take his photo.

I should bring Gulbasara a photo of Samuel. Poster-sized to put over her bed.

Thus, I am here—with Gulbasara, and each day another Gulbasara. Or like this same day, with 26-year-old Kurbangul. Also in ICU. Also as thin as thin. Also in pain and with fever. With that goitre in her throat which makes swallowing medication difficult. With that bad heart. And too weak to walk so also confined to wheelchair. And, of course, with MDR-TB.

Kurbangul reaches out with her stick-like arms towards me when I appear. "I missed you. I missed you." Alone here in ICU. Waiting, always waiting. For something. She pulls me in, holds me tight, cheek to cheek, heads touching. Her fever against me. This is Karakalpakstan where men never touch women unless they're married. Where it's a gossiping point if someone physically latches onto someone else. We talk. I shout to Aynur who shouts to Kurbangul so she knows we're both really talking. She smiles, winces at her pain, inability to eat much because of the medication. Pleads to go outside to be with other people.

Two hours later, I return to her. After having my lunch of bread and cheese and cucumber. After speaking with Achmed and promising to bring him 30,000 sum tomorrow in an unmarked envelop that no one will see, the money to tide his family over because the welfare office has screwed up their application once again for assistance. 30,000 sum. I'm your friend, I say to him as he protests, says his family will make do another 25 days until the next cheque day, that it has finally been sorted out. 30,000 sum is $15. What a big spender I am.

After speaking to Saperbuy about how to respond to the dread of taking the cacophony of daily drugs. How it is necessary to open to the drugs, to the necessity of them, to open to the adverse side effects, let them come. But then stay open and let them go. Let them go. It's all about stopping resistance, stopping the clenching and dreading and just letting be, letting the body rebound. Opening to the rest of the day, the rest of life, of one's own life. To his new baby. To the trees growing to green, to the magpies hopping from limb to limb. In theory it sounds so good.

After speaking with Altingul, finally giving up and agreeing to end her three-month refusal to keep on the drugs and injections that had been her life already for six months before, agreeing to go to hospital 19 kilometres out of town and 84 beds of everyone older than her and never having seen the place. After taking her to ICU to see Gulbasara and Kurbangul and Islam our boy with the beautiful eyes in the middle cubicle. We wanted her to see what thin looked like because she'd heard how one of the drugs made you gain weight. And we said please do gain weight because MDR steals the flesh from bones.

After speaking to Altingul and getting her to smile just a bit. After laughing with 20 other patients and snapping their photos out in the sunlight. Laughing some more with the three taking English from Murat and some others taking Russian from Altinay. Then, finally, I come back to get Kurbangul and wheel her outside into her sunshine And after Kurbangul on this same day as the one that Murat and I jump over the ditch with bananas, on this same day — Roza, Nazira, Sultana, and Erkin.

This is my letter for that day. And, of course it leaves out lots. Only tells a bit. But it tells where I am. Or more accurately when I am. I am here. Always here. Only here.

⌒ Tonight there is a half moon making leaf shadows on the hard earth road, still a bit warm from the day. Men are speaking quietly as they squat in the darkness near their homes. This truth is centuries old. The trees green now. Apple blossoms almost all limp on the ground. New flowers on the small cherry trees. All dark but for the half moon. All at peace as though each house didn't wait for the next death canopy to be raised for the next funeral. As though even I was safe and had a right to be here. The low roofs of the homes, the metallic or wooden double doors fronting the entrance to the courtyards and the living quarters of the many. Me walking as though it was normal for me to be here. In and out of shadow, the moon cutting its light over everything. Salt residue still on my shoes from crossing a field earlier in the day. Both Aziz's children with bad coughs.

⌒ Each Saturday at 6 pm I take an aikido class. It's wonderful. Aikido is a gentle, graceful defence art based on responding to the other's aggression, the other's movement and the nature of our bodies. Last week I was watching a kick-boxing class down in the main gym as our aikido class was happening. The kick-boxing was all about speed and power while the aikido is about gracefulness and thinking and opening and awareness. Of course I am hopeless at learning the moves. Male and female, there are over 20 in the class aged from seven to me. I am easily the worst student. I just can't master the moves. But I try, and it all feels great. It's great to be at the bottom, to feel incapable. And it complements my days when I have to be inside others and so intensely mindful. It also teaches me to be less sure of my judgements. My teacher Manas may be burning with anger at a multitude of injustices in his life, but as an aikido sensei, he is the epitome of relaxed compassion. I guess everyone needs the proper element to reveal their real selves. I no longer see him as an MSF guard.

$$\sigma$$

April 10

I have gone with my big counsellor Kuanish into the desert. He has written a letter to his dead father as I have asked him to. Aynur is with us to translate. Our driver, the portly, slightly balding Naeel, has driven us out of town and then off the road for a kilometre to this place in the middle of nowhere. Naeel speaks no English and doesn't know what to think, but he is curious. Naeel has already taught me to be aware of how my actions impact others who do not understand my ways. A month ago I hurt his feelings. I was yelling at a logistics fellow for ignoring my request for a car, and Naeel was the driver. He thought I was angry at him too. The next day, he had to sit beside me at lunch and ate so fast that I thought he would choke. I called him over later to apologize for my outburst and clarify that it hadn't been intended for him. He was shaking even then. But a week later we were good. Now he's driven us out to the desert shortly before the end of the work day. And he's been asked to wait while we walk away from him out onto the sand and disappear.

Kuanish and I are good too. He's entered into my counselling sessions with a keen desire to resolve some of the demons locked inside him. He doesn't care that, unlike the English speaking counsellors, he has to go through Aynur to bare his secrets. He's all focus, all intent. We sit on the sand and he unfolds his letter. "Dear Father," and Aynur translates. Kuanish talks of the times his father had disparaged him, had beaten his mother, had behaved as though there was no Kuanish, as though nothing he did was enough. He says he no longer wants to carry those memories, that this is his time and he wants it to be his. Kuanish cries as he reads the letter. When he finishes we sit in silence.

Then I ask Aynur to return to the Landcruiser. She walks back to Naeel. Kuanish and I walk together hand in hand farther out into the sand. When we look back and can't see Aynur, I gesture for him to follow me and I race down an incline with my arms out screaming at the top of my lungs. Kuanish races behind me, screaming, arms out. We arrive at the bottom, huffing and hoarse. We embrace. I hold out a box of matches to him. He opens it, takes out a match, and strikes it. Slowly he puts the flame to the letter he has written his father and watches as the bits of charred paper turn to flecks of ash and blow into the desert. We walk in silence back toward the Land-cruiser. As we come back up to the top of the rise, we see Naeel in the distance standing atop the Landcruiser cab. It looks like he has his hand above his eyes scanning for us.

As we come down the last low mound toward the Landcruiser, we see a new burgundy Dodge speeding towards us. Coming between Kuanish and me and the Landcruiser, the Dodge swirls about in a near donut and stops, sand flying up into our midst. Out jump three men. They come right to us. One guy puts his hand in his pocket and whips out an ID packet. "National Security!" he barks. "What are you doing here?" They are surrounding us. They look very serious. We are where? Where we shouldn't be? Aynur comes over. She says they are telling her that this is a restricted area and in the direction of the Kazakh border. The head guy wants to know what we came here for. This is an area where smugglers come. An area where men come with prostitutes.

I say: "Tell him we're with MSF and that I'm from Canada. I've only just arrived and I've never been to a desert before. That you've taken me out here to show it to me." I try to look earnest, open, innocent. Dumb. The guy buys it. He says don't come here again, and they pile back into the Dodge. And it swirls off just the way it arrived. We all jump into the Landcruiser and follow them back to the main road. They drive fast as though it's their desert and they want us to know it. Naeel drives fast to show he's doing what he's been told. Aynur is shaking just a bit. She says: "It's really lucky you got back when you did. How could I have explained what Naeel and I were doing alone out in the desert?" Her eyebrows raise. "Or they didn't show up when you, I and Kuanish were sitting together out in the desert. Two men and one woman. You know what they would have thought." We laugh.

Then as we drive back to town, Aynur tells about Naeel. When she came back toward the Landcruiser he was already standing atop it. He was staring out trying to determine what the hell we had been doing. He had suddenly stated: "Hey, they've started to run. Now they're screaming." None of us talk about how National Security knew we were out there.

⌒ I think of how those who live here are time bombs—the toxins and constant salt exposure working away in their bodies, the bodies of their young children, and waiting for the future to tell the results. This morning I picked up some papers on a table close to my bedroom window. I noticed there was a powdery covering—not visible but I could feel it with my fingertips. I tasted it—ahhh slightly salty.

And what is in my lungs?

⌒

April 13

Daniyar turns 20 in three days. Both Aynur and I want to buy him gifts. I ask him to walk with me alone out of the hospital grounds and over the fence into the bordering farmer's field. We go through the field and across a narrow road. At the road I use improvised sign language to gesture to him to turn back toward TB2 and throw out his infected lungs, leave them back there before we walk into the empty desert in front of us.

He puts his hands to his chest and then flings them outward. Once, twice, three times. Then abruptly he turns to walk with me up the sandy incline into the desert. We walk in silence, with no words to share. Just the human language that comes so easily once we shut our mouths and open our arms. We walk over the sand. Tiny blades of thin grass poke through the yellowy tan sand dunes, a blade every few inches. The paltry spring rains just enough to raise these slivers of green.

We walk alone out across the sand, brittle, prickly bushes jutting up every so often, goat droppings, the sight of small holes of desert rodents, the spring sun not so hot, but warm, a light, light breeze. We walk until we can't see where we have come from and then we sit together in a shallow dip in the land. We sit back to back. We feel each other's bodies breathing. Our lungs separated only by the fibres of flesh and bone. Breathing together in silence, the backs of our heads touching. Minutes pass.

We hold each other's hands as we sit back to back. We hold hands until we can feel the blood pulsing. Silent *whump, whump, whump*, so slowly, so persistently, our blood. No way of distinguishing whose pulse it is or if it is the two combined. We have just one pulse. We hold hands. We breathe. We sit together back to back.

And then we turn and sit looking at each other smiling. We stand and embrace for long minutes. Long minutes. We walk in silence back to the hospital grounds. Daniyar goes into the building back to his room on the second floor with five other men. I leave with Aynur in the Toyota cruiser. This time no National Security.

April 19

I'm spending more time at our wards in TB1. Kairat is alone there with the 50 patients. I was coming sporadically, but now I'm going to come every Wednesday and Friday. Monday and Tuesday out at TB2.

Thursday as is needed at polyclinics. A schedule is good. Keeps me in a rhythm, focussed, feeling like something gets done. Aynur is the hardest worker in MSF. Her mouth gets so tired. Yap, yap, yap. Counsellors are supposed to be about listening but I talk too much. And when I am listening which is more and more these days, she still has to talk. She's both patient and counsellor. Maybe this is the nicest meaning of a double-talker! Then in the trainings that I give the counselling team on Monday afternoons, it's mind shift and more blabber for her to pass on. Good thing she gets a break when I go to the project team and the medical meetings with the expats.

I like this one room of women at TB1. I've gotten close to them. There are six of them. Not like room 10 at TB2. These ones are livelier or maybe just a different chemistry, maybe because they are newer into treatment. I was the one who introduced two of them to this new world of MDR-TB and its drugs. They hadn't yet begun the drugs, were all smiles and energy. Young, only 21 and 23. Now, however, they know the drugs too well. Eyes more apprehensive, like deer who have watched others in the herd being shot and butchered. Yet, in the afternoons they crank up the music and dance. The six of them, embracing their time to let loose.

Gulsima, just 22, has two children, an infant son and an older daughter. That four-year-old is being raised by her mother-in-law, following the practise of giving the first born to the husband's parents. Gulsima hates it, says that she is not allowed to hold her daughter or address her as daughter in her presence. How the child cries when Gulsima leaves to go to hospital. Gulsima is pressed by her in-laws to get home and resume her duties. Husband is also frustrated. She loves him but wants to live with her own parents. She knows it will be easier to stay on the drugs. But what about the oldest daughter?

Azima is beautiful. Thirty and regally lustrous. I can't take my eyes off her, especially when she smiles. The others in the room all choose me as their counsellor. Azima hesitates. "You won't know our customs." But then she relents and agrees to take me on as well. She hesitates because she does not want interference with the path she has chosen. She has sized up her life and knows what needs to be done. She is so strong that she accepts the inequality in her home, in her life.

She has two children. They all need to live somewhere. Her sister-in-law also has MDR-TB. She's in TB2. Azima knows that, when they are both discharged, it will be she who does all the housework, the cooking, the serving and her sister-in-law who will be the beneficiary with the rest of the in-laws. And Azima accepts me as her counsellor because she knows she will only see me when and if she wants.

Gauhar is also beautiful. She speaks okay English. Her husband is a farmer but they come from good families. Her parents-in-law are both doctors. Unlike the norm here, Gauhar lives separate from them with her husband. Only four weeks on the drugs, she is always smiling but she is struggling. The nausea wracks her, but it is more than that. We speak privately. Her smile fades when I press her for the truth of what's inside. She cries. She cannot understand how she can have this disease. It is not possible. She has always been healthy. No one in her family has ever been sick with anything serious. She is ashamed. She does not want it to be true. Her body refuses to accept.

And she does not like crying.

Sveta is a dentist. Tall with flowing black hair, she could be a North American aboriginal. High cheek bones, eyes that survey what they see. A great smile of golden teeth. She thinks she must have gotten the disease from working on her own patients. Now, she too struggles with the drug intake. Vomiting almost every day. I tell her that can be stopped, that it needs to stop because it reduces the effect of the medication. She knows this. It makes her worry. I say instead of waking up each morning dreading the pills she might try waking up and wishing for them. I say to speak aloud and wish that they will make her nauseous. Wish that she will vomit. "I hope I will vomit today." She laughs and thinks I'm crazy. But she says she will try. Her husband is in prison in Moscow. He has been in prison four years. It happened because he fought with a policeman. The policeman started it. She talks with him on the phone sometimes when he calls her. Their son is four. She misses him. She cries. Her life is filled with loneliness. I ask her if she would like me to hold her. She says yes, I need the energy. She is the only one in the room that I have sensed will fit with this kind of holding. We stand and embrace. There is no hesitation, just melting. We breathe. I feel her strength.

After I finish my counselling sessions with the women, I go down to the first floor to see Oleg and on to another room of six men. Oleg is still managing. He is not gaining any weight but he is eating. The others on the floor share their food with him. They bring it to him in his room. He has no money but they share. Sometimes Oleg asks me for 3000 sum so he can contribute. One woman has told me that he sneaks into the lunch room at night and takes food. She says he should ask and not steal. Oleg is thin. An MSF photographer has come and taken an arty black and white portrait of him as he sits partially up and bends, naked torso and head face down towards his bed. It's a striking photo, the ribs and spine like the frame of a boat covered in parchment. I hate it, hate that we've taken this from him.

The room with the six men has a comedian. A 53-year-old mechanic with eyes that sparkle brown with insightful mirth. But he has told me that he laughs on the outside and cries on the inside. A man abandoned by his wife and stuck here in the basement floor of TB1. Yet he is wise and funny. "Did you ever really, really want something more than anything else? Something that consumed your thoughts so that nothing else was on your mind? Something you wanted so badly?"

I don't know, maybe.

"Well, I have."

What was it?

"I really needed to piss one time. It was terrible. And then finally I found a place to go and, *ooooohh*, was it ever good." He mimics the action of peeing with his hands in front of his fly and his eyes closed and a great smile of relief on his face. The whole room erupts in laughter.

April 24

I've gone to try to fix a mistake. It's Saturday, and MSF would prefer we didn't work on weekends and didn't ask National Staff to work. I don't see my counsellors as National Staff. I see them as free to care.

Aziz is with me. We've gone to Alfiya's house. She's a woman with whom I danced several days ago on the 1st ward in TB2. Later in the week, her husband came to see her. I introduced myself, said to him that she was a good dancer and a good woman. He looked at me half-smiling and shook his head. "No, no she's a bad woman." I laughed and repeated that she was good and that I was glad to see him out at the hospital visiting. I could tell he had been drinking. Later, I said to Aynur: "Look, they're over under the trees just sitting and visiting quietly."

Two days later I learned Alfiya had gone home, left the hospital and treatment. Her husband had been angry that she had impressed me. Later he had phoned Alfiya's 17-year-old roommate and asked of her behaviour, who she visited with. He wanted to know if she ever talked to the male patients. The roommate was caught by surprise, said yes, sometimes, why? He hung up. Next thing, he had ordered Alfiya home. We heard that he had beat her. Alfiya was angry at her roommate, who was scared and upset.

Aziz and I have come to Alfiya's home. Her husband is out. Good. She greets us. Her son appears. He's about 24. Alfiya looks toward the floor and goes silent. We are sitting in their living room on the floor mats. The son tells us to get out. "This is our family's business, not yours. We will handle things ourselves. Go away." I don't reply for a few moments. I try to look relaxed. Aziz is ready to leave. The hostility is palpable.

"Actually, we are all in the same family. The human family. We have come because we care about your mother. We know you love her. That's good. We know you want the best for her. That's good. She will die if she doesn't go back to the hospital and restart treatment. And while she is at home, she is infecting everyone else. We need your help. We understand that your father is angry. You can help him to understand. She is your mother. She needs you to help her to live."

He relaxes. He is not so sure now. "My father doesn't understand. He is very hard-headed."

I speak some more about the hospital, about treatment. About the hundreds in the region who have the sickness. The meaning of epidemic, how it kills.

"You can reach him. You are the eldest son. You are a man. He will listen to you."

He pauses. Then whispers: "I will do my best."

When we have finished explaining all about treatment to the son and explaining to Alfiya how we will try to help her when she goes back to the hospital, we get up to leave. Outside, with the son back in the house, Alfiya looks up at us and pleads: "Please, you have to help me. Get me out of here. Just take me to the hospital."

Aziz and I don't know what to do. I give her money for a taxi. We leave our number.

☙

April 25

They are going to declare grandmother Shakargul a treatment failure. She misses her drugs two or three times each week, spits others out occasionally. She has been here over a year. They say there is no hope. I tell the doctors to give me another month. She was in that room of three, my first friends in TB2. I will reach her, get her taking the drugs each day, stop her from avoiding. I will affect her immune system somehow.

I look into her eyes. They seem blocked, a dullness inside. Instead of going to the depth of her like so many others there is a cloud in them, as though something has left her and gone far away. I ask of her life. It's normal, she says. Two married daughters, two sons, youngest only 13. She lives with them in Chimbay. She was in hospital before and became negative then turned positive and had to return. This made her angry. One of her sons has MDR-TB also. She has three grandchildren.

Her life has been fine, she insists. But then she says that for most of her marriage her husband was a heavy drinker. She admits it has been hard. That things were so often in disarray. She lived in fear. The kids hated it. I affirm the strength she has had to manage all those years, raise her children. "Did he hit you?" Yes, of course. They all do. I say the drugs are not harder than what she has already been through.

She can do it. I ask her if she wants to live. Are you sure you want to live? Tell me. Say: "I want to live. I want to be cured." She says it. I ask her to say it again. She does. You can only get somewhere if you face the right direction. She promises to take her drugs. "I will try my best." I think her words are beautiful.

⌖ I have organized a picnic for this afternoon. I tried to hold it three weeks ago when the weather first began to warm. The hospital doctors freaked out. "No way. It's too cold. They might get sick." If it is too cold of course we will postpone it. We might hold it by the canal. "THE CANAL!!! That's impossible. A patient died there when they decided to go swimming. It is not possible to hold a picnic there." Okay, okay, I only said might.

Today the weather is warm, has been warm for a long time. We have started a fire out on the overgrown play area close to the fence that surrounds TB2. Patients dragged broken limbs and any sticks they could find. We have put potatoes in to cook. Everyone has brought out their cups and we pour juice. We hand out wieners. They peel the clear cellophane wrapping off and eat them raw. Two each. We wait for the potatoes to cook. We've brought Kurbangul out from ICU in her wheelchair. She's with her sister Sarbinaz who had been admitted only a week earlier.

Gulbasara is not allowed out. Everyone else sits or squats on their haunches. We are having a picnic. The first ever at TB2 in the seven years of its existence. Around us the trees are green, shrubs are growing, grass up.

I ask for some songs. The man who sang before after my first big hospital meeting steps up. His voice carries and fills the whole area. Others clap in rhythm. They sway while he sings, his arms outstretched. There is no such thing as tuberculosis, this must all be a sad joke. These cannot be sick people. Cannot be patients. Then another woman sings. She looks like a gypsy but she isn't. There are gypsies in Nukus but they are fringe people like everywhere else in the world. They don't qualify to come to this kind of hospital. The woman who is not a gypsy sings well and others join the chorus.

Then I say I will sing. I can't sing on key but I want them to hear me trying anyway. I sing a song I made up years ago. Aynur translates in the pauses. Everyone claps after I am finished. They know I am a bad singer, but they know I tried.

Finally the potatoes are ready. They get passed around. Totally black. The outside is peeled off and everyone munches. The nurse comes out and yells that it is afternoon snack time. The patients yell back that they don't want it. They eat their hot potatoes. Watch the fire, its orange bouncing flames.

Skin

I think I have figured out the inner workings of the patients that cause them to stop treatment. Imagine how most of us would react if we learned that we had a fatal disease for which we believed there was no cure. We'd feel pretty downtrodden, desperate. Especially if many in our community had already succumbed from the same disease. Then, by great fortune someone came and said there was a cure. That it was free. The hitch was that there were awful side effects and it took two years. Most of us would say, that was okay, we just want to live. Then we were told that, although there was no guarantee, the odds were very good. We'd be so thankful, and we'd hunker down to make it through the two years. So why isn't that the case here? Why does it become like a dyke filled with holes as, one after the other, patients miss treatments and flirt with defaulting, and in fact so many do default, at least a third of those who start?

Well, we're all humans with a context. We are never simply patients. We have homes and relationships. We need to make a living. We need the means to run our lives. With those afflicted by MDR-TB, their common socio-economic level often means there is not a lot of money available for something extra in their lives. While it is true the drugs are free and, unlike other medications and services in Karakalpakstan, one doesn't have to pay a bribe for TB treatment, there are costs involved. Being sick and on treatment, as evidenced by Achmed's situation, means not being available to earn money. For women, it means being more limited in their expected home duties. It costs money to get food to patients when they are in hospital. Once discharged, it costs money for transportation to and from their poly-clinics every day. Twenty months of fares. It's a constant financial drain, and it creates family resentments and patient guilt. Sometimes, there just is no money to sustain the transport.

Within families, jealousies, competition, ignorance, and animosities sometimes weigh against the individual's intentions to keep going on treatment. Domestic violence, marriage discord, others' health problems all exert a drain on the patient's capacity and will to stay adherent, suffer the relentless side effects. The role of stress cannot be overstated.

Then, there is the omnipotence of the grim reaper, the dark whisperer. Any patient who has already experienced premature deaths in their immediate family, especially from TB or MDR-TB, knows too well the reality of the dark whisperer and its message. When premature death regularly cleaves a family or community, the inevitable conclusion is that no one is safe, that death will come, that no one knows who is next. Similarly, grief over losing a parent, sibling, or child weakens one's own resolve to live. Aside from the heartache over loss, guilt about surviving enters in. The result is a fatalistic consciousness that reduces the necessary will to withstand for any duration the arduousness of the side effects, the arduousness of having to journey back and forth every day in every kind of weather just to feel debilitated, in the hope that the treatment will actually cure.

And lurking beneath all of these factors are the individual traumas in people's lives from which they likely have never healed. Each of these erodes that faith in oneself, that sense that one has the right to live, that one has a bright future, all of which one needs in order to persevere. In order for our immune systems to do their job, we need sufficient energy. Energy that goes into dealing with stress or that gets balled up or diminished by unresolved or unresolvable pain is not available to fuel our immune systems.

I have done a training exercise with the counsellors in which I set a pumpkin in the centre of the floor and told them to imagine the pumpkin as the child growing up. I said imagine that child's parents are fighting all the time and that makes the child live in worry and fear. Then I reached into a box and pulled out a sharp knife. I thrust it into the pumpkin. Then I said imagine the child's father is alcoholic and beats the mother. Stab, I thrust another knife into the pumkin. I carried on—a family death, a suicide, sexual abuse, physical abuse, emotional abuse, divorce, abandonment, great poverty, sibling brutality, peer rejection, and for each of these I thrust another knife into the pumpkin. I finished by saying that most of us have knives stuck in us. And that much more often than not, those knives have never been pulled out, never even been fully acknowledged. Those knives deep in our vulnerable child souls dictate how we live, and especially how we react to traumas and stress as adults.

The room of counsellors was silent, each of them again touching the freshness of their own wounds.

In order for us to make a difference in keeping patients from defaulting, we must get inside the walls of the protective forts in which they live. We must gain the amount of trust needed for patients to reveal their inner truths. It's all about building relationships. And it's about paying acute attention so as to discern what's really going on inside those forts because too often the patients aren't consciously aware of what is driving them or what eats at their resolve.

Patients focus on hating the side effects, but it's our job to figure out what underlies that. And then to figure out what can be done to lessen the power of the underlying factors. The great proportion of defaulting comes once the patients leave hospital and are on their way to being cured. The newness is over, the first level of commitment has been used up, and now the dull reality of so many more months to go and its accompanying drudgery settles in. They might start to feel fewer symptoms or the opposite, and magical thinking emerges to coalesce with the daunting daily routine of facing the drug war within their bodies. The notion to quit and hope for the best becomes ever present.

The counsellors have to counteract that. I say to my team that we all have to keep learning, keep developing our insight, go outside the box in finding creative ways to respond. A holistic and open-minded, constantly thinking approach is the direction.

☞

April 26

Deelya has phoned to say Oleg would like me to bring him some lemon green tea when I come next.

Guldana has called me over to tell me something. Her analysis has come in. She is negative. She's going home. I pick her up and swing her around. She smiles sheepishly. I tell her I will visit her in Hodjeli, the town just outside of Nukus where she lives with her brother. It is just the smear that is negative, and she still must await the culture results, but after a year of waiting, of hunching in the pose of vomit every day, what else is this but great news! Victory.

I visit with Erkin. She is 26 and arrived three weeks ago. Her father died some years back. Her mother died from MDR-TB in November. We don't talk about it. She looks straight into me. When she laughs or smiles her nose crinkles; to its sides are little lines that flow downwards. There is something very distinct about her. A bearing, a confidence. She says she has goals. Wants to live because she has goals. She is beautiful. I love her. I hold her. Then she asks what I felt after I held her. I'm the one who asks, no one ever asks me. I answer that I felt warm, wonderful.

Slohan is 31. She is in room 10. Still there. All the others that were first there when I did my chant are gone — the woman with the strong hand, Gulsara, beautiful Roza, Gulshat her ivory face and death-scythed family. All are gone but Slohan remains and now with several others and young Altingul. She tells me her story. This is her second go at TB2. She was here over two years ago. That time her stay was only two months and she was discharged. A few months later she felt so healthy she decided she no longer needed the daily ordeal of toxic drugs and she stopped the treatment. All went well. But 17 months following, she got sick again.

When she was 14, her grandmother died. This was a real blow because they had a special bond. Then her mom died. Then her dad. Then, when she got sick this last time, her husband left her and later divorced her. She loved him. Slohan wears a dark beret that tilts slightly over her brown hair. Her mouth curves downwards, eyes carry a hurt look as though waiting for the next bad moment. After six months she is yearning to get out. She sighs.

I have gone to a polyclinic to visit beautiful Roza from TB2's Room 10. Uncharacteristically, she is sad and distraught. She says it's the side effects, that they are getting to her. She has spent the last few weeks behaving as though she is more than the side effects. So much so that others chastised her, told her she would attract the evil eye if she behaved so, behaved happily like nothing was wrong. Better to wear the burden more visibly. Safer that way. She knew they were just jealous that she could stand the side effects so well. But now she's long out of the hospital, no more room 10 at TB2, and no more coming each day to OPD for her drugs until her culture results show she is for sure not contagious. She is on her way, and her body has responded well to the drugs. Why a problem now?

She says they're too much. I press her. She gives in, says she is having quarrels with her husband. He is angry. He wants more of her. Wants sex when he wants it, doesn't accept that the drugs are hard on her, make her sick. He is young. They had a small company that operated with him as head with his computer programming skills. That all stopped after Roza got sick and had to have the abortion. If you are pregnant when you get MDR-TB, they abort the foetus because having a baby taxes the system so much and because the risk of infecting the baby is so extreme.

Roza with her long brown hair, a face of candlelight, eyes quick with awareness, and a non-Karakalpak vision of herself. But she is with a husband who wants her to obey. Her mother-in-law expects service, badgers her to have a baby, listen to her son. So Roza lives at her own mother's home. When she was eight her father died. "He loved me so much. Even more than my brother." But he was an Afghan war veteran and prone to psychosis. He got TB, but recovered. Then he had a heart attack and died. Later, her mother remarried, but her step-father got TB and he died. Before doing that, he coughed a lot. That's how Roza thinks she and her brother both got MDR-TB.

At her wedding, Roza wanted to dance freely, joyfully. But her husband said no. Her husband is depressed now. And Roza says the drugs are hard to take. She asks me if one's soul will go to heaven if one dies by suicide.

❧

April 29

Kural is 31. He has been at TB1 for four weeks and tells me he has been waiting to have a turn with me. He has a goitre that is quite visible, some teeth missing, hollows beneath his cheek bones. And he speaks with a slight mumble. He's also a bit hard of hearing. Aynur doesn't like him. She has a harder time with anyone who displays too much need, either from physical impairment, mental impairment, or just a nature that doesn't shy from asking for help. She does not like helplessness. But there is something about Kural.

He tells me that he has been with TB for seven years. On and off treatment, it never going away. Now he has been diagnosed with MDR. He is finding the huge cocktail of pills too much to tolerate. When his mother died in 2003 he was heartbroken. There has never been a father and he became responsible for his three younger brothers. Finally, he got married but then, as soon as he was told about the MDR, his wife filed for divorce.

"What's the point of it all? Life just keeps going from bad to worse." And he adds that there is no way he can keep on the drugs. He also has developed an incessant ringing in his ears.

The talking is good for him. I can see the quiet intelligence in his mannerisms, his natural gentleness. He just needs some support, a sense that somehow he can keep going. I finish the session by holding him in a long embrace for a couple of minutes. Before stopping the embrace, I pat him several times gently on the back. He does the same to me. He has gentle, honest eyes.

❧ Oleg drinks a cup of the apricot juice I have brought him. He unwraps the block of pork fat which he also requested. "This will improve my appetite," he says, eyes twinkling. He has refused his drugs the past week and knows it's not a good idea, but he feels better, more alive. Death just nods.

Upstairs there is a huge kerfuffle. One of the TB1 doctors is pissed. She's ordered all the patients on that floor into the pill room. Thirty of them gather, some inside standing, leaning against the wall, others poking in from the hallway. She demands to know what the hell went on last night. The duty nurse reported that the women were having a party at 2 am and the noise was so bad that the other wards were awakened. The patients were all dancing and yelling. She looks over at me. "I know he told you it was good to dance but you have to be reasonable." She is particularly angry because the chief doctor of the entire complex has called her in and accused her of not being in control of her patients while her partner Dr. Zakir is on holiday.

The patients react instantly. Is she crazy? Why would they be up so late? Someone is making this up to get them in trouble. They were sound asleep by midnight as usual. They did dance until about 10 pm. Who said these bad things about them? Lies, lies, lies. So many attest to this version that the doctor isn't sure. Her face changes. She says more quietly: "I'll have to find out." The discussion moves to a broken toilet. The doctor suggests that they and the staff pitch in some money to get it fixed. And then we all reach agreement that any dancing has to stop by 10 pm. Later, I pat the doctor on the back, tell her what a good job she is doing, how important it is. I really am happy with her. She is the only doctor I've seen who listens to the patients.

In the evening, Deelya takes me to meet Adilbek at his home. He has been angry at her, and she is intimidated because he is older — 53. A university educated draftsman, he worked in the army as a physical education trainer. Now, Adilbek is agitated and confused by the system. He had TB seven years ago and was cured. Each year he has to take an x-ray to check that it has not returned. This past year he had a fever and some coughing. They did an x-ray and a spot was detected. An analysis was done. MDR-TB. Adilbek went to hospital and started the drugs. After a month he was gaunt and weak. His wife could not believe the change in him, how his robust condition had deteriorated once on the treatment that was supposed to help him.

Nonetheless, he quickly converted to negative, only spending 28 days altogether at TB2 before being sent home as non-infectious. For the next three months he continued losing weight and feeling weakened by the drug side effects. At home, he ate well which helped, but it was not enough to fully stop the weight loss. That very first sputum analysis had actually said XDR-TB which meant extreme drug resistance. In other words, good luck and don't get your hopes up. Yet he converted so quickly and was not coughing nor breathing abnormally. No further analysis indicated any infectiousness.

Adilbek had come to believe that either the drugs were in the wrong regimen or some other mistake had occurred. The last month he had refused to take the drugs and, since the community TB doctor was either on holiday or on cotton campaign, no one was available to discuss his condition with him. When it's cotton planting or cotton harvesting time, all government employees at every level and all higher school and university students are ordered to go for three weeks or more of service. Cotton campaign. Jobs are dropped as teachers, nurses, doctors, administrators of every ilk are transported to live in the fields. I listen attentively to everything Adilbek has to say. I ask him about his anger, about his relationship with his wife. I show him the OM, MANI, PADMI chant. We do it together. I tell Adilbek I will check with our head MSF doctor. By the end of the visit, he isn't yelling and his eyes aren't blazing. He shows me the medical books that he has been reading about tuberculosis.

April 30

Samuel, our head MSF doctor, looks up Adilbek's records. Strange. Not the usual pattern for XDR-TB. Odd that he would convert to non-infectious so quickly if he was so resistant to so many of the drugs. I wonder if the x-ray only showed a scarring from his previous TB. I posit that the analysis could have been flawed somehow. It is known that nurses put the wrong identification labels on the sputum sample containers, that lab techs write the results on the wrong line, that samples themselves get cross-contaminated. We make mistakes in the West all the time. Surely there must be more here where the training, pay, and management are of so much poorer quality? Our doctor says he doesn't know.

What should I tell Adilbek? Samuel says he doesn't know. I like and don't like that answer. I like it because it's honest and exactly what more doctors need to say, indicating a readiness to look deeper, search more. The patient can only benefit. I don't like it because it means it's up to me to go back to Adilbek and respond. If he has XDR and stays off the treatment he'll most surely die. If he doesn't really have XDR or any TB, if he is totally fine and only had a cold way back, then being on the toxic drugs for two years might seriously harm or even kill him. If it doesn't, then it might make him resistant to future treatment if he ever does get TB. What to do?

☞ At TB2 I'm with Shakargul. We walk out of the hospital grounds into a glade where we cannot be seen. We walk hand in hand. I'm a grandfather and she a grandmother. She has told me that her grandson is the best thing in her life. Instead of waiting for analysis results, for someone or something to decide her future, instead of holding onto the pain of her alcoholic husband's past behaviour, I want her focussing on what she wants. I want her connecting to her own will and to be aiming for something.

She has done some affirmations for me. I want to have 20 grandchildren. I want to be cured now. I want to live to 100. And now we are out in the field. She in her burgundy traditional clothes, scarf wrapped head, and I in my t-shirt and jeans. I ask her to close her eyes and breathe slowly in and out. In and out. I ask her to feel the air around her. To notice the sounds of the birds. Then I ask her to stretch out her arms and slowly turn in a circle where she stands. Slowly. Feel the movement, feel her breathing. This is her world. When she finishes and opens her eyes, I repeat: "This is your world. This is your life." I ask her to look me in the eyes and say those words.

Then we embrace and the two grandparents from opposite sides of the world hold on long and close.

Amangul is alone on a bench. I go to her. She arrived just two weeks before. I call her the new girl in glasses because she can hardly see without them. When she arrived she clearly wasn't in touch with how monumentally her life had changed. She is now. She cries as soon as I get over to her. She wants to die. She is angry that the disease has got her. Already her life sucks. She got married at 16 and has been married 13 years. Her husband is alcoholic and beats her regularly. Sometimes she flees across the street with her three children, but he goes after her. The neighbours are afraid of her husband so they give her up lest he attack them. He attacks his other family members if they try to intervene. Her life is one of waiting. Waiting for the next binge and the next eruption. Waiting to see how her three children will grow up, how this will affect them. And waiting now for two years to be cured.

So, she wants to die. Her cousin died from MDR-TB and, while dying, Amangul cared for her. That's the origin, she thinks now, of her present predicament. She is not able to sleep, feels nervous and anxious most of the day. Her husband asks if she is fucking anyone at the hospital. I shake my head and say why don't you leave him. She laughs and says she has. She says she owns their house and has kicked him out several times but he just comes back. I say what about going to the police. She says that she did that also. The police talked to him and even put him in jail. But when they let him out he comes home and in a few weeks drinks and beats her again. The police told her not to go to them anymore. "He's your husband," was all they would say. "I know they felt bad for me, but they knew they couldn't do anything else."

After an hour, Amangul has cried lots and talked lots. All I can say is to do it as often as she needs. We will support her. We care. And that since she has borne such a shitty burden all these years she has lots of strength and can push through the challenge of MDR-TB. "If anyone can, you can." Amangul is husky and looks younger than someone who has been married 13 years. She looks like a person who owns her own house.

Later, I go to Polyclinic 5. Murat has gone to Tashkent and I said I would look in on his patients. This is the first time I've been to this polyclinic. Many of the patients are curious to see me. I know some from TB2. Gulshat from Room 10 is here, still taking an hour to get through all of her pills. Then a fellow named Kutlimorat asks to have an individual session with me. He's got a fierceness to him. Penetrating eyes. Thirty-five maybe. Lithe, intense. He says he is nervous and scared all the time. He demands help. Wants to stop worrying. I do the usual simple counsellor routine — active listening and clarifying. Then I decide to do an exercise. I hold my cell phone out in my hand and ask him to take it from me. He reaches for it but I pull it away. I hold it out and repeat that he should take it. He reaches again and again I pull my hand away. I repeat the process. This time he grabs more quickly, but I snatch it away. Then again. He lunges for it so as to rip my hand off as well. I pull away just in the nick of time. He is annoyed. Then I hold my phone out one more time and ask him to take it. This time I don't move and he gets it easily.

I can tell he'd like to keep it now. But he just asks what's the point? I tell him that his symptoms and problems are like this. If he wants them to go they will, but if inside he doesn't want them to go then they will stay because he won't let anyone take them.

He doesn't especially like the message. But, unfortunately I have no more time. I have to go to another polyclinic. I shake his hand and tell him I will see him again. When? Soon.

✍ Finally, it's evening again, and I'm back with Deelya to Adilbek's house. He and his wife are anxiously awaiting my news. What did the expat doctor say? What should he do? So, it's like this, I say. No one knows for sure. It is your choice what to do. I think it's possible there's been a mistake. And then I spell out the possibilities and his options. He doesn't know it but I am too ignorant and too afraid to go further in helping him decide. He listens. He says that for now he'll still refuse the drugs but will pass in another sputum analysis, and he'll wait to talk to the community TB doctor when she finally gets to him. He is feeling better each day.

✍ This weekend, the other expats went to the Aral Sea — what remains of it — since it's a holiday weekend and they could make the outing. It's 200 km to Moyniak, that's the former sea port, fishing town that's now 150 km from the water. A big attraction are the rusted ship hulks scattered on the sand. Then the next day they go to the actual sea where they stay over night in tents. Last day they drive all the way back to Nukus. I didn't want to go because it means three days of driving in the back of a Toyota Landcruiser—bench type seats.

May 4

Our first concerts.

This week I have paid 40,000 sum to have a music concert at each of our two hospitals. A music guy came with his machinery to blare out tunes. And he sings on some of them. It was loud and all dance-able so the patients really liked it. It reminds them that they are full humans and not just patients, that they have MDR-TB but that they are more than that. Everyone was dancing. 20,000 sum for each of the two days—90 min in each hospital. All the patients in TB2 and our 50 in TB1 plus another 60 of regular TB patients in the other part of that hospital. The music blaring outside and everyone smiling. 20,000 sum equals $10. So for the price of admission to a Western dance club, the club came to all those people.

I use my daily food allowance to buy things for patients—food mostly but also other small items. Last night I had a dream that I had found a guitar on sale for $29.95 and I was really excited as the patients have asked for one. There were two on sale in the dream so I was going to get both, one for each hospital.

So little would make everything better for their daily lives. The hospital food, for instance, is so bad no one eats it. Relatives bring food. The problem in one hospital is that the kitchen is occasionally closed to save money on the gas needed for the one cook stove. And at the best of times, patients have to wait their turns to use the stove. For poor patients getting food is a problem. Other patients help but then that makes the poor ones feel ashamed.

MSF used to provide money for the hospitals to provide food but that stopped in January. On Friday when I went to TB1, a whole bunch of nurses and hospital personnel were outside in the furrows on the grounds, on their knees in their white uniforms pulling weeds and digging in the earth. They had been ordered out to do that.

But music is fun, brings fun to the buildings of sickness. Music reminds them of the lives they had before they got sick. Like Islam who is not in ICU anymore. He is in a room with his younger brother. Still weak and thin, but he comes out to sit on his haunches—strong enough to listen to the music from afar. Like Shakargul. She was only sitting and watching while others danced. I went up to her and beckoned her with my fingers, dancing in front of her, copying what I'd seen others do. She looked up at me and shook her head. I persisted. She refused. I took her hand. And up she stood. Hands out like sinews in the wind. Grace. Arching her torso, sensuality in her eyes, wild now and alive like I'd never seen them. No longer a grandmother, life seeping away to stillness, but the true Shakargul. Only one dance. But a dance of vibrancy.

May 5

Roza is confused. At TB2 she was a force for aliveness. Now, she is lost. The memory of her abortion troubles her. Her husband has become an irritant. She asks again about the consequences of suicide. Can one donate their organs if they kill themselves. I can see from her eyes that she is not right. She says her husband is a pig who does not look after himself if she is not there to advise him. She wants more support and understanding at home. He wants sex. She will donate her heart and her kidneys. And now she has red in her urine. She has trouble sleeping at night. Her husband won't kiss her because he is afraid of infection. But he wants to fuck her. She worries he is out with other girls. The wheel in her head is going around and around. It is whirling too fast. Like it was with Guldana.

I tell her she is like Guldana now. She must stop that wheel. She must breathe out of it. Do you remember the chant we used to do in room 10?

OHHHHHHHMMMMMM MAHHHHHHHNEEEEEE PAHD-
DDDDDDDDMEEEEEE HUUUUMMMMMM

I use those sounds not for their meaning but because they sound nice, sound absorbing, take the listener away from the part and into the whole. At TB1, the room of dancing girls say to me, do that sound stuff again, it helps us to sleep.

Roza remembers the chant. She says she has done it at home but has to do it quietly when no one else is around so they will not wonder or ask questions. She says maybe I should meet her husband and teach him the chant. Then she laughs. She says her husband might get jealous if he meets me. He doesn't want her to volunteer as a peer support and return to TB2 even if I pay her some money. He doesn't want her around other men. I talk to her about sex. I want to get her head away from dying. No one talks about sex in public here. It is to be laughed and asided about with close contacts only.

I buy her some ice cream. We have stopped at a restaurant. We are inside with her. Aynur is not happy because, even though Roza is negative, it's always possible she could reconvert. "I have a son," Aynur says. But we eat our ice cream and drink green tea. Aynur hates me sometimes. I guess that's appropriate.

✍ Murat and I have gone to Amontay's home. He left the hospital two weeks before. Ran away. He's the guy Aynur and I call photo man. Whenever I would take pictures with my camera, this 40-year-old would want to be in them. Alone, with that guy, with this other guy. With a group. Shit-eating grin. Big ears sticking out a bit. A simpleton.

Aziz laughed the day Amontay tried to run away from the hospital the first time. Aziz was coming in the MSF Landcruiser, bumping along the windy dirt road that heads 5 kilometres from the highway through the desert out to TB2. He looked over into the field and saw Amontay walking. Amontay had spotted the MSF vehicle coming and pulled his jacket over his head thinking it disguise enough. But Aziz stopped the truck and told him to go back to the hospital. Amontay did. But the next day he escaped again and never came back.

We are here to convince him. We exchange hugs. Sit around the low table on the mats. His aging mother is there. She wants him back at hospital. He refuses. He won't start the drugs again. Not much conversation. Just us blabbing, cajoling, reasoning and him shaking his head with an aw- shucks downward resignation that says *gol darn it I ain't going back for nohow.*

I take his hand. "Look me in the eyes, brother. I need to see your eyes. You will die if you don't go back. You don't need to die. You are still strong." His mother cries a bit. She exhorts him to return. He says he won't. I tell him we will see about home-based treatment. That we'll come again.

As we go back to the car, Amontay comes out to offer us a piece of round bread. That is the way. When someone visits your home in Karakalpakstan they must be offered bread. And it is proper to take at least a thumb pinch full. We take the bread. We hug again and get in the car. We wave. He stands watching us go, and he waves. "I like that guy, now," I say. "I didn't used to. When he was at the hospital always bugging me for a photo, I just found him annoying. Even though I know he is simple. Handicapped."

"You know," Murat says,"you know, he wasn't always this way. He was normal when he was younger. He was in the army. And one night he was walking home and some men jumped him. They beat him viciously. They used their punches, their feet, and finished it with bricks. He was in bad shape for a long time. That's why he is the way he is now."

☙

May 7

I am in the counselling room at TB2. There are nine women with me. I'm talking to them about women's roles in Karakalpak culture and about relationships. Three are 17-year-olds. Altingul is now 15. Gulnas, one of my first three friends, is 31, Jumagul is 27. Fatima is the 40-year-old virgin who still wants to marry and have kids. Amangul is 31. Erkin is 26. I want the young ones to learn from the older ones. I want them all to have the experience of sharing and thinking openly without shame. We discuss how it is to be married, to have to serve the husband's family. Each talks of their ideas and their past.

Jumagul says that coming to the hospital has helped her to understand herself and her life. She says that ever since she got married she has had to work from dawn to night. It was always about her duties and serving everyone else. It got even worse once she had her two children. Then it was the same duties but now caring for the children as well. "No one ever appreciated what I did. And I never appreciated myself. I just did what I was taught, what was expected. Now, I understand that I just got so worn down and that's how I think I developed this disease. Now, I'm really angry at those years. I don't want it to be that way when I get out of the hospital and go home. I appreciate what I did and how hard I worked. I appreciate myself now. I want the others to appreciate me too."

She is from Chimbay region, lives in an outlying village 50 minutes from the main town. Her eyes are strikingly beautiful. All the others always comment on her eyes. Now they see her mind as well.

Then, I decide to introduce sexual education. Aynur has been fore-warned but I can sense her gulping. I pick up a felt marker and move to the whiteboard that Murat uses to teach an English class to Gulnas and several other patients twice a week. I explain that having the full strength of one's self means opening to all of one's self. I mention how I know that no one talks about sex in Karakalpak culture but that sexuality is part of who we are, and by knowing about ourselves we have more power.

I draw the female genitals on the whiteboard. I draw the male genitals on the whiteboard. Then I talk about shifting sexual interaction from a strictly physical act into a fuller emotional act. I talk about how it is important to understand how sexuality can be fuller and can create greater confidence in women once they accept and value their rights. I mention how pornography, which is now available even there on satellite TV, has so wrongly influenced men in the West away from intimacy and away from understanding the fullness of sexual interaction.

The younger girls listen but look toward the floor. This is not in their comfort zone. Amangul, on the other hand, pipes right up. She, who has regular beatings from her husband. "Is it true that the TB drugs make you want sex more. I cannot believe how I feel when I go home on the weekend. When my husband and I have sex, one time is not enough. I want more. It wasn't like this before."

About pornography, Amangul continues: "Yes, I see what you mean about those videos but at least they show what to do. None of us knows otherwise. And if we know what to do then our husbands will be happier. They won't go looking for it elsewhere."

The hour wraps up. I'm feeling pretty good. The counsellors had said not to do it. But it worked thanks to Amangul and Jumagul. I grab the cloth and go to wipe the whiteboard clean. I wipe. The images stay. I wipe again more vigorously. They still stay. I look at the felt marker. PERMANENT.

"Aynur, you gave me a permanent marker!"

"No, I didn't, you took that yourself from the chalet table."

I carry the whiteboard, facing against my body, back out of the hospital and back to the counsellor chalet we've been allotted. Murat will have a more compelling English class.

✐ Alfiya is back at TB2. It took us another visit to her house and another session with her son but they brought her back. I walk with her out of the hospital grounds to sit in the sun. She recounts all the years of having to deal with her alcoholic husband. Twenty years. She cries. I hold her and say how proud I am that she has returned to treatment.

Counsellor joking with Deena and Gulsara at TB2
during a concert day. (Photo courtesy of Marcell Nimführ)

Gulsara – Nefertiti

Elder who sells onions at Nukus bazaar

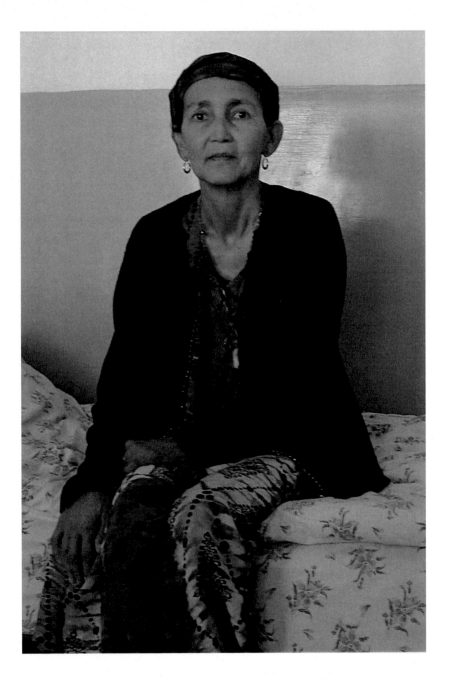

Shakargul on her bed at TB2

Kurbangul and her sister eating charred potatoes at the TB2 picnic

Kurbangul with apricot blossom at TB2

Old woman in Jalalabad whose home was burned to the ground

Last day of school celebrations for Nukus children

Nukus bazaar

A vendor at Nukus bazaar

Burned out homes in Jalalabad

Toilets at Karauziak hospital (Photo courtesy of Courtney White)

Islam and the author at TB2

Slohan on a happy day at TB2

Oleg and the author

Guldana at TB2 in the beginning

Moments in the Sun

May 10

When I visit Kurbangul and Gulbasara in ICU they always teach me about the possible. Gulbasara has been on her bed in ICU for more than four months. She has a sponge mat to place under her hips to counter bedsores. Her MDR-TB is in the back, lungs and left eye. Kurbangul, though only 26, looks much older. Both are thin. Bones within skin. Neither can walk, though Kurbangul is very agile and can fold and unfold herself into various positions on the bed.

I was the counsellor who first told Kurbangul that she had MDR-TB and that it meant months in hospital and two years of daily treatment with toxic drugs that cause dire side effects. Her face contorted with shock, and after stunned silence she smiled and said she would just have to be strong. Now, when I come to our hospital and enter her room, she stretches out her stick-like arms to me and pulls me to her for a long embrace. When we finish the embrace, I kiss her through my mask on her cheek. Neither of us can speak the other's language, and of course our cultures and upbringing are radically different, but we communicate fully. When the nurse or doctor see our long embrace, they can't figure it out.

Gulbasara is a different story. After we began to talk, I was always curious to find out what new musing or state I would get. Philosophical, fearful, disconsolate, energized? Could be anything. Every so often, her father and uncle would visit and I'd see them propping her up one to each arm and helping her walk the ten steps back and forth in the little aisle that fronts the three ICU cells.

One day, I was visiting as she was preparing some food for herself. Unlike Kurbangul who can easily move around on the bed, Gulbasara lies mainly flat on a very slight incline from a heightened pillow. She had a tomato and a cucumber beside her on the bed, having plucked them from her small bed table. In her hand was a paring knife and a cup just a bit larger than the normal one for tea. She began to slice the two vegetables. She had to look downward along her cheeks to see properly. The slicing was meticulous. One piece. Then a half. Then into quarters. The tomato got done. Then on to the small cucumber. She was making a salad. I had to hold back from grabbing the knife and doing it for her. Allow her this power and witness it, how painstakingly slowly the cucumber was sliced. Then just as slowly, she reached over for a small plastic bag on the table. She untied it. Salt. She sifted some onto the salad. Then with the knife she stirred it. All from the prone position she had been in for all these months.

Fifteen days ago, Aziz and I took them both out in wheelchairs. They crave to be outside and breathe and interact. Kurbangul's eyes open so widely once in the natural world. She takes everything in, examining the state of the grasses, the leaves on the trees, the clouds, the spraying of water from garden irrigation pipes. Gulbasara has long worried that she will never walk, and asked us to go farther, out of the hospital grounds compound and along the road to wind through the scrub desert pastures. We obliged. In fact, for a short distance we semi-raced the two wheelchairs. We wanted them to feel the motion, the air flowing against them, to know that they were as alive as anyone else and that we didn't see them as limited or forgotten. We wanted to spark them. The pebbles spit up from the wheels. The two women laughed. They thought we were nuts.

About 400 metres from the hospital, we halted and watched cattle grazing. Gulbasara joked that, when she could walk, we should go out farther in the day and buy some fruit from the farmer and then go back again in the night and steal some more. The four of us spent an hour together and it was great. Two days later, even though it hadn't been my first time doing so, the local doctors raked me over the coals for taking them out without permission, for racing them, and for going away from the hospital. Their spies are always watching. It's the nurses' responsibility for patients in ICU, they exclaimed. What if one of them had been hurt? Who do you think you are? You are not a doctor. Since I have to work with patients for many more months, I accepted the doctors' remonstrations and apologized.

Then about ten days afterwards, Gulbasara started to walk by herself. Her stick thin body moving slowly, carefully step by step out to the hall, dishevelled hair, worn pink bed clothes. A few days ago, she made it up two flights of stairs to sit and watch television. When the doctor found out, she ordered Gulbasara to stop doing it. It was too risky. Gulbasara felt defeated and cried when she told me about it. But she continues to walk.

As for Kurbangul, because I am very busy, and out of hesitation at the doctors' ire, I backed off and decided to let the hospital personnel take care of things. Now, today, fifteen days after I last took her and Gulbasara out in their wheelchairs, I ask permission and take her out again.

She loves it.

Naively, I ask when she has last been out. "When you took me out," she replies. "You remember."

I can't respond.

Kurbangul's eyes roam everywhere, and she smiles at all she sees.

May 11

Deelya and I have gone to Hodjeli to see my Guldana. We meet at the train station outside in the great, bare parking and drop-off area which would indicate a major city if we hadn't just driven along the ordinary street to get here. The station was a hub for most places in this country until change brought cars and enough money to drive them, make money from them.

Guldana gets out of a taxi with her brother. We walk towards each other. I am excited. This is how I told her it would be three months ago. We will meet together like real humans not patient and counsellor, meet together and have a drink and sit in the sun. I remind her, and we hug. It is good to see her in street clothes, to feel her embrace. Her brother shakes our hands. I am the first foreigner he has ever spoken to.

I pay for her taxi and we head over to an outside café table shaded beneath an umbrella. We order samosas and Coke and chai. What a joy this is to be out here with her. But there is some difficulty. She goes each day for her drugs but it costs taxi money and there is little to be spared for that. I hand over 15,000 sum. She hasn't asked, hasn't hinted. Guldana looks downward, usual sheepish smile, whispers thank you. Deelya and I leave them forty minutes later. Victory.

☙

May 13

We just get out of the car and are walking toward the MDR-TB patients entrance to Polyclinic 5. Kutlimorat sees us. It's like he has been waiting for us. "I thought you would come back sooner. It's been two weeks!" He sidles me off and asks if he can talk to me first about something really important.

He begins by relating his long years with TB and now MDR-TB. He talks of knowing the MSF mental health officer who was here before my predecessor. Over two years before. "Leo. Leo and I were good friends. He helped me a lot. I used to help him." Kutlimorat says that Leo helped him to craft a letter to the Karakalpak Minister of Health, how he later met with the Minister about patient concerns. "I know all about psychology," he says. "I have read books about it." Then he tells me how drinking has ruined his life, how he tries to quit but it is hard. He rubs his head in anguish. He puts his hand on my shoulder. Looks me in the eyes. Turns his face downwards. I can see he is struggling with something. It seems familiar.

"I have a problem, and I need some help. I will tell you about it." He is looking at me again. He tells me how his younger brother gave him a cell phone as a gift when their father died. It was a good phone. But Kutlimorat got drunk and gave it to a crony in exchange for some money. Sort of pawned it. Now his brother wants to see the cell phone.

Kutlimorat's eyes take on deep remorse, desperation. "If I can't get it back, it will create very bad feelings in my family. My brother will disown me. It is so shameful."

I now realize why this lead-up has seemed so familiar. Kutlimorat squeezes his fingers on my shoulder. The whole time he has kept me in grasp. "I know it is too much to ask for. I would never ask for it if I didn't really need it. You probably won't give it to me. But I have been thinking about you. You remind me of Leo. I know I can trust you. I will pay it back in one or two weeks when I get my pension money."

How much?

"I need 110,000 sum. That's all."

"Whoa! That's too much for me. I can't give you that. I don't have that much." I don't add the words — in my pocket or that I want to give away to you. Kutlimorat drops his hand from my shoulder in disgust. The earnestness is gone. Only his profound disappointment in me remains. His body gyrates to the left, to the right, his head becomes lower as he droops, looks up at me. Scowling, he utters: "I knew it. I knew you would say that. You are like the other expats. You just look at us. You aren't like Leo."

"Hold it. I will give you 5000 sum. And Murat will give you 5000 sum. Then you could just go after everyone else you know and get them to lend you 5000 sum. I'm sure you will get enough so that the guy with your phone will give it back temporarily until you get the rest and then you can show it to your brother. All will be well."

"No way. That's not good enough. I need 110,000. Only 110,000. 5000 is no use to me." He walks away agitated and shaking his head.

I call after him: "It's a start. You should think about it."

Kutlimorat stands farther away sulking. Then he whirls around, walks toward the clinic, goes right below the window to the room in which his fellow patients are taking their pills, jumps up and swats the plastic covering it. He continues on away from the clinic muttering. He yells back to me: "You could give that if you really wanted to help me."

Later, at TB1, Gulsima is waiting to see me. Her husband is leaving to work in Kazakhstan. He'll be gone for six months. She is feeling crushed. She knew he would leave but now it hurts. I hold her while she cries. The disease, the side effects, being in the hospital, and now this further aloneness. Unlike all the other patients, she does not have a cell phone. She won't hear from him except for when she goes to her home on the weekends. The doctors are angry now because too many patients leave on weekends after they take their drugs Saturday morning. They come back on Monday morning for the next drug intake. It didn't use to bother the doctors so much, but someone higher up has found out and complained and now Dr. Zakir and the other doctor are clamping down—or trying to. Leaving the hospital to go home means possibly infecting others. Gulsima is nervous that if she goes home on the weekend they might not let her back in.

She asks me if she can just not take her pills for a couple of days. Just so she can process the leaving of her husband. I tell her she can do whatever she wants, but when she stops the pills it just makes the bacilli stronger, means longer time in hospital. She knows this. She had to ask anyway. She says she feels better after crying.

Downstairs in TB1, I meet with the comedian and the other men in his room. As usual, his eyes are twinkling. Black mustache, black messy hair, smallish wiry guy, a smart 53-year-old comedian. His eyes really do twinkle when something funny is stirring in him that he wants to relate.

"Hey, you know I get headaches all the time. We had a doctor in the other ward who, when we'd tell him about having a headache, he'd never do blood pressure checks or even take our pulses. We'd ask why he wouldn't check us the way he was supposed to. He'd tell us: 'Oh, I can evaluate patients just by walking into the room and observing them.' He had no need for any equipment. And our doctor, Zakir, is the same. Those doctors have special powers, I think. See, look over at that guy on the corner bed. He never gets side effects. You know why? He's Zakir's brother-in-law. I bet he gets better drugs than the rest of us." Everyone is laughing. The comedian too, his partially toothed mouth grinning like he's got as many answers as anyone ever had questions.

In the other room, Oleg tells Aynur and me about growing up in a town in Russia, about how his mother died when he was six and his sister four. He had never known his father. When his mother was pregnant with him, she had married his sister's father. That guy abandoned them to an orphanage. They were together there for two years and then his little sister was adopted, but he remained. He left when he was 14. While he was there, he learned sign language to communicate with the deaf because lots of the children put there were deaf. It wasn't a bad place to be.

As he grew older, he was taught mechanics and got really good at fixing cars. That's what he was doing in Nukus when he got sick. He had come here because his mother and her family had been from here. That's how he met his natural father a few years before. They had lived together until the old man had died months back. He died from TB. Oleg tells us he wishes he knew where his sister was, what became of her life. Aynur likes Oleg, his unassuming cultivated Russian and his obvious graciousness.

Aynur wants to get more information from Oleg about his sister. She wants the details so she can write the case off to the Russian reality television show which tries to reunite long lost relatives. "It would be really great if we could find Oleg's sister for him, don't you think?" As a translator so regularly in the trenches of human need, Aynur has had a consistent practise of keeping her feelings apart from the job, and a wise practise it is.

Unlike me, she goes home to her own family each day, home to caring for her son and, after I leave in December, she will be stuck here with all these new humans in her life and their needs. For her to allow caring and emotionality into her would create immense distress. She would become overwhelmed because the sadness and the unfixable plights are too many. So, she tries to keep an emotional distance as best she can. But without even trying, Oleg, like Daniyar, has swayed her into personal caring. This emaciated man with the parchment skin that hasn't been washed in months, his long white hands tinged with green on the fingers, his scraggly cheeks, has touched her.

The main streets in Nukus are wide, four lanes, six lanes all nicely paved. The cars and marshrutkas zip along these arteries with the confidence and assurance that real ants would have. They flit in and out of lanes, passing on right or left, screeching to a halt and changing direction as easily as the chatter on their drivers' cell phones. The marshrutkas and taxis halt for passengers wherever the passengers are, halt for disembarking wherever the passengers want to disembark. A marshrutka trip is 400 sum. That's 20 cents. A taxi costs between 1800 sum and 3000 sum for practically anywhere in the city.

Lesser streets are a different story. No one wants to bottom out their vehicle or thrash the springs and suspension so the journey is careful, winding around the broken dips, emerging potholes, past piles of dirt, and always responding to the compelling dictates of the bumpiness.

Most streets are lined with trees, some of the big ones with flowers. Irrigation ditches criss-cross the whole city and spread throughout the vast surrounding desert wherever there are habitation clumps. The water inevitably comes from larger channels and canals originating from the great Amu Darya. The river that creates life here. Its water is the true blood of the land. And the streets of Nukus with their poplar trees and other robust trunks of green all derive from the Amu Darya. In winter, the branches fracture toward the sky in stark bareness. Arrivals at that time of the year could only experience a pervading sense of bleakness. The desert cold drops to 20 below and skiffs of snow can climb a few centimetres. But now in May, arrivals would not see the city itself as desert country. The full ditches, deep with flowing water, brim as though some sultan of old was demonstrating his disdain for wealth by flaunting its wastage. The constant blowing of the dunes at the city limits means nothing.

✍

May 17

I am in the foyer of the second ward in TB2. "Calvin, look. I can sit down now. Jumagul has shown me how." Gulbasara has walked out of ICU into the foyer. The doctors have warned her not to make the perilous trip up the two flights of stairs to the TV, but she won't give up walking out into the foyer. She stands beside the wall in all her thinness, her pink sweater. Hair dishevelled as usual. She places a hand against the wall and slowly, slowly lowers herself, bending her knees as she braces against the wall until her bum lands with a bit of a thud on the step up from the foyer to the hallway. She looks at me beaming. "See!"

☞ Grandmother Shakargul is to be sent home today as a treatment failure. The doctors didn't want to wait the full month they had given me. She was still missing drugs some days. It is enough, they said. I speak with her alone in her room. How do you feel, I say? She cries. I put my hand on her shoulder. I am tired, she says. I need a rest. It is good I am going home. Eat well at home, I say. Then I take three photos of her. One of her and me, one of her on the bed from the other side of the room. One of her face close up. I'll bring these to you in Chimbay.

☞ Kizlargul, the most recent arrival of those first three patient friends way back, was sent to ambulatory last week. Her smear is negative, so she has been sent to OPD to take her drugs there until the culture results come in and say she is fully not infectious. Kizlargul, the thinnest, the 34-year-old, on her second marriage and with a four-year-old daughter happy to have her home again. And Gulnas, the youngest of those three, is happy because she is taking English lessons from Murat and she is in the less infectious ward now. In her pink fleece jacket she smiles at me and says proudly in English: "How are you?"

☞ Erkin is crying. She has gone over to the cooks at the outside clay oven. Like the other patients she has smelled the enticing aroma of the bread baking on the inside of the clay ovoid walls. She has asked if she can have just one round disc of the bread to take back to share with the group of patients she has come from. The others were talking wistfully of how good it would taste. They considered asking the cooks but were too afraid. Erkin took up the quest. "Why not ask?" she grinned. "The bread smells good. They know we have little food. They will understand. They are like us, after all, Karakalpaks. I'll go ask. You'll see."

But they had only gotten angry at her for leaving the normal area for the patients and daring to approach them, daring to think she might deserve bread. Who was she to come over to them?

Erkin walks with me to a secluded place and cries. Her head is hidden in her hands. Her shoulders heave. "You are not crying so hard about not getting the bread," I say. She does not answer.

I hold her. "I am crying because they didn't even think for a second. They acted like it was incredible for me to ask. Like I was so beneath them. They were angry that I came to them. Like I was a dog."

☙

May 18

Three nights ago, I met Deena's body. I went to the home of a 17-year-old who had been pleading for two months to be admitted to hospital. She has MDR-TB again and has been reduced to skin and bones—a tiny, frail child who looked like one of the starving in the worst of African famines. She was in her bed and her counsellor, Deelya, and I came to see her. Her anxious father stood by the doorway watching us, hoping. His hands fidgeted at his sides as he listened. His gray hair, his sad, worn face, alone in his home with this young daughter and her smaller sister.

She was so weak, and there seemed to be no point in doing more than exchange introductions and small talk. I assured her I would try to get her into the hospital and started on treatment again. She knows she is dying without treatment. There was nothing more that I could do, so I asked her if I could hold her in order to pass some of my energy to her. She agreed and with her smooth, brown arms strained to push herself forward on the bed to a sitting position. I bent to her and held her. Within my arms, her body was like a casing of paper holding protrusions—her skin covering a spine and tiny ribs. She was fevered. I felt her cheek against mine and I cradled her in my arms and breathed. My breath long and easy and flowing, hers in short puffs only as brief as her, maybe as her remaining life. I held her a long time until I felt that we had been connected. Then I asked Deelya to do the same.

As I looked at her again, she was more relaxed and so I held her hand and spoke of dying. I said: "I'm going to tell you the truth, but I want you to listen to all of it." She nodded. Then, through Deelya, I spoke.

"You might die." Immediately her face contorted and tears formed. Even though it was her great fear, these were the words she did not want. I pressed her hand, put my finger to her eyes and said not to cry but to listen. There was not enough strength in her to now give away to tears. I continued: "You might die because you are so weak, but right now you are alive. And I might die, when I leave your home and get in the taxi to return to my own home. Crashes happen here all the time. You know that. We are all going to die. None of us knows when. That is what life means. Right now you and I are both alive. I felt your life in my arms. So, instead of thinking about dying, I want you to focus on living. To give your energy to living. Don't run away from the idea that you might die. But keep your gaze on the truth. Right now you are as alive as I am. You want to get into the hospital. You want to start the drug treatment again. You know how hard the drugs are, but you want to do it. That's who you are. You want to live. So go in that direction. Put your mind on living."

Then, I asked her to eat more, to eat small amounts all day long. Yogurt, milk, eggs, rice, fruit, whatever her father could offer. Make herself eat. To drink more. To pay attention to strengthening her body. That was her job now. Deelya and I left.

Outside in the taxi, Deelya began to cry. I asked her what it was like to hold the girl, her patient. She said she had been afraid. Afraid to come so close to someone with so little left of her. I said, that was what we could give. We could give warmth. We could give our love. We could give her human touch. A message, however unconscious, that she was worth being held by other humans, male and female, that she had value, that she was wantable. To experience through the physical intimacy of another living human her own aliveness, her own presence, her own heart beating. That was what we could give. And if she would die that night then she would have died at least with that.

Deelya cried because the girl's mother had died only two years prior from MDR-TB. And the girl had reached out to Deelya two months ago for help when she showed signs of having MDR-TB once again; how Deelya had tried to get the doctors to re-admit her for treatment—this little girl who had already gone through two years of treatment and was designated as a completed case. Two years of taking those toxic drugs believing they would give her salvation, trusting the system, the doctors. So many waver and default but this little girl had started at 15 and never wavered. And she was begging to do it all over again. Deelya was overcome by her own sense of failure because she had not been able to convince anyone to re-admit her patient and had last seen her three weeks before. And now how severely wasted away she had become. This little girl who Deelya had cared about for months and months while she was first with MDR and who was now on a death bed and so thin as almost not to be a body at all.

And ... the next day Samuel was able to overcome the Ministry doctors' reluctance and the little girl was admitted to TB2. They didn't want her because, if a patient dies in hospital, then the doctors are grilled and feel blamed.

And now ... three days later Deena is still alive. I have looked in her eyes again and there is a difference. She sees hope. Today, I asked her if she would like me to hold her again. She smiled, looked away and replied that I should make my own decision. Deena. I have met more than your body.

May 21

At TB1, Kural has not taken his drugs for a week, but he took them today and now his ears are ringing. He is afraid, thinks the drugs are going to set him off again. A week ago he had a bad reaction, didn't know where he was and tried to jump out of the second-story window. He was trying to escape the craziness in his brain, he said. And after they grabbed him and calmed him down, he felt like a fool. Dr. Zakir took him off the drugs for a week to let his mind settle. He is afraid he will make a fool of himself again. It's the little he has left. He doesn't want that to go too.

Gulsima has had one text from her husband since he left for Kazakhstan. She is glad he is safe there, and thinks she will avoid going home on the weekends for awhile. That way she won't miss seeing him so much. And it will prevent conflict with the doctors over leaving the hospital. She has rethought her daughter's situation. When she is discharged she has decided to live with her parents and bring both daughters there. She is going to reclaim her eldest, be her mom.

Sveta the dentist is vomiting in the sink. We were having a counselling session and she said she had to stop. I said just go to the sink right here. I put my hand on her back as she vomits. Aynur sits back on her chair and looks out the window. This is not the translating work she expected when she answered the ad five months ago. When Sveta is finished, we resume our session.

Then after Sveta's session, when we go out in the hall, a cleaner is mopping up some other vomit. Azima is wiping her face. I pull her in for a session. She looks beautiful even after vomiting. Her olive green eyes. She went home last night to be with her children. It had been too long since seeing them last. She only returned at 9:30 this morning, rested in bed a half hour, went to take her pills and injection, then in minutes they came right back up. Useless.

I ask how the home visit was. She cries. I suggest that her heart and mind were still at home when she took the pills. That her body wasn't here to accept them so they just got ejected right back out. Protest.

She nods. "Next time when you go home, come back and wait a few hours before you take the drugs. Give yourself some time to adjust. Some time to be a patient again and ease away from being a mom who wants to be with her kids."

Gauhar has vomited also. An hour after ingestion, so at least there has been some benefit. It's hard enough swallowing all those pills, downing the granules of two packets of pazor and then spewing them all back out, having to do it all again. That's if the nurse will do what she's supposed to do and allow it. It's more tempting to just let the disease win that day.

☞ The MDR-TB outpatient department, OPD, is in the same complex as TB1. Outside there are two benches for patients to sit. One is beneath a tree. They come here from all parts of Nukus and environs. They are the in-betweeners. Not safe yet, if they will ever be safe, but maybe on their way. The culture has to come in and show not enough bacilli to be infectious. There is no predictability. If it comes back positive, then the patient must return to hospital. Out and overjoyed and then back in and despondent. A giant hand yanking them. And, of course, they don't realize that the culture results could have been in error, nor will anyone ever check. Here in Karakalpakstan all is a matter of faith. We have faith that the drugs are potent, faith that the prescribed regimen fits, faith that the sputum analyses are accurate and actually belong to the patient who gets them, faith that the drugs will be available every day and not have a supply break, faith that the x-rays are accurate, and faith that the patient even has MDR-TB.

☙ Nitbek is in OPD today and asks to talk to me. Nitbek is 50 something. A big guy, Aziz was told to prepare him as a treatment failure a while back because he had been in TB2 too long and had not become negative. Aziz was upset because Nitbek had become a model patient. In the past he had started and stopped, gone periods without taking drugs but then in the past few months turned a corner and become super adherent plus a positive example for all the other patients, joking, holding court, encouraging. Aziz dreaded having to inform him. Then all of a sudden a smear negative analysis came. Nitbek jumped in the air and hollered when he was given the news. And since then, he has been coming each day to take his drugs at OPD and waiting for the culture results.

I saw him a couple of weeks ago in passing. Dressed in smart clothes for the warm weather, he looked as fresh and energized as a man on vacation. Today it was a different visage. Still looking robust, his face showed something serious. "I won't take the pazor anymore."

"But Nitbek, if you don't take it then the drugs don't work. That's just the way it is. You know that. You have to take all the drugs all the time. If one is missing then the bacilli win; they get stronger."

"I don't care. Then you have to give me the pazor and I will take it at home."

This is not done. There are many stories of discarded pazor packets scattered outside patients' homes. The policy MSF follows here is called DOTS+. DIRECTLY OBSERVED TREATMENT FOR TWO YEARS. It's the only way to be sure they take the drugs properly. Each day the nurse records who came, what drugs they took. Sometimes the nurse will lie. Sometimes the patient will bribe the nurse to say they were there and took all the drugs. Sometimes with or without a bribe the drugs or just the pazor will be handed out to be taken at home. When the record says all is in order, that the drugs were taken, no one gets questioned, no one blamed. All can smile. Everyone does their magical thinking that way. The disease becomes secondary to the immediate relief of no side effects, no criticism. And if there's been a bribe—a few thousand sum, a gift of some kind, well then the nurse goes home with something more than her paltry salary. It's even been known that a nurse will withhold a drug to sell it. Pazor comes in two small packets. It is the most hated drug because it is most likely to bring on nausea. And it must be taken with an acidic liquid. If it goes down with just saliva or water, the absorption is too quick and the effects are drastically minimized. The patients must take it with orange, tomato, lemon juice or with yogurt.

I lie to Nitbek. "We can't do that. Everyone has to take the pazor in front of the nurse." Even though I have watched nurses nullify pazor's effect by pouring water into the spoon used by the patient. I always speak as though the rules are followed, as though everything works, as though everything is known. I'm a good liar. But this time Nitbek doesn't care.

"Look," he says in an emotional, agitated voice, "I'm 52. I have a wife and family. My sons are grown. Each day it takes me 45 minutes to an hour to get here from my home and the same to get home. I have to take two marshrutkas. If I have to wait on the road because they are full, it can take longer. The sun is hot. Do you understand? The pazor always makes me nauseous.

"Yesterday, as I was going home in the marshrutka I started to feel really sick. I knew I was going to vomit. I had to ask the driver to stop. I climbed out from the back seat. And just as I got out, I started to vomit. But I got a little on the side of the marshrutka. The driver was furious. He jumped out of the van and began yelling at me. He called me a dirty drunk and grabbed me by my collar. He threw a rag on the ground and ordered me to wipe his marshrutka. I heard other passengers saying I was a disgrace, that the police should be called, that I should not be allowed in the marshrutka in future.

"You know I can't tell them I have MDR-TB. They would be even angrier and word would get around and no marshrutka would pick me up. I had to get back in and ride the rest of the way. Of course I still felt sick. It's the pazor that causes that. It's the same every day. Other times I was able to make it. If I was able to take my drugs at the polyclinic close to my home, it would be okay. But I have to come every day to OPD. Tell me. Tell me, Calvin, what would you do? I am 52. How do you think it made me feel?"

Nitbek wipes the tears forming in his eyes. Looks at the ground, whispers: "I won't take the pazor anymore."

☞ Slohan, the last of my originals from Room 10, is also finally now at OPD. She is glad to be smear negative and out of TB2, but she is troubled. We talk. She is angry at her sister-in-law. Right now her brother is away and she and her handicapped sister are at home with the sister-in-law and her children. They don't get along. Her sister-in-law resents them being there. She locks the food away in her room. Slohan is not eating. She has to use her money to get to and from OPD each day. She is hungry but she is more concerned for her sister. All she can do is ruminate on how unfair it is, on how she wishes her parents hadn't died, her husband hadn't divorced her, wishes she wasn't sick so she could work, that her brother had married someone else. Why doesn't she understand? Why is she so mean to us? What have we done?

I give her some money. "Buy some food. Make sure you are eating. When you need more, tell me. And each day look for something that gives you joy."

They all tell me their stories because I ask. And because I really listen. I tell them stories back. The words all evaporate in the heat, become imaginary molecules. What's left? Them and me. They are sick. I am not. For now, anyway. We each carry our stories, words constantly forming and evaporating. Money lasts just a bit longer. Tastes better. Sometimes.

May 24

I am at Polyclinic 2 in the counselling room with Tamara. Her long hair is in one braid that extends all the way down her back to her waist. She is elegant, eyes large and aware. She is neither short nor tall, about 35 years old and has four children. She reminds me of women I have seen on the train in India travelling alone with their children, completely in control, relaxed, sure. Tamara could be wearing a sari right now. The lines in her face ready to curve into mirth at any moment. I am a novelty for her. She is only three months away from finishing now. It has been hard but she has done it. I want to learn how she was able to adhere so well, what gave her the strength. I am educated, she says. I want my children to have a future and I want a future. But it has been hard. Sometimes I want to die. I think about hanging myself. Her face becomes dark. She looks away. I control my impulse to pull her back from the darkness, say something funny, get her to smile as she was only moments before. Sometimes I just want to only hear happiness. But I do my job. "Tell me about it."

"I have been married for 15 years. I should have had five children but I only have four. I love them. But my life is not good. At home I am the servant for everyone. Sometimes I think I will die of exhaustion if the disease or the drugs don't kill me first. My husband likes to hit me."

Her regular counsellor, Nazigul interjects. "She has come sometimes for her drugs with bruises all over her face." I wonder why Nazigul hasn't told me this earlier. Looking at Tamara I would never have guessed.

Tamara continues to tell of other events of pain and demeaning. It is hard to listen to. I can see the paleness in Aynur's face as she is forced to translate. There are few words I can offer back in this first unplanned encounter that will have the meaning to fit such gravity. And yet, this woman with the long braid is almost free from the disease that takes so many. I want her to make it. Not to have some punch be the one that finally breaks her now when she is so close.

I ask Tamara if I can do something, if I can touch her face. She nods. I begin softly running my fingers lightly over the skin on her face. Her forehead. A cheek. The other cheek. Over her eyes. Down her nose. The space between her nose and upper lip. The space beneath her lower lip. Her chin. The side of her throat. The other side. Slowly, softly. Then each part again. I touch her eyelid so that it closes and I stroke the closed eye. Then the other. I tell her she is beautiful. I tell her this is the touch her body deserves, what her face deserves. I tell her she is a warrior, that I cannot understand how she has had the strength to make it this far. How she can take the drugs each day as she does. I say, you will make it. You will make it. And your life will be better. I say, you can do anything.

When I finish, I ask if she would like me to hold her. She says no. I ask if Nazigul can hold her. She says yes. They embrace for long moments. Breathing into each other.

⊘

May 26

Now Alisher is refusing to take one of the drugs. The one that causes the skin to darken. Two of the other patients in Polyclinic 4, young men, are teasing him. They call him Samuel's son. He is frustrated. When he looks in the mirror he sees dark skin. It's summer now, I say, of course your skin is darker.

"No, it's one of the drugs that causes it. I know," he says. He's right of course.

"But it will go back to normal when you finish the treatment."

"Right, a year from now." He won't look at me.

Eighteen years old and he is thinking about what others say. We talk. I ask if maybe this is not just what he can focus on, that maybe he is at a low point, that maybe he is so lonely, missing his mother. No dad. And stuck with the disease. He cries. He says that he is struggling to take all the drugs every day and that when he can't he knows the disease is winning. He feels like a failure, like he is failing himself. Alisher never has a problem letting it out. I wish I could be Alisher.

He doesn't even think about how the other two guys are actually as dark or darker than he is. He tells me not to come to his house looking for him anymore. He doesn't want an MSF car or a foreigner in a taxi coming after him. At least he wants some control. His street doesn't need to know he is sick.

⌒ Today, I am on my way to see Batir. He lives out beyond the subdivision. The road ends and bumps off to the left across sand. Rectangular mud houses are in a spread out line. We pull off the road into an entrance. There is a yurt in the back yard of the neighbour. It is windy. Aynur and I walk across the sand to Batir's house. There is a dog in front of it, barking, hair raised on its hackles. We stop. There is a chance the fucker knows the one that bit me months back; word has spread. Aynur says she isn't going any farther. "I am afraid of dogs," she says. We wait while the dog barks. Someone comes out of the neighbour's house and calls the dog.

We knock on Batir's door and enter. He comes to the entry way and takes us into his living room. He is 20. His father and brother are away at work. He is home alone. I recognize him somehow. "Do you know me?"

"Yeah, I remember you from TB2. You used to come there just before I got discharged." He has the brightest smile I have seen. He makes me smile just looking at him.

"You have stopped taking your drugs. Why, now?"

Batir still smiles, looks at the floor. "It is too hard to get to the polyclinic each day. I have to walk across the desert for 20 minutes to where I can catch the marshrutka and then it takes another half hour to get to the polyclinic. Coming back is the hard part because by then I am feeling sick. And it's so hot out now. It is too hard. I cannot walk very well." He points toward his feet.

"What do you mean?" He pulls up his pant leg and stands. His foot is twisted and misshapen. One leg is shorter than the other. Ahhh, I see. No one told me of this. They only said that he was refusing his drugs. What can I say?

"If we can get home-based treatment for you, will you take the drugs? Every day?"

"Yes, why not. I want to live. The side effects are not that bad. I can handle them."

I don't understand why some patients, a very few but some, get a nurse to bring the drugs to them and others don't. Nazigul says it will be hard to arrange a nurse to come here. How will the nurse get here? No marshrutka comes this far. They stop at the sub-division two kilometres back.

She is right of course. The notion of DOTS—TB drug intakes that are directly observed—is fine in theory, but how can it work in poor countries where people are spread out and there is inadequate transportation? I tell Batir that I will see what I can do. He smiles a beautiful display of mirth.

I hope the dog outside doesn't know how powerless I am.

May 27

Nargisa crouches down on her haunches as close to the floor as possible. She waits on the steps in the short passageway between the first and second wards at TB2. Silent, her mind floating, fluttering. I bend down to talk to her.

I am happy to see her here. Unexpectedly. We have tried for over two weeks to convince her to come back. She lives with an older male cousin and a younger sister in a hutch of small rooms on the third floor of a stark block of Soviet era flats. They are all Soviet era flats in Nukus. The stairway up to hers reeks from the foul waste water that underlies that end of the block.

We have tried for many days to get her back, squatting beside her in the tiny kitchen only large enough for the stove and a sleeping mat. Nargisa is 17 and lost in her own world of ogrely or wraithsome demons. We don't know which. She does not or cannot tell us. Nargisa herself is a wraith. We know that.

Aziz had already convinced the doctors to let her come back to TB2. This little patient who wets the bed sometimes at night. This little girl who flinches, who cries easily, whose eyes dart about. This little girl who only unlocks the door at her flat after we have stood outside and called with repeated variations trying to caress her into letting us in.

Today, she has suddenly appeared and I have been the first to encounter her. I have brought our new Project Coordinator, Sonya, with me to experience first hand the world of patients. She has just arrived from the Philippines. Sonya knows nothing about this reality having neither met her predecessor nor been a PC before. Now she's the head of MSF here in Nukus.

I bend down to Nargisa. I stroke her hair, speak softly. Her eyes flicker about. She responds in few words, only hesitatingly, to my queries. Did you bring your things with you? No. Did they give you a room yet? No. You were really brave to come back. I'm proud of you. You've done the right thing.

Then, suddenly as if from some awful cue from the god of unfairness, Doctor Ayeesha appears. Clad in white, her eyes flash with anger as she sees Nargisa. Paying not the slightest attention to me or the new expat, Ayeesha launches into a loud tirade at the tiny, huddled girl. "What are you doing here? Why did you come back here? You can't just show up like this, come back when you feel like it. You need to have the proper papers signed from your community TB doctor. You can't stay here. Get out of here!"

I am stunned. Ayeesha leaves, still continuing to yell. I call back at her half-heartedly. Nargisa hasn't moved. Still hunched in her small pose of nothingness she stares at the floor.

The hospital has recently decided to enforce an old policy that says any patient absent from the premises for more than three days can only return with a signed request from the community TB doctor who first sent them to hospital. It is to teach the patients a lesson and to have them see the hospital as a serious place, try to make them adhere to the treatment. But in practise it's an absurdity, somehow believing that the rule can be more convincing than the disease. The counsellors are trying everything to keep patients in hospital, on their drugs each day, going to homes to assuage the sufferers back to hospital, back to daily side effects. And, when they return, the doctors kick them out again. So, normally, one of the counsellors goes to the community TB doctor to get the form signed. Another of the many disconnects and absurdities in this land.

I reassure Nargisa. Kneel beside her, get her to look in my eyes. "Don't worry, we will have someone bring the form out. You can stay. It will be okay. You are wonderful to have come back. Don't worry about Ayeesha. Her anger is nothing to do with you. We are with you. Aziz and Murat and I will be with you. Just go visit with someone you know here. You have done the right thing. We care. I will find you in an hour and we will get you a room." She doesn't move. Aynur and I go into the other ward and I phone a counsellor to gather the form, get it out here ASAP.

An hour later the form arrives. Yes. Now another soul can be helped. The system can be out-manoeuvred. We go looking for Nargisa. We can't find her. I go to the latrines, to all the nooks on the grounds I know of. We ask if any have seen her. Yes, she was seen leaving the hospital ten minutes ago. Over there on the path beyond the latrines, through the bushes.

I run after her. Out of the hospital grounds and along the path to the road. Jog down the hot desert road all the way to the marshrutka stop. There is no one. It is too late. Nargisa has beat me to a marshrutka and made the 19-kilometre trip back to her small flat, to the ghosts of her dead parents, to the strange welcome of her cousin, and to her own slow drain into death.

Later, I hear Ayeesha has exclaimed with satisfaction that Nargisa has gone off. "We don't need her here," she says.

I know we will never see Nargisa again.

☙

May 31

We are having another concert at TB1. On Wednesday, we'll have one at TB2. With all the trees in leaf, some in flower, the expanse of these grounds give it the feel now of a summer rock concert. Groups of the regular TB patients are scattered everywhere; they don't realize MSF has made this happen and are amused that a concert is taking place in this staid complex of TB wards. Our MDR patients stick together. All are outside except Gauhar who is upstairs looking out the window. She has seen her former classmates, Aziz and Kuanish, outside and feels ashamed for them to see her. She still doesn't like others to know she is a patient sick with MDR. Her whole life her parents told her she was special, treated her like gold. She lived up to that. Then with her parents-in-law she had to learn their expectations and live up to them. At first it was not easy, but in time she accomplished that. She only knows what she is supposed to be, not who she is. MDR-TB is not who she is supposed to be.

Our singer is Sarita, arranged by Sergei our National Staff education guy. "She's a famous Karakalpak pop star. She's very good," he told me. When I thanked him for arranging it, especially that she is to only be paid 30,000 sum for each concert, he said: "Thank me after the concert, once it has actually taken place." He's Karakalpak and he knows that what is agreed upon doesn't always transpire.

But Sarita is here and she is good. And glamorous. She has brought a traditional musician as well who will do a short set of songs and music with her stringed instrument. But it is Sarita who is the show today. In a leopard pattern suit and matching pill box hat she holds the hundreds in thrall. They dance with her who has come to sing to them.

And Kuanish, Aziz, and I dance too. This is something we all need. Blue sky, warm sun, tree leaves tasting a soft breeze, a beautiful singer, and all of us becoming movement together.

✺

June 2

It is June now and Guldana has gone back into TB2. Her mind would not let her rest. She became more and more frantic, continuously stewing that she wouldn't be cured, wouldn't be able to take her drugs every day, too much money to take the taxi in Hodjeli to get to the clinic, on and on. She kept phoning a TB2 doctor and so he readmitted her. Culture results not in yet, so we don't know if she's infectious or not. She is in ICU now, her lips more purple than usual. Her limbs a bit swollen. They say she has low blood pressure, that her condition is severe. I don't understand how this has occurred. She was fine when I had sodas with her and her brother not long ago. What has changed? There are no answers. No one cares anyway. She is just a patient. With MDR-TB, it's always just what it is.

When I enter her cell, she is in an oxygen mask. A nurse is strapping a blood pressure wrap on her arm. Guldana sees me and motions with her fingers to sit beside her on the bed. We embrace. The nurse almost jumps back in shock. I tell Guldana she is crazy for coming back. She says she knows that. But what to do? It is the only way to keep with the drugs each day. Her head hurts and she has a fever. But she is happy to see me. I love you, I say. Me too, she smiles in her mask. I can see in hers but mine is opaque.

Guldana was in my arms as I swung her around out in the foyer just a few weeks back after she was told she would be discharged, and now she looks worse than I've ever seen her. If I could get inside her mind and just turn it off, put her into neutral for three months I am sure her body would heal, her lungs repair. It is that constant churning of invasive thoughts, worries, doubts, negatives which wear her down.

☞ And now, they also tell me that Gulbasara has been discharged from ICU to a psychiatric hospital. I'm shocked. Why? Because she was threatening to go upstairs and jump from the second floor balcony. They don't want problems at TB2. So she was shipped out yesterday. I will check on her tomorrow.

☞ Ahh ... in Ward 1, Deena is walking. And smiling. Her body has rebounded. The drugs are working. Deena is a poet, and she shows me her notebook filled with the poems she has written, the delicate illustrations that go with them. This little girl is ready to live. Her spirit beams. The drawings with her poems are crimson roses with long green stems that sinew around the page. Deena is a crimson rose. As delicate. Her voice, a voice of mirth and optimism. A tiny rose pushing her way through a crack in the concrete, defying the hardness to reach toward the oxygen of sunshine. Everyone who meets Deena loves her.

෮ I have brought some montey from Cafe Svetlana to Islam. To make room for Guldana, he's been moved out of ICU and back into Ward 2. He likes montey, a dumpling type of dish with small bits of meat mixed in. When I bring food to patients I sneak it in by putting it in the small pack I always carry. That way no one feels jealous or left out. Others in MSF think it's not fair for some to get and others not. I say I don't have enough money to feed everyone. And I bring the food not just for the nutrition but as a vote of affirmation and as an expression of connectedness. Islam looks okay. He is holding his own, and now his brother keeps him company.

෮ Achmed has been discharged to OPD. Erkin has been discharged to ambulatory in Chimbay. Sarbinaz is staying in hospital to be with her sister Kurbangul even though she also can leave to OPD. Daniyar was discharged a while back and is home in Hodjeli and taking his drugs each day from the polyclinic. Lots of little victories. For now.

෮ The concert at TB2 goes well. Almost everyone dances. The singer, Sarita, wears the same leopard patterned outfit. They have all seen her on TV music videos, so now TV has come to TB2. Everyone is happy. Kurbangul is outside in her plastic wheelchair with her sister. Guldana, not allowed outside, listens from inside ICU.

After the concert, we go to Chimbay to bring Shakargul her photos. She is weaker and has gone to live with her own aging parents. This grandmother just a daughter again. Her voice is failing and it is difficult for her to speak. Her eyes look farther away.

෮ It's mulberry time here. Trees of three varieties. White, red, and black. I ate some for the first time in 30 years.

I'm about 10 lbs lighter now. Face thinner. Heat and the lack of appetizing food. This must be the one bloody place on earth with no Chinese restaurant. That would save me. When I eat out I can only eat the same dish each time—three fried eggs, mashed potatoes, and a Greek salad. It has worn thin like me. There is one other place where I can get the same vegetarian pizza again and again. I like the food that Jonathan and my other housemate Maru cook at home best but it's still not exactly my taste. They wait for me to take my serving and then douse it with the hot spice they need to make it familiar for them.

Fruit is a going concern now. Strawberries have come and gone. Cherries are nice now but $2 a kilo for good ones. Apricots are at 75 cents a kilo. Soon, melons maybe.

We have no internet at our house but for some reason we now have 400 channels on our TV. And a porn one!!! No internet but free pornography. Maru is a Sri Lankan Muslim and he prays several times a day. He likes to watch the channel with live streaming from the pilgrimage site in Mecca.

Jonathan didn't go to work today due to a bad stomach. A second bathroom is being built at our house. The contractors work at it and a guard/driver from MSF comes to make sure nothing untoward happens in the house while the workers are there. Jonathan came downstairs and there was the guard watching the porn channel—the door to the rest of the house where the workers were working was closed. He didn't know Jonathan was at home. Jonathan didn't say anything but carried on to the toilet. When he returned to go back up to his room, the TV was off and the guard gone. That was how we discovered all the options on our new TV set-up.

σ

June 3

Gulbasara's father has brought her back to TB2. He is conferencing in an office chalet at the back of the hospital with the doctors. I see Gulbasara sitting on a chair next to where the other patients take their pills. She is sitting upright, straight-backed, looking like she has just come from an accident scene. Her father rescued her from the psychiatric hospital after one day and is demanding a different placement. He wants her in TB1.

I greet Gulbasara. Am happy to see her. "Oh, Calvin, it was awful. I don't know what they were thinking here. I was angry because they wouldn't let me walk. They wanted me to stay in the bed. I couldn't stand being stuck in ICU anymore. I couldn't stand it. So, I told them

I was going to jump out of the second story. I was crying, and they took me serious. So they sent me to the psychiatric hospital." I have never seen Gulbasara more present and alert as now. Her whole countenance is animated and clear.

"Calvin, it was like a nightmare. They are all crazy there. Everyone is walking around making noise. Singing. Acting strange. When I got there I was so afraid. People kept staring at me. Some tried to touch me. Others were singing to me. I didn't know what to do. I covered my face with my hands. I thought they might kill me." She is looking at me intensely, shaking her head as she recounts this horror.

"I won't go back there. They can't make me go there. I called my father. Thank God he could come. It's a long way from here. But he came this morning. He saved me. Last night, I couldn't sleep. I was afraid to. They stay up all night. They don't sleep either. One man started touching me and massaging my legs." She is almost crying but then she giggles and her eyes change: "Actually it felt kind of nice."

I tell Gulbasara that she doesn't have to go back.

☙

June 4

Guldana has phoned from ICU. Her vital signs have improved. She phoned me this morning before work. I had Aynur phone her back. She called to say she wanted three kabobs, some tomatoes, a banana and a radio. Yes!

☙ We are sitting in Oleg's room on the bed across from him. He is happy we have brought him the fried chicken he asked for. The way Oleg says thank you, the look in his eyes makes us proud of ourselves. Tempts us to bring food every day just to receive such a thank you. He is also sitting up, just wearing sweat pants, bare torso better to handle this early summer heat. His pale skin a perfect crepe over bones, the angle of each delineated better than any Leonardo da Vinci drawing. His face is covered with short brown bearding, soft and full. It hides the thinness of his cheeks, he says. He tells us he has washed his hair twice today to beat the heat, but hasn't washed his body in four months. He has enough strength to make it to the washroom and toilet but not enough to manage the process of full bathing. He will wash when he leaves here.

As we talk, I suddenly notice I can see his heart moving in his chest. Not just the pulse but the full *falloomp, falloomp, falloomp*, a rhythmic undulation like in a film documentary. A Leonardo da Vinci heart in motion before my eyes, only the mere parchment of skin shielding it from full exposure. I mention the sight to Aynur. "Oh my God, you're right. I've never seen anything like that before. It makes me feel uncomfortable." Oleg asks if we have heard anything from the TV show that finds lost relatives.

☙

June 5

It has turned hot. 43 degrees Celsius yesterday. At midnight it was as hot outside as I have ever experienced at that time of night. This is such a crazy place — in the middle of the desert but this city of 300,000 is green. The water is released into ditches. People turn their taps on and let it pool in their yards. Rice paddies grow out by our TB hospital. No sprinklers, just sitting water everywhere. As though there will always be water. And in the 4th and 5th floors of apartment buildings there is no water because the pressure has fallen. All so screwed up. Yet all looks modern here. Orderly. That's the irony. The absolute backwardness of how they handle the water would be more under-standable in a primitive setting.

I'm bracing for the heat to come. Tonight I went to my aikido class. I go every Saturday. This time I could only last an hour because of the heat in our small dojo.

Each day when I walk down my dusty street to go to work, these little kids come out of houses almost as if on cue. Little kids, maybe three-to-six years old, teeth missing, the girls with their heads shaved for the summer. They skitter out from the ornate wooden doors that mark entrance to the otherwise nondescript walls of their family home. Or from the pale blue metal doors that open to other homes. Always homes with large inner areas of hard clay or greenery or rows of vegetables, a cow tied, or a dog with pups, and then other doorways to other living areas for the large extended families.

These little children clamoring at me with the perfect blend of "hello! hello!, photo! photo!?" in both daring child innocence and sweet child respect. They come closer to touch my hand and smile and chirp on in elegant wonder at my strangeness. I look at them and wish I could pick them up and put them on my shoulders or stop and tell them stories of bears and otters, wish I could grab hold of that universal beauty, that universal charm that is all children at that age when there is no culture, no gender, no difference at all, simply joy at being alive and seeing something new. To stop and stay with that moment and not be anything but there with them forever.

Earlier today, I was watching another small boy by a big leafy tree, straining his arm upward for one of the few ripe and sweet white mulberries low enough for him to reach. I stopped with him and tried myself to reach some of the sweet fat ones curling off the higher branches, also straining to get them. For these interjecting seconds it was easy to forget about the thick heat of mid day here on the other side of the earth, to forget about everything that needs forgetting about. There are many children here. An easy thing in this land of fear and sickness in which the Aral Sea has been stolen away to leave a plague of misery. Bear more children. Bear more innocence, more joy, more beauty. As long as it all can last.

⌖

June 6

Someone phones to tell me that Shakargul has died at her parents' house in Chimbay. Her grandmother's voice trailing to childhood whispers in her own mother's arms and now to silence.

Her last dance was with me.

⌖

June 7

Gulbasara got her wish to be free of TB2's ICU isolation and has made it to TB1. She's in a room with seven other women. No longer alone. She looks fantastic, beaming, a full human once again. She is weak but walks now without admonishment, without threat. The plastic lawn chair wheelchair an item from the past. The route to sanity is through the Nukus psychiatric hospital and the insistent determination of an aging father. Even her nightgown is new.

❧ The MSF doctors have asked me to speak to my Oleg. His analysis has changed from the lesser PDR-TB now to MDR-TB. That means his drug regimen will increase. There will be more side effects. The treatment will last a year longer. He has already often balked at taking the drugs for several days at a time. The doctors want to know if he wants to go to TB2 or to stop altogether and be sent to TB3 as a failure. Wait his days out there.

I know they don't like having Oleg here. His emaciated frame is a constant reminder of what they cannot change. They also don't like that he is his own person and only complies with his own daily needs and moods. He is 40 after all and has no one. He has wanted to die so there is no sense of fear for the future in Oleg, just living by the day. The doctors are uncomfortable having him in their hospital. Better for him to be somewhere else. But Oleg speaks with such smoothness, graciousness. The expat doctor has asked me to give him his options and see what he wants to do.

I sit with him, relate the worsened diagnosis. He thinks. This is not what he wanted to hear. This means going further than one day at a time. He lies back down on his bed. How many patients are out at TB2? What is it like there? I tell him I will give him time to consider everything, that I'll come back before I go home to get his decision.

Later, out at TB2 I sit with Guldana in ICU holding her hand. Her hair is wet and she is fresh though her feet are still swollen. An aide has helped her wash her hair. I ask her to write a letter to her dead mother. In it, I want her to tell her mother about her life since she died those 12 years ago. And most important, I want her to say good-bye to her mom. That when I come in a couple of days, I will ask her to read it out loud to me while Aynur translates. Guldana agrees. I search for any shred of intervention I can imagine. Maybe, Guldana's immune system is repressed because she yearns for her mother, deep inside thinks to follow her. Do any of us know what pulls at us from the deepest parts of our psyche? I know that this woman who welcomed me so openly in my first visits, who welcomes me still through all her discomfort, deserves to live.

  ❧ Islam sits on his bed, head shaved and with a blue, traditional round cap. He wears a new yellow t-shirt. This weekend was his birthday. He and his younger brother Kamil left their room in the hospital after Saturday's drugs and returned to their home for the celebration. He's 25 now. I've brought him some cherries. He says he's badgering his brother about taking his drugs every day. Kamil looks down at the floor, looks back up grinning sheepishly. Islam smiles at him.

  Then just before the work day ends I return to Oleg in TB1. He has made a decision. His eyes are bright. How many are in each room at TB2? Usually four, maybe more. Can you swim in the canal out there? Yes, but it's a 10-minute walk. "I'll go to TB2. At least I won't be lonely out there." His gold teeth grin at me.

  "You have to take the drugs out there. Every day. It will be harder than it is now."

  "I know. I am ready to try," he says, blue eyes brighter than his smile.

  Death moves uncomfortably, not knowing what to think. The man in line has chosen to leave the line. Death shakes its head.

  ❧ I'm going to Takhtakupir once a week. We've placed Kuanish there to be the supervising counsellor. Patients have been coming from Takhtakupir and Karauziak to TB1 and TB2 for a while. But there is no counselling or program set up for when they become ambulatory and need to take their drugs at home. Karauziak is about a half hour past Chimbay and Takhtakupir another half hour more. All spread out around them are the various hamlets. It's a huge area to service and we haven't properly understood that logistical reality. We are going to interview for a team of new counsellors there. We'll hire eight more to work under Kuanish.

When I chose Kuanish for the job it wasn't appreciated by some of my MSF colleagues. "Who is Kuanish?" they reacted. I said: "He has been a counsellor for two years, much of that under my predecessor, and he will be a fine leader."

"But he doesn't speak English."

"Neither do the patients out there, nor anyone else who lives there."

It will be a challenge for us—to get to see everybody in such a spread-out place and with meagre transit. Somehow, the new counsellors once hired are expected to find their own ways to all the health units no matter how distant from each other. Every expat has an MSF car whenever needed to do whatever job or excursion desired. National Staff, on the other hand, sometimes can have a car and other times not. In this new project, only Kuanish will have a car sometimes.

Plus, MSF has decided we should minister to the regular TB patients as well. A Canadian nurse is coming in. And later a Bangladeshi doctor. At first I thought I was just being included in the planning as a consultant. Then I figured out that I was supposed to be in charge of the psychosocial situation there. I have to run it. So I was happy to transfer Kuanish there as my right hand person. Good for him. Jump in pay from 600,000 sum to 750,000 sum. $375. A really good wage for here. I asked how he'd feel about being away from his wife, daughter, and infant twins since he has to live there and only come home on weekends. He smiled. "Less work."

✐ I think I'll become more empathetic to the donkeys that live here. This is donkey land. Along the side of the road will come a string of eight carts all heaving with great bundles of branches maybe four metres high or other great loads and being pulled by a donkey. On some of those donkeys there will also be a man riding. Born to pull until time to die. I have been happily pulling a cart here in Nukus and Chimbay. Tired at night but happy tired. Now, it will be another nine counsellors to go with the nine I have already plus the five others we'll hire later in Nukus. The medical team thinks we already aren't doing a good enough job. Now we'll have all these new bodies so we can see patients properly, and still the default rate mightn't drop so much if at all.

The drive to Takhtakupir takes two hours. If the driver goes by the MSF rules of no more than 90 kph and plenty of caution. I might be a donkey but I prefer to be a fast donkey. We now have two extra cars for the psychosocial department. I use Jenya most days and especially for my trips to Chimbay and Takhtakupir. He used to transport cars in Belarus. Point A to point B. Don't stop. He told me if you stopped you got hijacked. Pedal to the metal. So, now I say to Jenya: "I need to get to such and such by such and such time. Can we do it?"

"No problem."

I may be a donkey, but I travel Air Jenya.

June 10

They had a consillium today. That's the weekly meeting held by the Ministry of Health doctors and the two MSF expat doctors to discuss various patient situations. These may be ones which require a change in drug regimen due to onerous side effects, or that someone has missed so much treatment that they will be listed as a defaulter, or someone has not responded to treatment and needs to be declared a treatment failure and taken off the drugs. Sometimes community TB doctors attend if it's their patients at issue and sometimes a counsellor will attend. I sent Deelya to this one because they were to decide on Oleg's situation. I had talked to the TB1 doctor and Firoza our MSF doctor and told them Oleg wanted to go to TB2 and accepted that he now had to fight full MDR and was ready to take the larger drug regimen.

I was an idiot.

At the consillium, Deelya was overpowered. The chief doctor at TB2 wanted to know if Calvin could guarantee that Oleg would take his drugs every day. Deelya replied that there are no guarantees any patient will do that, but Calvin thinks Oleg will do it. What Calvin thinks is not good enough. Oleg will be sent to TB3 as a treatment failure. They wiped their hands of the problem. No more drugs.

No more hope.

When Deelya tells me the outcome, I am devastated. I want to tear the walls down. They asked me to help him decide, but now I see it was a lie, there was no deciding. No one wants Oleg. I frantically phone Samuel. "Yeah, it was too bad. You should have been there. Deelya tried but they would not listen to her. I think if you had been there then the decision on Oleg would have been different."

I want not to be in my skin. I want to rip it off and disappear. This is too much for me. Oleg has no one. Not even me.

June 11

It is Saturday and I've gone with Deelya to see Oleg in his new room at TB3. I am ashamed to see him and scared. I apologize for failing him. But, of course, Oleg knows who I really am. Just another person in the big river that moves us. He was shocked to be told it was all over. He said he had cried when the doctor left. But he has resigned himself now. No more drugs. And a new place. I give him the apricot juice I have brought and the montey dumplings still warm. He bows his head.

We talk about Massor and Natasha in the other rooms, how they were sent here over a year before and are still doing fine. I say I will make sure he has enough food. I will come out to see him two or three times a week. Whenever I leave Oleg, I always bend to him, shake his white hand and touch my head to his. Today, I do it with more humility.

Refugees

June 13

I'm in the middle of interviewing prospective counsellors in Ta-khtakupir. We have gone through three candidates so far. My house-mate Maru, who has become Project Coordinator for this new project, insists on being the one to start each interview, talking about MSF, etc. He's the boss. Then we take turns with the questioning. If I start to feel strongly that an applicant is not suitable, I say that I have no more questions. That's the signal to Maru and we close off the interview.

> *Candidate 1:* *Do you know what a counsellor is? No*
> *Do you know what TB is? Yes*
> *Can you tell us what TB is? A disease.*
> *What strengths can you bring to this job? I will do my best.*
> *Candidate 2:* *What made you apply for this job? I need a job.*
> *What strengths can you bring to the job? That's for you to determine. I can't be the one to say.*
> *Candidate 3:* *Why would you like to be a counsellor? It's better than sitting at home doing nothing.*

Candidate 4 is a 21-year-old man. He is super alert. Smiling, every utterance filled with energy and enthusiasm. He needs the money. He likes people. He wants to help. He will do everything to learn and help. This would be his first job. We thank him. I tell Maru he is like the Energizer bunny from the TV commercials. Maru has never heard of that commercial. We agree he is a great kid and we'd like to hire him, but ...

Now we go on to the next ones. Candidate 5 is just thrilled to be there because both she and her older sister applied but only she got the interview.

Candidate 6 is a 47-year-old teacher. He is clearly the old guard authority type but with a nice open face and obviously intelligent. I doubt he will fit our needs. But then I ask about what kind of struggles he has had in his life. His demeanour changes. He tells us about his wife getting seriously sick and almost dying, how he had to stop work to look after her and nurse her back to health. His eyes moisten, and he says it was a great learning experience and helped him realize what mattered and what didn't, how scared he was that he might lose her. He'll do.

Candidate 7 is a 25-year-old man. Smart guy. Personable. Good answers. I ask him how he would handle a situation of a female patient who is being beaten by her husband. He pauses, reflects. "I would meet with her to learn about what she does that makes the man want to hit her. See if there is some actions she could take to change that." I'm thinking oh no, he sees it as the woman's problem, her responsibility. He pauses. Thinks. "Then, I'd meet with the man and find out why he is abusing his wife. What makes him want to do that, why he thinks it's okay, and try to educate him that it is wrong and that his wife needs support not beating." Hired.

The phone rings. It's Stefan, Head of Mission from Tashkent. There has been a crisis in Kyrgyzstan, another former Soviet Republic just to our east. A coup took place last month. Now there has been an outbreak of violence in their southwest right on the border with Uzbekistan. Kyrgyz have attacked their Uzbek neighbours in the Kyrgyz cities of Jalalabad and Osh. Thousands of refugees have streamed across the border into Uzbekistan. Camps have been set up and MSF is sending help. They need a mental health specialist. I am to leave that evening for Tashkent with my counsellor Deelya as translator.

Interviews ended.

June 15

After the one-hour evening flight to Tashkent, Deelya and I spent the next day pinching ourselves to be sure it was all really happening, going from the non-news of serving MDR-TB patients in the desert to being on the way to an international story.

Stefan filled us in. MSF was already in Andijan, the major Uzbek city closest to the Kyrgyz border through which the refugees had fled. Reports said at least 75,000 had come across various crossings and were now in over 40 camps. The refugees are mostly women and children. Medco Jorge was there with some of our logistics people. MSF was in the process of donating a Landcruiser, and the other agencies there were saying the great need was for mental health because of the trauma and so many refugees.

And Deelya and I are going to be that mental health, or so it seems. Today was exciting. We have just arrived, and happy to say that. It is eight hours or so from Tashkent to Andijan. Soon after leaving Tashkent to go east, the highway begins its climb into the mountains and then winds its way up through rugged terrain, alpine villages, down along crumbly, rock gorges and eventually out into the Fergana Valley, a lush, fertile agricultural plain.

We travelled by taxi. The driver's name was surely Michael Schumacher, because no one else could drive like that. Eight hours soon became six, and that was because I asked Michael to slow down. The half Nepalese half Austrian Alps Grand Prix was exciting for Deelya. She has never travelled any distance in cars, doesn't know speeds. The hairpin corners meant nothing to our driver. The potholes meant nothing. Jenya, my regular driver, knows how to slow down when necessary. Not this guy.

Deelya and I looked across at the stunning verdant hillsides climbing steeply from the other side of the gorge and imagined ourselves on a leisurely picnic. But no matter how much energy I put into the fantasy and the incredible scenery, my fright panel kept lighting up. It seems to be located near my bladder because every forty minutes I was compelled to ask for a stoppage in order to urinate. Perhaps it was merely subliminal strategic responses at work. I did ask Mr. Schumacher to keep the speed close to 90 kph, citing MSF regulations. (I wasn't just going to tell him I was afraid!) And he did slow down, going from 140 on the curves to 120, but he was clearly more comfortable at 160 on the straight stretches.

"This is not fast," he declared. "I know this road well!"

I don't dispute the latter. I wonder if he knows the car. The ball joints, the tie rods, the wheel bearings, any of those mortal parts that could break and send us somewhere even more quickly. I could not help but gaze at the scenery so beautiful, wondering if it was indeed, to be my entrance to paradise.

At our hotel, the reception lady is a bit slow. She can't quite figure out who we are. There are supposed to be three of us checking in. But there are only two. She isn't sure if she should proceed or not. It takes a half hour to convince her that it's okay. Our rooms smell a bit, but they will do.

❧

June 16

We are introduced to Abdulla and Miradin. They are to be our hosts and handlers. Abdulla is a linguistics professor at Andijan State University. Miradin is the driver of a red marshrutka which normally transports Abdulla about and which will be our transport while we are here. MSF is welcome in Andijan. There are several other agencies here—United Nations, Red Crescent, U.S. Aid among them. And several news agencies—BBC International, CNN, Associated Press, and Uzbek media. Everyone has a handler. This is a country with a government which understands hospitality and control.

Abdulla does not speak English and, though normally employed by the university, these days he is a government official. Both our hosts are affable and accepting. Our first order of business is to visit one of the refugee camps. We drive 15 kilometres along pleasant rural roads to the gates of a cotton factory. Within its grounds are U.N. tents set up in long orderly rows on the concrete padding behind the factory's administration headquarters. There are 1400 refugees here.

We are presented in the administration building to the camp director. He quickly tells me that all is working just fine here. He is a psychology PhD from Moscow University. He insists there are no mental health needs here whatsoever. They take care of any issues which arise. He has several psychologists working under him.

Next, we are taken for a jaunt through the rows of tents. All is calm and clean. Abdulla ushers me to the canopied dining area. It's like a linear outdoor restaurant. There are set meal times, but people can come here whenever they want after those times and order food or drinks. We are introduced to four psychologists who sit with us as we drink tea.

The leader of the foursome is a lady of about 40. She goes into a fluid exposition of all the services they offer, how many psychologists per refugee, the number of other volunteers who help out, what kind of activities are held for the children. I ask some more specific questions. MSF wants me to assess the need. These people are telling me conclusively that there is no need.

I feel a bit frustrated. They make everything sound so good, yet I know that real psychology in terms of counselling is hardly existent in Uzbekistan. They might have studied theories but there is no practise to speak of. I think that they can't possibly be treating the Post Traumatic Stress that has to be here in significant numbers. But every time I probe or suggest something, they have a pat answer.

I am thinking, I will go back and tell Medco Jorge that all is in hand and Deelya and I should return to the patients who need us. I start to say words to this effect when a distraught woman comes toward us. Someone introduces her as filled with flashbacks and nightmares, unable to sleep.

Suddenly, I am doing a counselling session right there at the lunch tables. The woman begins to calm down. She relaxes. I hold her hand and talk. She goes through her ordeal from a week before. The psychologists listen and watch raptly.

Then as we finish, a young boy of about ten is brought forward.

He is agitated every day. We do a session together. Only 15 minutes. But it seems to help.

Then an old man comes over and begins to show us how strong he is, how he can do deep knee bends. I greet him warmly. We exchange conversation.

When it all finishes, the psychologists are very animated. The woman who does most of the talking is totally different. The end result is they are excited to have us and want us to teach them what we know. I suggest that we do a 90-minute training session for all their crew the next morning. Abdulla says he will set it up.

We have been told how hundreds of people were indiscriminately killed or injured in the communal violence in the nearby cities of Osh and Jalalabad and smaller towns right across the border in Kyrgyzstan. And the number of Uzbeks coming across the border —now at 75,000—is increasing. After up to two weeks in the camps, my sense is that there has to be a dire need for proactive counselling.

☙

June 17

9 am: In a large room at the university, 35 "psychologists" have arrived for my 90-minute training seminar on fundamentals of psychological post-trauma responses in refugees. These "counsellors" are a mixture of educational psychologists, psychology students, and ordinary teachers. They are all volunteering in various camps during this crisis. A mix of genders and ages, all are committed to help the refugees and keen to participate.

After explaining that we aren't claiming to be know-it-alls come to tell others how to do it, but MSFers offering to share what we have learned, I begin by having them all stand up and hold hands in one large circle. I ask them to close their eyes and I do a brief guided visualization.

The bulk of the training involves helping them understand the nature of post-traumatic stress, and how the vast majority of the refugees cannot help but have it in varying degrees of intensity. I expand on how therapy is most effective when it is done as soon as possible after traumatic events so as to prevent the patterns of response getting entrenched. We go over a few simple approaches to therapy which if done will shift the direction for both individuals and the entirety of the camps, and how they can prepare those groups dealt with by them to share the strategies with others in their families and tents.

I explain how, with so many thousands, it won't be possible to intervene directly with each but that enough can be done to empower the refugees themselves, making it easier for resolution and healing to come.

I also explain how holding people who are especially suffering the symptoms of PTSD or who are in immediate emotional distress can help them to centre and regain contact with their own inner strength. I explain how I often do this with my patients in Karakalpakstan in order to ground them in the present and convey a deeper experience of support than what can come from talk therapy alone.

The whole session goes extremely well, though Abdulla has come to me at the mid-break and asks me to speed it up. He is not fully comfortable.

In closing, I ask if they would like a further seminar the next day. All heartily agree but say they would defer to their coordinator. It is not clear if that is Abdulla or someone else. Before I sit down, the PhD from Moscow University comes to the front of the room.

An older man who is a professor of psychology, he thanks Deelya and me, saying we have imparted some useful ideas. He then tells the participants that much of what I had said was not valid for Uzbek culture and traditions! They all give us a round of applause.

Later, several participants come up and privately say not to pay any attention to that guy, that they don't see it the way he said nor do they think anyone else would agree with him.

☞ At 12 o'clock, we are taken by Abdulla and Miradin to link with the deputy Prime Minister of this large district. To our surprise, he happens to have an Associated Press duo with him. He has been asked to take this media contingent to a hospital to see wounded refugees and has decided it would be added PR to include the MSF specialists.

Deelya and I can't figure out what is to happen. Abdulla just says we are to accompany the convoy to the hospital. A police cruiser with flashing lights leads the way. At the hospital, it becomes clear that we are to be part of some kind of international showcase.

We are gowned, and led toward the wards of the wounded. The AP photographer goes before us crouching down to video upwards as we move down the hall. Swinging doors fly open and the gowned foreign Doctors Without Borders specialists enter a ward. This is some kind of strange, crisis reality show. There are beds of bandaged, wounded men. Some are unconscious. All look to be in serious shape. The cameraman goes around the room to shoot from different angles.

This is not what I anticipated. I have no idea what to do, but there is no way I want to be a hollow shape for the camera to insinuate the illusion of medical attention. So, I decide I will do what I know. I will be present with some of these victims even if for a few minutes.

Several are being treated for gunshot wounds and in one case stab wounds to the head. Deelya has never seen this kind of trauma before. Me neither, but I get to initiate the talking. She can only translate and follow. With each, I hold a hand or touch a shoulder. I smile. I speak of how they are safe now, how their time of fear is over. I look them in the eyes and tell where I am from, that I care about them, and that I hope for them to get well. "Just relax now. You are safe. You will be cared for. You will heal, and then you can return to help your loved ones. Let yourself heal now."

In response, a young man with bullet holes in his side and arm whispers to us his determined affirmation: "I will live."

As I leave the first ward, one man flat on his back, arms to the sides, flashes two thumbs upwards. Deelya goes to a window in the hall before we move on to the next ward. She is crying. The man with the stab wounds in his head, all bandaged, the iodined scars criss-crossing his scalp has been too much for her. She needs only a few minutes, and then we go on.

Two wards later we are in a room with only three men. Two are bed-ridden and one sits on a chair over by the window. After visiting with the two in their beds, I go to the man sitting. He has gunshot wounds to the leg. I think to chat, seeing how he looks like he's quite content all things considered. He greets me with a hand shake. I say that it's good to meet him, but express my condolence that it's in such circumstances. He is very placid, relaxed sitting by the window, looking out into the garden area.

I joke that I guess a month before he didn't imagine himself here with a gunshot wound in the leg. He smiles a bit, saying no he could never have imagined it. I mention that it's good he made it here, how he's safe now and can heal. Then I ask of his family. He looks down and replies that his wife and two kids are dead and he doesn't know about his other kids. Quiet tears slowly, slowly emerge and softly run down his cheeks.

I sit there in silence with him then, just keeping my hand on his back and shoulder. Sitting with no words to say.

After the hospital visit, the district Prime Minister takes us for lunch at a nice expansively treed outdoor restaurant. The tab's on him. The AP people and I talk about what we've seen and done so far in Andijan, how we keep hearing the official script from everyone we encounter. All is under control. Everything is working well.

I wonder if inside they are asking themselves what it's like to have your wife and children die before your eyes?

Following this we are driven to another clinic to visit three sexual assault victims — all sisters aged 16 to 23. But they have been released before we get there and have gone to a prosecutor's office. The doctor in charge says they have been here for three days of treatment.

The decision is then made to go to the camp to interview their mother. When we get to that camp, we are told that the mother has gone to be with her daughters. The AP duo interviews refugees while Deelya and I tour the facilities on our own. There are 2,200 people in this park-like area. Tents are packed and the main building, also housing refugees, is very crowded. Order is good. Children are playing. There are young volunteers present who are helping out in sundry ways from preparing food, to leading groups of children in activities, to picking up garbage. The natural surroundings add to the positive atmosphere.

However, it is also clear that stress is building. A group of refugees are pressing the AP duo for help and express much fear about their future. One older lady speaks with me of her troubles and in the process whispers to Deelya that it was not only girls who had been sexually assaulted but that some of the boys have as well.

In the case of sexual assault during communal violence, it is likely to be more widespread than reported and, due to the stigma involved, less likely to be addressed therapeutically. My guess is that in all Uzbekistan there is no developed program nor skill set to offer effective therapy for victims of sexual assault. I will suggest to Abdulla that I can train his local counsellors in how to do rudimentary therapy for victims of sexual assault.

The deputy and the head of the camp come by and insist all is fine and good and that no help is needed.

The AP reporter interviews me on camera for five minutes about impressions of the refugee situation. Abdulla quietly asides to Deelya to tell me to say good things about the camps. He is obviously concerned for various reasons about what his "expert" for whom he has responsibility will say to an international audience!

I know what I am to say to keep MSF welcome here, but I also can truthfully affirm the good job done for the refugees' external needs by Uzbek authorities in the three camps we have visited. Nevertheless, I also express the serious need for longer range planning and extensive proactive responses to the psychological/emotional needs of the refugee population who all suffer from post traumatic stress.

Afterwards, Abdulla is disgruntled that Deelya did not translate the interview for him while it was being conducted. Apologies and reassurances are made. Now, he will have to wait to see if he bears any repercussions from some negative assessment given in my words.

We finish the day by my offering to do daily training for people who can work as counsellors. I say that we can call in the whole Nukus team and we could train hundreds of locals—teachers, medical people, whoever could volunteer for psychological intervention. That the training could change the lives of thousands for the better.

Abdulla says he will ask his bosses.

June 19

9 am: We meet at the airport where the Uzbek government has set up its command centre for the crisis. This is all very professional. In one corner of the large room a TV continuously replays news coverage and interviews of the carnage in Kyrgyzstan. Computer banks flank two other sides. Tables and chairs are up for conferencing. The Uzbek government knows what it's doing and wants everyone else to draw that conclusion. They also want it made perfectly clear that the Uzbeks of their neighbour country have been victimized and that they now, consequently, are doing good by their ethic kin.

Most of the personnel from the other agencies here as well as the five of us from MSF are divided into assessment teams to go to camps in order to conduct refugee questionnaires.

Our first camp is Xanobod in which 3,575 refugees are registered. For some reason, the U.N. guy who devised the questionnaire says not to bother doing it here, so Deelya and I meet for some time with the woman who is the psychologist for the camp. She is very receptive to our idea of bringing in our Nukus team of Uzbek counsellors to conduct training sessions for those who could work as camp counsellors. We assert the growing need for proactive and intensive psychological intervention and programming within the camps and the capacity of the Nukus team to train effective crisis and trauma responses.

This camp is situated within a sports facility of some kind, surrounded by walls. The population seems primarily to be of those not directly encountering the violence but more running for fear that it could reach them. The psychological response happening so far is primarily providing warmth and attention in the form of greetings and enquiries as to any need for help. Evidently there are 64 counsellors that come to the camp on a regular basis to check with refugees. The atmosphere is stable. However, when an Uzbek media team arrives and begins interviewing, a large crowd gathers and stress stories begin to unfold. This kind of occurrence is problematic as it stokes already latent fears and insecurities. It can easily escalate and permeate the camp.

The need here is to begin a systematic schedule of daily group meetings in which refugees are guided in the direction of self-care and problem solving. At the same time a system of quick identification of more acute PTS victims needs to be set up. As each day passes, the sense of desperation and fear will increase. Uncertainty and boredom will erode the social balance that is currently here. At this time there is no awareness of this coming risk. The positive note is that the psychologist is totally onside about bringing in training to address these needs.

Our second camp is called Alawaddin. It is totally different in that it is situated in a summer recreation camp. When we arrive, kids are dancing to a speaker system, while many others are playing on swings and other play apparatus. It is as though we have walked into a great summer program. The whole atmosphere is relaxed and calm. Lots of space. At a feeding centre there is a line-up to get ample portions of plov, the traditional rice casserole, that our MDR-TB patients would have been thrilled to receive.

Again at this camp it seems the population of 2,000 are primarily of those who fled because of the stories of threat rather than the actual experience. Here, they are just waiting for the opportunity to return home. Deelya does two questionnaires and I converse with a young woman who can speak English. She says that she was told they could start returning home on Monday, that official processing for that had already started. Her experience in Osh was not one of discrimination. She says many of her Kyrgyz friends have phoned her and are worried about her. She thinks that, when she returns, she has hope that all will be as before the crisis.

Abdulla shows up. He wasn't with us earlier because we had gone in the teams and had no need for his involvement. He is happy to see us but he says our offer of bringing in the Nukus team is not needed. Nor is it necessary for me to do any further trainings in trauma counselling or sexual assault therapy, but he is happy to continue taking me where I'd like to go in the days ahead or to show me other places of interest. He says there is sufficient psychological expertise already here and that refugees will all be returning in a few days.

Inshallah.

Our third visit of the day is to an obscure border crossing farther away in the rural area. I don't know why we were brought specifically here. No one ever explains it exactly. The Uzbek TV crew has come along also.

The border seems to be marked by a ditch about three metres deep and five metres across. Armed soldiers with machine guns patrol the Uzbek side. An injured man is being helped across—a rough wooden bridge having been thrown over the ditch for the man to reach a waiting ambulance. There is a crowd of refugees on the Kyrgyz side. A medical person helps support the man as he teeters across the bridge.

Deelya and I walk with him to the ambulance, his head fully bandaged, one eye covered over, blood stains soaked in the fabric. I'm not a hundred percent sure that it isn't staged because it seems strange that, just as we arrive with the TV crew in tow, a casualty is crossing the border. I hold him under one shoulder and his brother holds him under the other. We get him to the ambulance and put him on the stretcher. I put my hand on the brother's shoulder and tell him the wounded man is safe now. The brother starts crying. I guess it is real alright.

The crowd gathered on the other side starts yelling for help. It is a scene from a war movie for sure. An old blind man is then led onto the Kyrgyz side of the bridge. With a young girl at his hand he begins a long oratory for mercy and support. We all listen as he speaks. Soldiers, doctor, camera crew, those hoping for sanctuary. His words finish with a morphing into heaving shoulders and muffled sobs. The girl leads him back into the crowd.

Then Deelya is comforting the young female student doctor who had been attending the wounded man in the no-man's strip on the other side of the ditch. On our side, she had been giving an interview to the Uzbek TV crew. The doctor tells us of the rapes of girls in a nearby madrassa school by Kyrgyz security forces. She says she had been telephoned by her friends at the school who were crying. They said they had been raped also. Deelya holds her as she cries, and we express our admiration for the work she is doing.

She goes back across the bridge. The soldiers pull it over to the Uzbek side. We drive away in the Landcruiser all silent. No questionnaires here either.

☞ Our day ends with a group meeting at the airport of all the international agencies on the questionnaire assessment. There is a follow-up meeting organized with the federal Minister in charge of the crisis. The spokespeople for the international assessment team outline their findings and at the end mention that the refugees have a need for psychological help. They seem nervous in the presence of the Minister who is obviously a man of authority and confidence.

Despite my earlier clarifications in the group meeting, to which all agreed, the spokespeople fail to directly articulate the specific need for trauma/crisis counselling expertise nor our capacity to provide it. The Minister listens to each comment and responds. The gist is that the Uzbek authorities are handling everything properly and fully. They can use more money and food. They have sufficient psychological expertise and practitioners. Nothing more is needed. The meeting ends with lots of congratulations.

☞ The day concludes with our being taken to the bazaar and later for supper at a nice restaurant by Abdulla and our driver. Their warmth is refreshing following the stalemate in the meeting with the Minister. Neither Deelya nor I nor any of the other MSF people have any clear idea about what we are to be doing here now that the Minister has spoken.

☞

June 20

Another camp.

The old man has been listening patiently for over half an hour in this canvas tent for refugees. He started us off with a prayer and blessing and for the rest of the time I don't know what he has been thinking as my eyes have been only on the 24 young men gathered in this tent. This group and I have not had enough time, I know that. Not enough time for each to tell me their stories, how they fled for their lives, the fear they felt, the shame they felt for running away. Not enough time for the shock they have swallowed to now be spewed back out, the events locked inside from a week ago to be released. Not enough time even to tell me their names.

But we did meet. We touched hands and saw into each others' eyes. We sat together body to body in this tent. One or two spoke for the others, how they hid in their homes when the assault began, how homes burned, how gunshots rang so loudly, and how they crept away in the dark to trudge the miles to come across the border. They talked of how hard it was to be so separated now from the rest of their families and the uncertainties they lived with. I listened and watched and then it was my turn to speak.

I asked them to nod as I spoke if anything I mentioned rang true for them. I began by repeating some of what was just said by the first speakers. Then I said how none had anticipated such carnage erupting, how they had been caught totally by surprise. The fire bombing, the sniper fire, the mobs all had just emerged out of nowhere. They had been helpless. They had done nothing to bring it about, could have done nothing to stop it. All they could do was to run. The danger and the fear was immense. And they nodded, each as it applied to them. Lots of nodding. This was the movement of voice, the movement needing no translation.

Then I spoke about their wisdom and courage in coming to safety, how this safety meant a future. They had given themselves a future by running to safety. A future over which they will have some say. I spoke about crying. How many of you have cried? I asked them to raise hands. And hands raised. I said that the crying they did and will do was the natural response, the healthy response to trauma. Like sweating is to a day in hot sun. Don't resist it. Invite it. And with the crying tell others your stories. Those are your stories. You did not choose them, but you can choose to release them.

Now the old man has asked to speak. Everyone is silent, listening now for his judgement maybe. All in white, Muslim hat, his aged wife seated beside him, at the entranceway to the tent like the leaders of a clan. He looks at me and begins to cry. "So much killing," he whispers. "Snipers on rooftops, rat-tat-tat-tat!" He points his hands as though holding a rifle. Then he touches his arms and legs and the sides of his neck where he says the bullets struck people running away.

I interrupt. I look to the young men, half of whom have not directly witnessed shooting, and advise them that they can leave if they
wish, that I won't be taking any more of their time. I don't want them
being unnecessarily re-stimulated by the elder's distress. They all
rise. Most are leaving in minutes to make the trek back to their
homes. I watch their youthful readiness clasp hands with each other,
their acceptance of the unknown embrace each other, their innocent
belief in life pat each others' shoulders.

After they leave, I turn back to the old man and ask him to continue. Several women have left their places on the outside of the tent
where they have been listening, and have come to sit on mats behind
the old couple. The elder starts talking of the rapes that he knows of.
The worst was his neighbour's 11-year-old daughter, her vagina torn
open. Better she had been killed rather than to live with that, his
neighbour had told him. His wife and the other women all begin sobbing quietly. And the old man breaks down again. I reach for him and
hold him while he cries. Then I do the same with his wife. In this land
where no one touches, let alone a stranger, the normal rules have
been cast aside.

☞ So far, the Uzbek government really has done a great job of addressing the refugee needs. We've been to five different camps and
each is filled with order and services. However, they won't be able to
sustain it if the crisis lingers as we think it will and the ten days become weeks. The so-called counsellors in the camps mean well and
are doing some things but they aren't trauma or crisis trained. All are
volunteers. And they are getting tired. Many have told us that.

For Deelya and me, this experience has been absorbing and dra-
matic. If the authorities wanted the help we could really contribute a
lot, but even as it is, it's all very intimate for us here. As in Nukus, we
are received into people's lives. The counsellors, the refugees, and
Abdulla and Miradin have opened to us. The latter two guardedly, of
course. Abdulla made a comment at lunch that all would be good
because of "Our great leader, Islam Karimov!"

I do have this nagging impulse to go back to Nukus, however, because I know the authorities don't really want us here. They humor the NGOs—U.N. outfits. I see how it works—a crisis erupts and all these groups arrive with varying degrees of cluelessness. They need crises to justify their existence and to feel good, but they may or may not have any brains. The locals understand this. The international groups can do good things but it happens with lots of unneeded running around and self-importance.

Our Nukus patients phone us here on the other side of their country wondering when we will return. That epidemic oozes along. We have no chance there—a better one here ironically. I expect to return to Nukus in a few days or sooner.

Andijan is very beautiful—green, orchard area. 400,000 people live here. Unlike Nukus, it all feels rich, easy, friendly, developed. We now stay in a nice hotel. Good per diem for food. Host and vehicle every day. What an irony our daily existence is considering why we are here and where we've come from. What a disconnect.

It's Sunday and Abdulla and the driver have this day off, so that means we do as well. For the past days we have been driven from camp to camp to see how all is being managed. Abdulla has been true to the custom in this part of the country and has been an impeccable host. Each day he takes us for a nice lunch at a different restaurant. He's our host but also our guard of sorts, and must control as best he can what we see and do. It's clear that all the "counsellors" we meet are aware of his position.

But today we are on our own, so we ask a taxi driver to take us to a river to swim. When he finds out that we've come to help the refugees he decides to lower his fare and not charge us while he waits an hour so as to drive us back when we are finished. The place he takes us is a fast stream of rushing brown water. It is from the mountains but has been warmed by its flow through the wide valley bottom.

There are lots of others frolicking about in the day's heat. But there are no females here, so we try to move away from the others, hoping Deelya will attract less attention. We sit in the fast rushing water. Deelya cannot swim, but she holds up handfuls of water to her face. "Ahhh, it smells like my village did when I was a child. It smells really good. Can you smell it?"

☙

June 22

The longest day of the year is over and there are still 75,000 refugees in these camps, maybe more. And we have stopped our red marshrutka on the high point of this road to look over these fields and far off to those of Kyrgyzstan in the distance. Smoke billows there—one large and two smaller areas. Neighbourhoods still burning or something else? Abdulla doesn't know. Both he and our driver gaze at the rising plumes with anxiety. Is the killing to continue?

Right at our feet, though, the grey fields of cotton slope downwards into the wide expanse of valley floor. This is a hot sun. Thirty-seven degrees today, but with a slight breeze. I ask Deelya if she hears the silence. She does.

Before stopping, we passed the swollen Black River, wild and thick with swirling mud water, an angry river carving the land on its way from the Pamirs to the great Su Darya.

After the Black River came rice paddies. Bright green. Brilliant. An expansive, fertile breadth straight from the movies of Vietnam, they undoubtedly gave us the heaped dish of plov that we ate yesterday.

And before the river and the rice fields, and the quiet people squatting at the side of the road with their pails of apricots and apples for sale, and the lone shepherd higher over in his field lounging in shade beneath the one tree while his goats ambled at their graze, before stopping to look across at the plumes of Kyrgyzstan smoke, we were at the camp.

Forty-five hundred and more still arriving at this other cotton factory compound where Camp Pahtazavod was set. The tents, row upon row pitched on the concrete. All those women and children there now over ten days, unsure of what time means. Husbands and fathers still in hiding back in Osh or Jalalabad away from their burned homes.

Their crying has changed now.

Outside the gates, scores of relatives were gathered, all trying to peer into the compound, wondering what was there, but not allowed in past the security check points. Abdulla got us in easily with just our signatures.

Deelya and I did a 75-minute counselling session for 16 women plus two camp counsellors and Abdulla in the factory laboratory. The women ranged in age from approximately 70 to 25. All had run from threat of violence and vicinity of burning homes but most not from directly experienced violence. As well as trauma experiences a common issue was fear about their future.

Mats had been laid out for us. Deelya and I at the front, and the women in two rows before us. Behind them various large lab machines for testing and sorting the cotton. One woman spoke more than the rest. She said that she came from a town outside of Jalalabad. Both her home and shop had been burned. As she spoke, she cried. I sat in front of her, hoping to control both her emotions and how it affected the other women. And, as important, to give her the personal attention she needed. When she finished, I gave her a short hug. My theme was that this kind of release of stress and sadness was necessary. I asserted that each should pick a time each day and go off somewhere in the camp either alone or with a friend and talk about what they experienced, what they were feeling now and before, and let it flow. I said to make sure that the kids aren't around because they don't need to hear their elders in such distress, that once the adults have released their own inner turmoil they can turn to their children and then help them do the same. They were all mothers, and they understood.

Especially fascinating was a young man who had been watching, a volunteer. At the end he said in English: "I found it very interesting. But I am a man and I am not able to cry. I would like to." I responded and we talked a bit. Then I got up and went over and hugged him Uzbek-style — a hand-shake and touching the side of our heads together. None of the women could understand our talk but they were mothers, and they nodded at the embrace.

June 23

The guy in the blue camouflages is big enough to break boards with just the meanness in his eyes. His partner not so huge but still equally serious. This isn't Checkpoint Charlie. We are at a small gate into the Kaozak refugee camp. Only a bit more than a kilometre away from the Kyrgyz border, in normal times there wouldn't be any military at this summer retreat, its large walnut trees, corn field just a few metres away. In normal times the creek that cuts through the property and stretches into tributary rivulets would be just as swollen, just as keen to move the old metal water wheel as it does now. In normal times there would be hundreds of children here just as there are now, but they would be thinking only of play, only of excitement at being away from home.

These are not normal times. This is June 23, 2010 and there are 2,000 refugee women and children squeezed here in their UNICEF tents, the big ones of dark green canvas, and their United Nations Humanitarian Relief tents, the Quonset rounded white ones, smaller but just as packed with sleeping mats, just as packed with fear. They have all fled their homes a few hours' walk away to come here to their ancestral Uzbek land for safety and, as it would be, acceptance and sustenance. As in every camp we've visited, it's obvious there is ample food and shelter and medical attention.

But still these people have been here two weeks now in their unexpected summer camp with all these unexpected neighbours and each day many live with the images of homes burning, of screaming in the street, of explosive sounds from weapons they could not see. Others live with the simple fear of what comes next, what now, where will they return to. This is the common experience of all refugees. Safety is great, a place for shelter and food is great. But what of the future? How does one continually only live in the present, especially when there has been so little choice of that present? It is like having one's eyes to look only so far and then stop seeing.

And the children, of course, they keep asking questions. When do we go home, mother? I want to sleep in my own home again, mother. I want to see father. When? When? When?

These are easier than the why's.

All these women—young, old, hobbling, the spring of youth in their step—are a great joint family now, a family of fear, of hope, of waiting. And no one knows for what. One young mother stands over me, dark eyes staring a hole into my face, and asks rhetorical questions: "If we go home how can I go away to work and know my children will be safe? Our jobs must now be taken by Kyrgyz since someone will have had to do them, so how will we work again?"

There are nods. Another woman speaks with more urgency, emotion, rawness: "They went wild. We lived together all these years and they just went wild. How could they do that? What did we do? That is our home. We have been there for generations."

Another says: "They killed my uncle. Then they burned his home where he and my aunt live. They are both dead." This woman is young and pregnant. As she speaks she touches her belly.

Around us more have gathered. All listen. All watch the interaction, this discourse of no answers. The large, leafy trees surround us. It is cool here away from the hot Andijan sun of late June. We are one small group in the midst of the earthen paths, the rivulets, and trees, the rows and rows of tents, the hubbub of humans busy with waiting. I have come here for these minutes. These minutes during which nothing happens but the flow of words, the exchange of eyes, the forming memory within each of us that I have been there.

This is the way of us. We are only what we are. We give only what we can, what we know to give. Often it is only other than nothing. All our faces will disappear from consciousness rather quickly, in minutes if not sooner.

Refugees are there for themselves. The rest of us come and go. With the great, great emphasis on go.

❧ While we are here, I want to take some of the women for individual counselling sessions but Abdulla says no. He is nervous. Some authority in a uniform has come into the camp and Abdulla hurriedly informs us that it's time to leave.

❧

June 24

Last night, we decided there was no more to be done. Abdulla insisted that the camps would be emptied soon, that the Uzbek government had negotiated with the Kyrgyz government and the refugees were to return home in the coming days. This seemed suspicious to us and decidedly unsafe. Most of the refugees we had met with certainly wanted to go home but they were afraid and didn't want to be forced home prematurely. Maybe, that's why there has been such great material attention to all the needs of the 75,000. The Uzbek government was pulling out all the stops to help but knew early on that they would not sustain it.

Just like that, for Deelya and me anyway, our refugee crisis is over.

Now we must find another taxi to zip us back to Tashkent. Hopefully it won't be Schumacher's brother-in-law.

Guldana's Voice

June 26

It's good to be home. At TB2 the patients are glad to have me back. I go to see Guldana. She is still in ICU, blood pressure still not right, legs still swollen slightly. She sleeps sitting now, folded over onto her knees, facing away from the pillow. The curve of her back moving slowly up, slowly down as she breathes. I sit beside her on the bed trying not to wake her. I want to put my hand on her back, want to feel the breathing, feel this young woman who has become my friend. But I will let her sleep and come back later.

The day before I left for Andijan, she read out the letter to her dead mother which I had asked her to write. She had it in an envelope, with a flower on the outside, that she was keeping beneath her pillow. As she read, Aynur translated and struggled to keep from crying. A beautiful letter.

> *Mother, I miss you. I have been sick for many years now, but I am still okay. I got married, but my husband divorced me when I got sick. That was okay because I never liked him anyway. I am happy with my brothers and sisters, but I miss you. I wish you were here, but I know you are in some other world. I am an adult now and even though I am sick, I am okay. I love you, but I will say good-bye to you now. I can live on my own. Thank you for being my mother. I will leave you now. Your daughter, Guldana.*

She folded the letter and placed it back in the envelope.

Now she is sleeping. Peacefully sleeping in a position she has become used to, a position which makes it easier to relax, give in to weariness. On her bed table are a small clear plastic bag of tomatoes, a disc of bread, and a tea cup.

✍ Kurbangul is still in the cell next to Guldana. She says she walked three steps yesterday.

✍ Slohan has been sent back to TB2. I am surprised that she looks so happy. She is still angry at her sister-in-law, but she is clearly more relaxed, happier. We go for a walk. Being back at TB2 was a shock at first, but then the security of the routines took over. She no longer can worry about her handicapped sister. She no longer has to feel the rejection from her sister-in-law. Here she can just be. I have never seen her this happy. It makes me wonder if she has seasonal depression, that once the sun and weather warms, her whole system charges up.

✍ Achmed has phoned. He said he saw me on television with Deelya when we were in Andijan. He's glad I am back safely. Right now though, he has a problem. His daughter is trying to get admitted to the Pedagogical Institute to study to become a teacher. Achmed is proud of her. But there is a problem. She can't get into the Institute unless she pays a 150,000-sum bribe. He doesn't know what to do. I tell him we should go to see the director of the school. Aynur thinks I am crazy. What can you do? What will you say? Hey, I say, I have just returned from the crisis so I am feeling confident.

Outside the Institute, we meet Achmed and go right up to the director's office on the third floor. The secretary says her boss is in another part of the building but she'll call him. This is surely the first time a foreigner has come into this office. After a few minutes, the director enters. He looks bewildered. Come in, come in. We go into his office. Aynur and I sit in the chairs close to his desk. Achmed stands back by the door, dressed in a nicely pressed orange, short-sleeved shirt and a look of wariness.

"What can I do for you?"

"Thank you for seeing us." I explain who I am and what I do. "I need your help," I say.

"Of course, but how can I help?" he says, with a puzzled look.

"This man is Achmed. He is one of our patients, and I know him well. He has been taking his treatment for eight months now. It is a terrible burden. The drugs make him sick every day. But he takes them. He is a warrior who is fighting to defeat this epidemic. If he stops the drugs he will make the bacilli stronger and then the epidemic worsens. I am really proud of him." The director listens attentively wondering what this has to do with him. How many times do I call patients warriors? And does it ever matter?

"Achmed cannot work while he is on the drug treatment. And right now this has created a huge problem for him. His daughter wants to attend your school to become a teacher. I know how things work here. But she does not have enough money to get in, and Achmed cannot provide her with that money. So I am asking you to help. Can you make an exception for her?"

The director hesitates, looks over at Achmed. Then he replies that in Karakalpakstan education is free of charge. There are only very minor expenses for one's books. Everything depends upon whether someone qualifies to get in. There is an exam to pass. If his daughter can pass the exam then she can attend.

I am unsure what this means. Is it just cover-up, trot out the official script and then after we leave business as usual? But then the director goes on. He picks up a pen and asks Achmed his full name, his daughter's name, their address. He finishes by saying that he will do what he can but she must pass the exam. Achmed says that she is smart and he knows she can pass it. I thank the director for his time and for his help. We shake hands and leave.

This has been a first for all four of us.

June 28

I am at OPD. A phone call has come from Aziz who is out at TB2. Guldana cut her wrist last night and was taken to the psychiatric hospital. Aynur and I call for the car and immediately head there. It takes us 40 minutes. I am upset and worried. I did not see this coming. I know she ruminates. I know she is frustrated at being sick for so long. Before I left on Friday I went to see her. I held her. We talked about Andijan and the refugees. I told her I was glad to see her eating so well, that she was not getting thinner. She said she was tired most days. It seemed like the usual Guldana.

At the psychiatric hospital, the nurse in charge is surprised to see us. She searches through the register of admissions for the night before. No Guldana. We go to another office where patients actually come when they are assigned a bed. No one there has heard of her. Back to the admissions nurse. She looks through the list of patients again. The list for the whole hospital. No Guldana.

We don't know what to make of it. I phone back to Aziz at TB2. He says he will check with the doctors. Is there another psychiatric hospital?

Then after an hour, we hear. Guldana was sent by ambulance to the psychiatric hospital. But the doctors would not take her because she was a TB patient. TB2 refused to take her back, so Guldana had to phone someone who came in the night in a taxi to get her. Apparently she has gone to stay at a relative's home but no one knows where or with which relative.

I ask Aynur to try phoning her directly.

Guldana answers. I say how happy I am to hear her. "How are you? I am really worried about you. I want to come to see you right now. Where are you?"

"No, I don't want you to come. I am not able to see you. I will let you know when you can come."

I continue asking, then assert that I need to see her. I tell Aynur to say I will get in trouble if I don't see her. Nothing works. She won't tell us where she is. I am glad she is alive.

🖎 We go to TB1.

Gulsima wants to see me. As soon as the door closes to the counselling room, she starts to cry. Doctor Zakir has refused to give her the drugs this morning. He is mad at her because she went home after Saturday drugs. She knew the patients were supposed to stay over the weekend and no longer go home but there was a problem. Her in-laws were pressuring her to come home and do some work. Her two children are there. She misses them so she agreed to go home. And she was missing her husband in Kazakhstan. At home there was lots of criticism of her for not being there more often to do her work. *How long will this treatment take? You are supposed to be fulfilling your obligations here. What kind of wife and mother are you? Who do you talk to in the hospital?*

Yet she was happy to have seen her daughters and had strengthened her resolve that, when she got discharged, she would take them to live with her in her own parents' home. No more discord. Both daughters with her again. Then, when she got back to TB1, Zakir was furious. He told the nurse not to give her the pills. He said he would decide if and when she could resume treatment. He told her she was lucky to be there and that he could send her out of the program any time he wanted.

I tell Gulsima that I can phone Samuel and get him to intervene. She says it is better not to or else Zakir might find another way to make problems for her. She decides she will go find him when she calms down more, apologize again, and say that she needs the drugs. After all the crying, she tells me she feels a bit better, that she needed to get it out.

We do everything in our power to keep the patients taking their drugs every day, the drugs that make them sick for hours and which they dread so much so that more than a quarter officially default and die while many others miss so many doses that they too die but not as official defaulters. Yet this doctor is sure he needs to teach a lesson by withholding her drugs.

Another doctor at one of our other wards has told a patient that, instead of the MDR drugs, she will give her an alternative single drug to cure her. And charge a bit, of course. There are no such thing as alternatives. I've been told the same doctor has prescribed various fringe treatments for regular TB patients in the past ... one of which was an exercise of repeated walking around a tree. This same doctor irritated Samuel by refusing to open beds for some patients. He surmised this was because she was frustrated being on the negative MDR ward where she could not make enough money as bribe taking in the MDR wards is so seriously prohibited.

Another patient wants to talk also. She tells me she is drinking donkey milk and eating dog fat and the yolks of four eggs every day. She has heard that will help her get healthy and cure the TB. I smile and tell her to keep doing it, that it can't cure the TB but it will add good nutrition to her diet and strengthen her. She says she will also drink camel milk on some days. Good. I think that is much better than what the patient who left TB2 to go home and follow another traditional cure has chosen. She is drinking a cup of her toddler grandson's urine each morning. Not sure of that one.

The day ends at TB3 and visiting with Oleg. I bring him a meal of fried chicken, hidden in my pack so that Natasha and Massor won't feel offended. Oleg is doing okay. He is interested to know of all the goings on in Andijan. Maybe Death won't find him now that he has moved.

☞

June 29

He is lying in a fetal position on his bed in Room 1. I only mention Room 1 because it suggests some meaning to these moments, having a definite place seems to imply a bit of identity beyond the inhale and exhale of breath. This is what Islam has come to now, the metronome of breath. He is the boy I first met four months before and sat with on his bed. He was not particularly happy to sit with me then. But not particularly annoyed either. Indulging me, the foreigner, maybe with a fraction of curiosity.

From that first meeting until now, we have been close, Islam and I. Never talking much. Me urging him to take his drugs, urging him to go into his anger and grief of having lost both parents and a sister to MDR-TB, him nodding. And me asking what kinds of food he might like me to bring to feed both his body and his spirit. Visiting him at home, getting him back to hospital, his time in ICU and then an upswing back to a normal room.

Now he seems close to death again. The x-rays show no lungs left. He needs the oxygen ventilator to breathe. His bones protrude from the tan skin stretched over his angular frame. His black hair, cut short, stands out wanting to be touched. If he was a Buddhist on retreat it would be ideal, each minute of his day a concentration on breaths. But he is dying.

Across from him is his younger brother, also with MDR-TB, also thin. The day they got back from Islam's birthday seems long ago. He looks over at Islam, worry replacing face. Kamil has stopped eating. This will be another dead part of him and so now he too doesn't want to live anymore. This young fellow is not bright like his sicker, older brother. This young fellow is ordinary, maybe a bit simple. He has no idea about what life is or what his life can be. He watches Islam.

I go to sit beside him. I tell him that it is true that Islam might be dying. That I know it is hard, that I know it scares him, hurts him to see his brother waste and stop. But I insist that this is his time to fight, to eat, to take his drugs, to live, to carry on. This is the time to serve his brother and all the rest of his family who bring them food several times a week even though they have little of their own. I touch his head, caress his back, put my arm around him from the side. I have never been close to him, never given him attention but he needs it now. This room should not bear two deaths.

Then I go back to Islam. I hold him. I whisper in his ear, talk about dying, how if it is his time that he can let go. But that I still see life in his eyes, still the same brightness, so I whisper that he should keep breathing, keep living, keep thinking. Over on the other bed, Kamil has lain down and is quietly sobbing in his own world of despair.

I squeeze Islam again and tell him I'll come back to see him before I leave, that I'll bring him food, that he should make himself eat, try to get stronger, that he has been in this shape before but rebounded.

Then I head out the door. Aynur is walking faster in front of me. We are both going to the same place—outside. Outside to go our own ways to cry. We leave behind the other two new counsellors whom I have brought along to train and who have just now met Islam and Kamil.

Aynur and I go out to the back of the hospital facing the field. She stands 30 metres from me. I can see her body slightly heaving with the waves of emotion. Mine does the same. It feels good to be so sad, though I tell myself that he is not dead yet.

After a few minutes I return to our chalet to check on the two new counsellors. They are just coming out in a hurry. They have gathered food into a bag and are intent on taking it to Islam and his brother. I ask what they are doing. Bibigul starts to explain and then breaks down. I begin to cry and walk over to the window. The other new counsellor turns her back and I can hear her crying. We are all in this together. It is the way it should be.

In the afternoon I come back with melon and meat. Before I leave, Islam is perched on his bed, head down and breathing into the oxygen ventilator mask. He looks up. His eyes as bright and deep as ever before. We shall see.

<hr />

June 30

Concert day at TB2 with ... ta da! Daniyar!

"Ladies and gentlemen, boys and girls we are privileged today to have one of the world's greatest performers. Here from Caesar's Palace in Las Vegas, Nevada, U.S.A. please put your hands together and help me welcome the incredible D A N I Y A R!!!!!!"

And everyone smiles and cheers and Daniyar takes the microphone from Aynur who shakes her head thinking I am just too much for her.

Yesterday in Hodjeli, I took the two new counsellors to visit Daniyar. He had taken his drugs earlier in the morning and we came to his uncle's home. He spread out the mats for us. After the opening greetings, I decided to try something different. Instead of having the counsellors Bibigul and Ana just observe as I did a session with Daniyar, I gave the floor to him. "Daniyar, tell these two new counsellors what patients need from counsellors."

For the next twenty minutes, he talked. I lay back on a pillow and just relaxed listening to his voice and watching their faces. I told Aynur there was no need for translating because I knew what Daniyar would be saying. He is so aware, so connected to himself, I knew he'd talk about being present with the patients, about not lecturing, about getting to their level, seeing them as the same humans as themselves, about listening, and raising their mood.

Then I told the two to ask Daniyar some questions. They did.

Now, he is holding a microphone and singing in his first official concert. Each day he goes to his cousin's small home recording studio to work on songs for another DVD. Now he's live at the hospital where he lived and worried and longed for the bacilli to forgive him and set him free. As he sings, I see him in my mind's eye those months before sitting back to back with me out in the desert. Me hoping and wondering if the drugs would work for him.

His first song is "Anajan," the one about his mother, about missing mothers who have died, about how they stay inside us. Everywhere people start wiping at their eyes. The TB2 chief doctor is there and crying. Counsellors Altinay and Aziz are there and they are crying. It is both the wonderful lyrics and the vulnerability of this 20-year-old as the melody stretches and curls and enters every pore.

The song finishes and everyone claps. Then Daniyar mentions how he lived upstairs for so many months in Room 5 and how just this morning he took his drugs as he does every morning. He says he knows now he will be cured. He straightens out his arm and, pointing, moves it towards everyone standing in the hospital grounds: "And so will each of you."

Then he launches into the next song and people begin to dance.

I look around and see that 14-year-old Altingul and 17-year-old Nazira have disappeared. I ask Aziz if he knows where they are. He says that, when Daniyar started to sing about his mother's death, they ran back into the hospital. I go looking for them and find them in their room upstairs. Each lies on her own bed face down. Each is wailing. Each has a dead mother to wail over. I listen. What to do?

I go to Altingul, place my hand on her back, say: "Good, good. This is exactly what you should be doing." I have spoken to her often about grieving for her mother more but she always shrugged it off. Now she has fallen apart. I bend down to put my face against the back of her head. "Good, good for you."

I go to Nazira. Sit down beside her, put my hand on her back. She shrugs abruptly to get rid of it. I take it away. Sit silently beside her. Nothing to say. Just let them be. After a while I get up and leave.

After more than an hour of Daniyar's singing and recorded dance music blaring out from the amp, it is time to close it down. The patients request a popular dance number that hasn't played yet. That finishes. Then a man asks for one more song from Daniyar. Sing "Anajan" again.

"Yes," yell others. They want to hear the song about his mother once more.

&

July 1

Concert day at TB1 with ... ta da!! Daniyar.

The patients here don't know Daniyar. To them he is just a performer. And TB1 is huge. Lots of regular TB patients also gather. This is a pop concert. The trees, the benches, the sun and shade and friendly soil for everyone to rest on and enjoy. Daniyar starts with his regular songs. Love. Relations with family. Easy-going songs. He doesn't mention that he is a patient.

Then half way through he sings "Anajan." Everyone goes silent. Tears. When he finishes, people from the audience come forward and place 500 or 1000 sum notes in his shirt pocket. Gulbasara also has come outside to watch and listen. Thin in the chair, she sits in her pink sweater. She knows Daniyar from TB2. And she calls me over to ask a favour. "Can I borrow 1000 sum from you until after the concert?"

I give it to her, and she gets off her chair and slowly makes her way over to Daniyar to place the money in his pocket.

Daniyar tells them he has MDR-TB and took his drugs this morning. Just like them. You can see all the eyes open just a bit wider.

☞

July 2

I have been asked to leave for Kyrgyzstan tomorrow. I didn't expect this. They won't allow Deelya to go. It is too dangerous there for Uzbeks, and MSF Switzerland is in charge of the mission there and they won't agree to her coming. I will be given a translator from there. I am afraid. The last time it was so successful because of Deelya. She is a counsellor and she knows everything I will likely say. I am nothing by myself. I plead, but I am told it is not possible.

I phone Guldana again. This is the fourth call I have made, one every day since she left TB2. I say that I have been waiting to hear back from her, that I need to see her. I want to go to the place where she is staying. Tell me the address. She refuses. Same response. Not now. I will let you know when. Not now.

I insist. "I need to see you Guldana. I miss you."

"No."

Finally I relent: "Okay, I am disappointed, but I accept your wishes. Good-bye."

The phone rings. It's Guldana. "I hope you are not offended. I really want to see you also, but just not now. I need to feel better first. Then I will call you. Is that okay?"

"Yes, of course. I understand. I love you."

"Me too."

☞ I go out to TB3 to bring Oleg some plov and apricot jam. He is lying on his cot snoring. I sit on the bed beside him, the movement on the thin mattress causes him to open his eyes. "Ah, Calvin." From the beginning whenever Oleg has said my name it does something to me.

He is glad that someone, he doesn't know who, has tacked up a mosquito netting over his window. I ask if he has gone swimming out in the canal. Of course not. It's too far, and he is too weak. "In time, then, when you get stronger. I'll go swimming with you." He smiles that wry golden toothed grin that he has as if to say: *Yeah right, that'll be the day but it's a nice thought.* Oleg asks for 4,000 sum to give it to the nurse so she can buy him some extra food.

He tells us that his neighbour came out to see him with some papers about the house that he lived in with his father until he died. The neighbour wanted Oleg to sign them. It was something to do with legal ownership. He refused because he couldn't be sure whether it was a case of the neighbour trying to help him with the title or trying to cheat him somehow. Maybe next time, he says, I will be there to talk to the neighbour with him.

He tells me to be careful in Kyrgyzstan, not to take any risks.

  Today is my birthday. I told Irena, the head cook, not to announce it at lunch. The custom is that everyone contributes 5,000 sum for someone's birthday or wedding, and then at lunch it's presented in an envelope. They all sing "Happy Birthday." But expats are expected to hold an additional celebration to which all are invited for food and drinks. I use all my extra money to give stuff to patients. I asked Aynur to tell Irena that I am really superstitious about birthdays and that it would be terrible for it to be announced. I said to Aynur to give her a 5,000 sum bribe not to announce it. Irena agreed but didn't want the bribe. She did give me a kiss on the cheek later.

Kyrgyzstan

July 4

I'm in Tashkent at the MSF guest house on a hot Sunday—40 Celsius. My bedroom though is air conditioned. So I am doing my part to destroy the atmosphere. Tomorrow I get a Kyrgyz visa to fly to Bishkek, the capital, and then make my way to Osh and Jalalabad in the south where evidently there are 400,000 homeless from the communal violence. It's unclear exactly who is behind this problem—amid speculation that the deposed former President is trying to foment civil war or even that Taliban sympathizers have been involved. For sure, though, it is nutty and sad.

To see and be with the people here, especially in Karakalpakstan, you could not imagine violence of any kind occurring. I'm sure it has to be similar in Kyrgyzstan. The blend of modernity, and quiet, polite traditions, produces a beautiful civility. I always say this place is more civilized than Canada—meaning that, as a populace, they are more civil and live more civilly more warmly together than we do. The culture is very strong. The good part of that is the civility. All expats want to stay here. Me too. The bad part is that women are so often doomed once they get married. Too often it brings much misery. And there are other cultural elements which bring about individual restriction. This does not aid the common good but is just a carry-over from old power needs. I often talk to the counsellors about good and bad culture. Bad culture is not really culture but habits or power practises that don't further civility or communal strength. There is much agreement.

So I am to go back to the crisis area. MSF Switzerland is in Kyrgyzstan. They need a mental health specialist for as long as I can be spared. I have agreed to be gone from Nukus for a total of two weeks. But I don't know what to expect. I am always confident in every situation I'm in. Part of the brain damage I suffer from. But this time, because Deelya isn't with me, I feel much more hesitation. Also, I don't trust NGOs and don't want to simply be another person playing foreign aid worker on the prowl. A simple translator won't be able to convey who I am or what I really mean, won't be able to see the truth of the others and the situation. Deelya could. I wonder if I alone can do anything worthwhile. After all, I don't really know what I am doing in the first place. On the other hand, if I was back with my MDR-TB people I could be useful. So I really had to think hard about losing the two weeks to go to Kyrgyzstan.

Four hundred thousand is a big number. Bigger than 75,000 from the last time. There will be lots of U.N. and Red Cross, etc. Lots of pain, closer to the threat and the rubble. Again I will be part of the paradox of helping and not helping. The useful gesture within pointlessness.

This is in contrast to the young man I counselled last night who recounted in anguish how he was anally assaulted at the age of eight by an older male relative, described how much it hurt, how the man threatened him, how his parents left him home to care for his two younger siblings and thus the man could arrive and do his deed, and how the same man once finished then assaulted the younger sister.

It was a horrible situation and the eight-year-old lived that horror for several years until he finally screamed the truth out to his mother. The perpetrator ran away before any of the adults could get to him, but then no one ever mentioned it again. It was as though the boy had never told. He still suffers the confusion about why his parents never broached it, never sought out the culprit.

This story and all the others I hear from the patients are of sadness but the telling of them means the regaining of authority by the victim. The power to tell truth. To have it witnessed and understood. They mark the occasion of humans moving as honestly and fully as possible in this life that they are given and thus are not really sad at all.

So, I hope Kyrgyzstan is worth this.

July 7

Osh is bigger than I thought. A divided city now. Kyrgyz and Uzbek. How does that work? One day living and doing one's daily routines just as for the past decades and the next a bomb blast of change. Us becoming us and them. Not really possible. But that's our way, isn't it?

Misha and I flew here from Bishkek in a small Red Cross plane with some other aid workers and two Australian pilots. Young guys. I was glad I didn't get air sick. Misha is a good fellow, an MSF logistician from Turkmenistan though he doesn't speak Turkmen only Russian. Weeks back he was supposed to go to Andijan after me but then all the refugees were sent home so MSF cancelled its plans.

Seventy-five thousand refugees in all those camps and then poof all sent home. Now the tension is back in Osh, Jalalabad and the other small towns where all hell broke out a month back. In retrospect it makes sense why the Uzbek government was able to put so much effort into caring for the refugees, immaculate effort, and why they didn't want our services. They knew it was temporary. Knew that they were sending them back. Head guys in places talk to each other, but don't tell the rest of the world what they are talking about.

I can see that Uzbek Minister in my mind's eye back at the control centre in Andijan, looking everyone in the eyes, all us international do-gooders, and as confident as glass saying thanks but no thanks. And the women in the one camp saying how torn they were, desperate to go home but anxiety driven about what they'd find there, how they'd be received. They knew that if one day normalcy could turn to savagery without any warning then there could as easily be another day. The Minister knew something too.

Flying over the mountains and green terrain from Bishkek to Osh was like being on a vacation. Such a tiny plane able to crash at any time but that thought pushed away by the delightful assumption that being a helper grants immunity. Excitement trumps risk. And, of course, new terrain geographically means the same as every other trip and just as safe.

We were told how nice the drive to Osh is. We were told how a bus load of Uzbeks had driven out of Osh to travel to Bishkek and been stopped after less than a hundred kilometres by armed Kyrgyz and forced to return. So we flew.

And Osh? Another green city like Andijan, which across the border is not so far away. But Osh MSF? Pandemonium. I am in this compound with twenty or more other MSFers. It makes me nervous. Pockets sitting here or there talking, others eating, drivers standing by the Toyotas, others at computers, others lying on beds. This house has been rented for about two weeks now. Misha and I are the newcomers. Our accents joining the rest. We wait for our briefing from the PC, a sturdy, bald guy. This guy is French and worried.

In his serious French inflection he pulls us in closer, the three of us on rickety wooden chairs outside and under a cherry tree away from the chaos of the rest of the compound. Everyone is nervous here. No one knows what to do. Security warnings are high. Don't do this, don't do that. Never go there. Never alone. Don't talk. Misha and I listen uncertainly. The PC is so serious, like a radio news announcer slowed down to tell what he really knows. "This is ethnic cleansing."

On the streets of Osh and Jalalabad in the Uzbek areas, there are lots of soldiers and militia out with their Uzis. There are frequent police/militia intrusions into Uzbek homes to interrogate, beat or take away people, create fear. The resounding questions are whether there will be renewed attacks and whether once their traditional forty days of mourning are up the Uzbek community will strike back in retribution?

Misha and I leave the briefing looking at each other. The MSF compound is nuts. That's obvious. We both want to get out of there, and fortunately we are told we will be going to Jalalabad, two hours away to the smaller MSF project there. But how precarious is the communal situation?

It is becoming evening so we are taken to the guest house — our sleeping quarters. I meet a young Brazilian/American psychologist. She has been counselling trauma victims the past ten days. She relates some of their stories. Her speech becomes more rapid. Then it shifts to expressing her own trepidations. I can see she is screwed up. She also talks about ethnic cleansing, says she was in Kosovo. She is looking forward to her end of mission in another two weeks. In acute emergencies MSF keeps missions short for its people. I think it's too bad her mission didn't end tomorrow. She is shaky.

At supper there are nine of us around the table. No one is present. Conversation is muted and detached from inner bodies. I catch Misha's eye several times. We wonder where we've come to, who these people are.

☞

July 9

Thank god we are in Jalalabad. This is relaxing. Our project is based out of two houses separated by an alley. The houses are owned by the same extended family. There are seven of us. Half sleep in one house with the family there. The other half sleep in the other and we have our work rooms there also. Each day we have our breakfast made for us in our respective houses and alternate each two days back and forth for nice suppers prepared for us. For lunch, we are on our own. Prepare individual food or jump in a Toyota to be taken to a restaurant. Easy living. A bed and breakfast. And relaxed energy.

But what are we here for? Fear dictates all of our movements. Kent, the Danish PC, is a lawyer and a nice guy. But he sees danger everywhere. He got angry at me this morning for asking a doctor that we met at a madrassa what he thought would happen next. The guy said he was really afraid and that he'd sent his own family to Kazakhstan. Kent is following the MSF party line. Invite no controversy, be seen as more neutral than the letters on the page, and expect the worst. By asking the doctor what he foresaw I was entering into a political discussion, taking sides, and endangering our translator should she ever be interrogated. Plus, she could be an informant. I think Kent's a bit overboard. But what do I know?

We can only move about carrying a radio phone/walkie-talkie type thing. Call in our movements. If the notion of ethnic cleansing is accurate then there is a certain degree of legitimacy to this security obsession. If not, whoa, let's get a grip. In either case, the whole point of being here is to get something done. We knew about the risk in the first place. But we stay safe. Armenian female doctor, Australian nurse, French nurse, Greek psychologist who is also Kent's wife, Misha, and me. Electra, the Greek psychologist, goes out to a clinic in Bazaar Korgon, another smaller town 40 minutes away each day to counsel trauma victims. The rest stay in the houses, counting supplies, writing reports, waiting. I think about the work I could be doing back home in Nukus.

I am the only one who has worked with Uzbeks, the only one already from the region. The others have been parachuted in for a month to six weeks. Jalalabad is a town of 70,000. About 200 homes were burned here while 2,800 were burned in Osh. I want to meet with any local Uzbek authorities to see if I can train their people as lay counsellors. But when I make this request, it's like my words have no meaning. But soon maybe, Kent says I can go out on the streets where homes have been burned to see if I can make any connections.

☙

July 10

I am in Bazaar Korgon with Electra. We are doing a joint counselling session with a man who has been sent to our room in the polyclinic because the doctors think his symptoms are the result of post traumatic stress. Electra has come here each morning since arriving at Jalalabad. She has set it up with the clinic administration to see all those they believe need psychological help. She was told that the Uzbeks have some trust of this polyclinic because there are many Uzbek staff working here. She says Uzbeks won't go to other clinics in Jalalabad for fear of being mistreated by the majority Kyrgyz staff or otherwise set up for repercussions. Here there is usually a line-up outside Electra's door.

The two of us work well together interacting with the man before us. He is scared all the time, cannot sleep well at night and is afraid of sounds. His stomach has pain as though there was an ulcer.

We ask him to tell us of the night of terror. When the shooting began, he and his wife hid outside in the courtyard of their home. The house next to them was set on fire. They wondered if the flames would spread to their home and if they would be burned alive. They didn't know whether to run and take their chances or stay and hide. They crept outside and made their way undercover of bushes at the roadside. They saw mobs of armed men firing weapons. Rifles, pistols, automatics. They saw soldiers with them which told them the attack was part of an official act.

The man began to cry as he recounted that night—his fear and his deep worry that he might be leading his wife to rape and murder. I said: "Yes, good. Good. Cry."

Then Electra interceded. She spoke sharply to our translator, a middle aged lady. "No, he said to cry. Tell him it's good to cry." Electra looked at me with her eyebrows raised. "The translator told him not to cry."

Good thing that Electra knows some Russian.

☞ Later, I meet Jamila. She's 26 and a lawyer, has been studying in Moscow the past two years and has come home to see her family and to help during this crisis. We have hired her to be my translator. Her father is Uzbek and her mom Kyrgyz. She is fluent in both languages and in Russian. Her English is good, her heart better. Ahhh, I am saved by fate.

☞

July 11

The charred structures stretch like old rusted ships on a strange street sea, in a way almost as though they should be so forlorn, their windows exploded, walls broken, roofs torn, and ghosts, of course, always ghosts. Weeks before, a young mother, and pregnant once again, stood with hands on her hips in the ironic serenity of the park-like Kaozak refugee camp, and with blank, staring eyes told me how her uncle had been shot by militia bullets, then burned with his wife in their home in Jalalabad. I listen for them now in this street of death.

But instead I hear other stories. In one courtyard are some twenty boys and young men at work chipping and tearing away at the sooty rubble, some of them with the insight to wear surgical masks as they climb the damaged walls. As soon as we arrive, they gather intently around. We are someone who will listen. We are other than the sadness of their task, other than the greater horror that might yet arrive in a few days after the traditional 40 days of mourning are finished.

Then the owner of this building is among us. Her squat, weathered face of contorts in tears as she describes the night of the attacks. How the militia-abetted squadrons of destroyers moved from Uzbek house to Uzbek house and beat and shot and wrecked, then burned. How the smoke infected the night. Children screaming. And eventually the tens and tens of thousands who fled this region for the border and beyond. Fled for something other than helplessness.

As the emotion escalates and too many voices grow about us in urgency, we ask to leave and visit again another day. The Australian nurse, tired of staying at the office counting supplies, has asked to accompany Jamila and me on this walkabout, and she is especially nervous. We climb back into our vehicle and drive 200 metres to the mosque and madrassa. In those compound walls, we talk with a Haji, a short man with warm eyes and a small white beard.

These Haji are respected and beloved. They've been to Mecca and come back to show it's not a dream for others in this far away town. He made his pilgrimage only three years before and still beamed for that privilege.

He tells us that many need our help. They have trouble sleeping, diarrhoea, high blood pressure, stomach ailments, and nightmares. They fear to go to the regular clinics. Only amongst themselves do they feel secure. And of course, they are waiting for the next attack. As we leave the compound walls, a car with tinted windows on the back drives slowly by and eases to a stop right before us at the gate. I wonder if someone is going to get out for the mosque, but no, I am told. No, it is one of the others just showing his power, reminding all that a mosque is only another structure.

Jamila and I walk over to a side street to talk with a group of women waiting to meet us. They tell of ailments and not being able to get medicine now. How they fear going to Kyrgyz shops, how it has all changed. As we talk, the tinted car cruises by once again on the bigger street, slowing to a crawl as it passes our side street. Jamila asks if we can leave. She is scared. She says she saw the man's eyes when it stopped in front of the mosque. She knows she is at risk for being seen to be helping Uzbeks with a foreigner.

And then we are driving away once again. The immensity of that protection not lost on any of us. Neither they nor us. Along this main street, interspersed with the black, empty homes and business-es, are other store fronts and homes intact as usual. People walk about as though there is not a thing strange about carnage. Watermelons are stacked in long mounds. Smaller, yellow melons in heaps beside them. This is July, and all around us in the vast fields of this wide valley outside of town are crops of sunflowers. Their yellow heads moving gently in the breeze like great open hands of sun.

Back at the office, the Australian nurse is angry at me for staying too long talking to the boys rebuilding the house. She is angry that I am "risking" the mission. "Risking" Jamila's well-being. She and Kent want to know what I was talking to Jamila about for so long after we returned to our own compound. I know they are thinking I was talk-ing about the political situation, asking her opinion, getting her in-volved, and thus, in their perspective imperilling her. I say the truth, that I was debriefing her, getting her to express her feelings, that she had been shocked and hurt by the appearance and behaviour of the scout car. "Oh," they say. "Is she okay?"

Later, I tell the Australian nurse that it might be better if she doesn't accompany me anymore. Kent pulls me aside later and apolo-gizes for her aggressiveness, says he will talk to her. I reply that I don't mind, she is young, that he doesn't need to say anything to her.

᠄

July 12

Electra had advertised at the Bazaar Korgon Clinic that MSF will hire counsellors to do outreach work in the town. We are to interview today. Electra, bless her heart, has advised Kent that I should interview them and start the training while I am here and that she can take over when I leave. That way everyone gets the most from my time here. She will do other community liaison work until I leave.

A large crowd signs up for interviews. They know that a job with foreigners will provide a fat paycheque. Then, an unexpected delight occurs. The work that Deelya and I did in Andijan has a moving response. It was kind of dark in the hallway when we arrived. But as my eyes adjusted, there in this big bunch of people is one of the refugee women we counselled in Andijan. She was in the group we did in the cotton factory lab. The one who spoke the most, cried, and whom I moved closer to in order to limit the effect of her emotion on the rest of the group. The two of us cry out excited greetings—half hugs, then a full strong embrace. There are at least 20 other women in the room all wanting an interview for counsellor positions, plus Kent and Jamila. They all are shocked at the intimacy. The pair of us are not. There are many burned homes here including her two.

I get tears in my eyes looking at her afterwards. I had wanted to see one refugee that I knew while I was here and now I have got my wish. The connectedness of the heart.

I hire her. So now she has a three-month job. Odd life, we live.

And the last interview of the day is a man. Just as we are leaving, this sweaty, pudgy guy runs in. "Wait!" he yells. "I want an interview." His name is Mahamet. He immediately sits us down and tells us that he is smarter than all the others he has seen come and go from the clinic. He tells us he has a computer business. Tells us he needs this work and that he would be good at it.

I ask him how he would handle it if he was counselling a man and the man started to cry. He replies that he would tell the guy not to cry. "I'd say, don't cry, you are a man." We talk more and tell him what we have told everyone else. The names of the successful applicants will be posted tomorrow morning on the wall at the first clinic.

Kent and I don't think he is appropriate. Plus, we are miffed at his pushiness. But ... he is the only male who has applied. We decide to hire him.

So, now I feel useful. The morning before hiring the counsellors, I did a two-hour training for local professional doctors and psychiatrists. Jamila was great. My purpose was to give them a solid grounding in the basic principles of trauma and how to begin alleviating the accumulation of post traumatic stress. They were very interested and a sense of good will abounded. Some of them were Kyrgyz, so I had to be very delicate in my phrasings about what had happened. Kent is correct in emphasizing how vital it is that MSF doesn't be seen as siding with Uzbeks over Kyrgyz.

Already, there are news reports coming out that say how Uzbeks started some of the conflict. We know that is not true, but it plays to the Kyrgyz need to not feel they are blameworthy as the villains.

☞

July 14

First training session with nine counsellors. Eight women and Mahamet. Mahamet is ten minutes late. He comes in sweating. And he smells. The odor is so strong the room fills with his B.O. Kent is there for the start to explain about salaries and get photos, signed contracts and photocopies of their ID. He tells me in an aside before he leaves and I start the training that I will have to talk to our friend about his odor.

I start the training by having them tell their experiences during the carnage. Mahamet goes last. "I was at home reading when I heard the shooting. It was farther away from my house so I went out to the street to see what was going on. I walked a ways and then I saw the crowd coming. I could see some of them throwing fire bombs into houses on the side of the street. Then people started running. So did I. We were too far from my house for me to get back before the mob got closer, so I ran down a side street. Shots started. I saw my neighbour fall in front of me. I ran to him, and he was covered in blood and dead. I got up and ran over into some bushes. I believed I would be dying in the minutes to come. I kept praying that they wouldn't go to my house. As it turned out they didn't. They all came down the side street that we fled on. They didn't find me. When it was over I snuck back to my house. My wife and two kids were okay. I have never been so terrified in my life."

All the while he spoke, he was rubbing his hands together, head bowed, filled with memory of the terror. A couple of the new women counsellors cried. With his honesty and open show of emotion, Mahamet had taken his place amongst them. He was now one of them. The odor no longer mattered.

July 15

In the mornings, I do PTSD counselling at the clinic and then after lunch do the training of the nine new counsellors. These are good days.

This morning, I broke Kent's rules a little. When the people waiting outside my door for counselling sessions finished, a nurse at the clinic asked me if I could go to see her brother because he was too afraid to leave his home. He had been unable to go outside since the night of the carnage. She was very worried about him.

Jamila and I walked a kilometre to his home and spent 40 minutes with him. He was a tall guy, grey-haired, maybe 45, Russian looking. His eyes still showed shock, fear. He was broken.

The good thing about seeing all these trauma victims is that, since I know I only have one session, one chance to add something that might shift things, it takes away all the hesitation and pressure. I just plow right in, trust my instincts, and try to put my heart inside theirs for just the few moments. I see it as a counter experience to the hate heart put inside them on the night of the trauma.

So, with this poor guy, here he was previously in charge of his life, happy with his wife and family, and very nice home—and then suddenly reduced to cowering, a bundle of nerves and unable to leave his yard. So, we talked. He told me his story. I affirmed the horror of it all. We talked of having no control, no power that night other than to run and hide. I explained that now he has some say over what he does with the memories.

We talk of how he needs a safety plan should another eruption occur. This is something I do with each that I counsel. It's one thing to work with the past trauma, but it's not faulty thinking for them to still be scared. They have good reason to be scared. MSF is scared. So much more so for the ones who have actually been targeted. So, part of all my counselling sessions has been to validate the current fear, to acknowledge the threat, and to help them prepare emergency plans. "What will you do, if the violence starts again? Where will you go? Have supplies and an escape route prepared for you and your family."

This is key in working with trauma victims. They need to know that everything they feel is valid. And counsellors always need to pay attention to the actual threat still out there. The past is stuck in their head, but the present is real. Both need to be addressed. And by them putting energy into current safety plans, the past helplessness is massaged and integrated with current practical capability to protect self.

So, after spending the time with him, I sent the women out of the room and held him in silence. Just like my patients in Nukus. Relax, breathe, be in your body. Afterwards, he was beaming. No longer so alone. No longer so confused. Fascinating what bodies can tell each other.

We all walked out of the yard and into the street in the sunshine.

I like these nine counsellors. Two 20-year-old girls, both university students, a Russian woman, two modern Uzbek women, and three traditional middle-aged Uzbek women, and Mahamet. We are a team. They are eager to begin. I tell them that, after my one week with them, they will begin working, and Electra will take over training them a few afternoons a week. They will go to homes of victims and begin the proactive addressing of the internalized traumatic responses.

Jamila is sweet. She has started to copy my body language and voice inflections when I do the trainings. I pace, throw my hands out, shake or laugh to demonstrate something and then she does the same.

Today, I got to the training room upstairs in the polyclinic a little early. The door was locked and the Russian woman was sitting outside on a bench in the hallway. Jamila wasn't back yet. I waited, and then the Russian woman asked if I wanted in. I nodded. She came over and unlocked the door. I started to go in. Ahhh, all the other women counsellors were on the floor at their prayers. I went back out and waited. This area is Muslim.

☙

July 16

9 am: I do a 40-minute trauma response and personal stress management session for health care professionals at Sputnik Clinic. They are all Kyrgyz doctors and nurses. This is not a very friendly audience so I make it short. The chief doctor has agreed to let MSF come in. I use it mainly to convey that we are here for Kyrgyz also.

Then it's up to Bazaar Korgon again and more trauma victims.

A woman comes in with her small infant wrapped in a blanket. She looks at me filled with earnestness.

"How can I help you?"

She indicates her tiny son, a few months old. She was worried about him. I don't quite understand. Has he been somehow affected by the violent events? He looks up at me and smiles. Cute little guy. I waggle my finger at him, shake my head and flash a toothy grin of delight to answer his little smile. I ask why she is worried about him?

"I have gone to many other doctors and they say there is nothing that can be done. I want him to get help?" I don't understand. How old is your baby?

"He is five."

I ask Jamila to repeat the question. Either she or Jamila must have misheard.

"He is five years old. He is a really good boy." She smiles lovingly at her son. "He understands everything we say, but he has never spoken. And he has not grown. I have to carry him everywhere. As you see. I am tired. I have two other children who are normal."

I realize that I am just another hope for her. A foreigner that must have answers or magic the local professionals don't. I start singing to the little boy, stroking his hair. He beams.

I say there is nothing I can do to help, but that she is doing an exceptionally good job as a mother. She gets up to leave and thanks me. She ends by saying that she will try to take him to Bishkek in the months ahead and maybe they can do something.

☞ The second person waiting is also a woman. She is about 23 and comes in with frightened eyes. She tells how ever since the night of killing and burning she has been unable to sleep properly. Often her body will go numb on one side or conversely tremor. Her husband is worried about her and she finds herself being unpredictably angry with her two small children. She is hoping I can help. The doctors suggested she wait to see me. I have her recount the night of terror in detail.

She does. I validate what she has experienced. Then I go over a plan of safety for her should violence break out again.

Next, I ask her if I could take her physical symptoms away would she allow me to? She nods. I ask again if she is certain that she would let them go, to really think about it. She goes silent and thinks, then nods again.

I have learned that, with trauma, a huge defence that we have is to identify with it and claim it as ours in order to feel an inkling of control. We develop adverse symptoms which cause us grief but we accept them because it maintains that sense of control. So, the key question can be: will the person truly let the symptoms go? Does the person truly want them to go? Yes, means being willing to be out of control.

She had nodded so I come closer and ask her to go limp. I wrap my arms around her and ask her to give me the trauma. At first I can feel stiffness, her reaction to the strangeness of the behaviour. I continue speaking softly and Jamila matches my tone. "It's okay. You're safe now. You can give me the pain in your body. You can let it go. Relax. Close your eyes. Let it go."

Her left side, the side that troubled her begins to shake. As the seconds pass the shaking becomes more intense. Then it is as though her whole body has an electric charge running through it. I hold her snugly, holding on for dear life actually. Minutes pass. I wonder how long it will continue. Then suddenly it eases and comes to a stop. I keep holding and then loosen my embrace. I thank her, and tell her that when she feels the fear come into her in future that she should walk or run. That if she can't walk or run then she should scream into a pillow. I say that she no longer needs to store it in her body but can release it.

Will this work? Who knows. I know it makes her feel better. I know she has experienced attention and caring. I know she has experienced going outside her norm in a parallel way that the trauma night invaded her norm. I know that now she is pointed in the direction of accepting and releasing. I know she has gotten something. And that is what I can do. Give something.

◌ Today, I do a counselling session with Mahamet so that everyone can watch and experience first hand how to give attention, listen, invite feelings to come out, accept the truth and the inner strength of the client despite the presenting needs. Mahamet is great. He recalls his terror and how sure he was that he would be killed. His readiness to be vulnerable and go deeply into those events touches me.

I end the session by reaching out and holding him. Some of the counsellors cry.

Now I smell like Mahamet. I never did talk to him about his body odor. And now I don't care anymore.

◌

July 17

This woman stands near her green U.N. tent — with her daughter and sister. We are three women, she says. No man. Then she cries. She points all around to the broken and charred walls of her home. She says she hopes she can have at least one room re-built for them before winter comes. The bricks stand like the ruins of an old abandoned granary.

She has no documents left. All burnt. Molotov cocktails will do that. Now she can only hope that the Kyrgyz government will do something to make it right, something to bring back some of what was.

The neighbours had told me about hiding in the shrubs of their courtyard as their house burned. The heat, the shooting. Expecting to be found and executed. That their neighbour was a single woman whose husband had died years before. Help her, they said.

The green canvas tent is neat and arranged for the three women. Inside it is sweltering, the canvas locking in the July intensity. I feel my sweat dripping down inside my shirt, covering my belly. It is like having a hidden bath.

The woman asks if she can make Jamila and me a cup of tea.

July 18

> the rivers here
> are brown and swollen fat
> like thick lines of blood
> tying the land together
> brown blood
> carrying the only truth
> these people know
> their burned homes
> their burned homes
> filled with chips of emptiness
> like their night dreams
> chips of emptiness
>
> the rivers here
> carry truth
> that there is always life
> will always be life
> whether we live or die
>
> like love
> true love
>
> whether we live
> or die

We are at a river up in the mountains about 90 minutes from our houses. Misha has arranged for an outing so we can forget the crisis. I will be going home tomorrow anyway. Electra will take over. When it took so long for me to get here, waiting for a visa in Tashkent, and then the piddling about from fear in our compound, I couldn't wait to get back to the patients where I could be of use. But the last five days have been worth it. The people who came for trauma counselling will stay with me. The beautiful nine counsellors will stay with me. Sanaya, the one who I met first in Andijan in the camp, will stay with me. And I guess, I will stay with each of them.

But today, we are at this churning mountain river. Several hundred metres from us, higher along the road, are scores of Kyrgyz weekenders also here to enjoy the warm days by a river and picnic their Sunday away. The young Australian nurse has gone off by herself to wallow in the shallow, cold water farther away down where it is flat. Electra, Kent, and the Armenian doctor lounge on a blanket and contemplate the large watermelon brought by one of the drivers.

Misha and I and the two young drivers have put on our shorts and clambered down the bank to the cascading water crashing through large rocks. The two drivers have found a perch from which they can jump out to a deeper part but not dangerously close to where the swirling current might sweep them over the cataracts. We watch them jump. Their brown skin is bright in the sun. Misha joins them. I watch. Then one of the boys decides he will dive. It makes me nervous. His youth arcs into the air. Momentarily he becomes more than himself. Movement. Freedom. Belief. Now. All of these in this idyllic mountain scene, no bodies interred back in his town, no burned homes, no sadness. He dives beautifully and enters the water. We all watch. He re-emerges, whips his head side to side to splay the water from his drenched hair, strokes rapidly to pull himself back into the pool and away from the torrent.

Misha and I clap.

In a few minutes, the same young fellow goes over to a ledge a little higher ready to dive again, but this time farther out into the current. I look around. Only me to offer caution. I choose to offer it. "Hey!" I shake my head. Misha says something. The boy grins and climbs back down and over to his original dive site, arcing once more to the same place as before. We clap and smile.

I go half as high as the rest, almost two metres, plug my nose, and jump gingerly out into the pool. Strikingly cold. Strikingly. But I did it. No one claps.

Deaths

July 19

Tonight, I am in the MSF guest house in Tashkent. Kyrgyzstan is over for me. I walked across the border early this morning and got picked up by an MSF car. Then off the six plus hours across the Fergana Valley and up through the mountains. It was a good trip.

But now, I have had a terrible reminder of the truth. Samuel arrived on his way home for two weeks of holiday. We were talking earlier after he had gotten to the guest house. In the midst of our conversation he calmly said: "And the patient Oleg died."

I could not believe my ears. I was in shock. He said it just as a tidbit of information from Nukus. It had happened the day before. He explained how counsellor Deelya had gathered left-over rice and meat from lunch at our MSF headquarters to give to Oleg. When she got there, she was told he had died that morning. He was still lying on his bed covered by a sheet when Deelya and Aynur had arrived with the food. Because he had no relatives, the hospital didn't know what to do with his body. They asked Deelya what to do. She had phoned Samuel in disarray.

I had to hold on to my feelings. Samuel and the other expats just have no idea how close I am to the patients, how well I know them, how much time I spend with them. That kind of intimacy is not on their radar.

I am still in shock. I keep the photo of me and Oleg on the fridge back at Vostachnaya. I look into our blue eyes every morning when I prepare my breakfast. I had no expectation of this. No idea. Of course I knew he was thin. I connected him with Death right from the start. But we were friends. I never fathomed he could die while I was gone.

I want to scream. Scream at how fucked up they are for sending him out to TB3 and over-ruling his decision to try the MDR drugs. Oleg was so elegant, so real. Every time I visited him, his presence spoke.

When I get back to Nukus tomorrow I will go to the office for some privacy since it's Sunday. I'll ask the guard to leave and then I'll mourn. I'll wail. I am in shock. Samuel just said it so matter-of-factly. I could feel my whole face disappear from its connection to my body. Like a light coming over me and washing me away.

I am in my shorts on these polished hardwood floors. At 11 pm, it is hot, and I am lost in my own world with the spirit of an emaciated man with laughing golden teeth, blue eyes, and gentleness.

July 21

Today is a good day. I am back. Everyone is happy to see me. They missed me. But they didn't miss me. That is the way it is. All just keeps going forward whether or not someone is around.

I go to Chimbay to see Nazira, who has been sent home negative from TB2, and Erkin. Nazira lives 40 minutes from town along a hot, hard dirt road. When we arrive she is out in the field working with her father. They come in wiping the earth from their hands. What is it like for a 17-year-old to live so far away from town? It must get lonely? Nazira smiles. Nothing to read. No TV. Three-kilometre walk to the medical post for drugs each day. It is good to see her. Now that she is home, she is uncomfortable about being hugged, showing too much affection around her family. When we leave, Nazira walks out of the house by herself to watch the car go. I can see her getting smaller and smaller still watching until we are out of sight.

Erkin walks each day to the big Chimbay hospital with its smelly toilets to take her drugs. She is not so glad to be home. There are 10 in her house plus children. It is her mom's sister's house. Erkin feels overwhelmed by it all. The drugs make her sick. There is no money. No privacy. No mom. No dad. She has been missing her brother who also died. She tells me she wrote many pages in a notebook about her mom, but then burned it all. I said that she's probably not ready to accept all the truth in her life. That she needs to let go. Let it all flow out. Needs to find her deepest pain and release it. Erkin has this beautiful face. Eyes that look into whatever she sees. If I had a spell to cast, I'd arrange it for Daniyar to fall in love with her. I know she, like all the other girls, finds him very appealing. Their wisdom would complement each other. But all I can do is promise to bring her a book to read the next time I come.

⊘ Last visit in Chimbay is another foray out into the countryside. We stop along the side of the road, leave the car and enter a gate made of wooden sticks. A young woman comes to meet us. Her name is Sayura. She has a dusky voice, syllables emerging as under protest, as though not used to finding themselves in the air. We walk for 50 metres along a path that winds through waist-high green grass in a field until we come close to a mud brick house settled in a meagre farm-like setting. A young man eyes us as we arrive. Sayura takes us past the house and down another path to a bench underneath a tree. There are some sitting mats folded in a crate. She spreads them out for us.

"So, your counsellor Gulishan says you are struggling now to take your drugs." She nods, doesn't answer. I continue that it is unusual for someone only five months from finishing such long treatment to struggle now. She looks down, says nothing. "Is there something else troubling you?"

She picks at small pieces of grass growing by the mat. I can see nervousness in her eyes. I have heard from Gulishan that she is having difficulty with her brother. I ask her if it is true. She nods. I ask if she can tell me about it. She says that he beats her. And that he won't let her go in the house, that she has to sleep outside right there where we are sitting. I rise to look back to where we saw her brother. He is standing in the same spot, looking at us through the bushes. I can sense his suspicions. Gulishan has told us that he has mental problems.

With more prodding, Sayura tells us that he also beats her father and her mother. They are all afraid of him. I ask if he has touched her sexually. She says no. I ask again. She says no again.

Then her father arrives. We greet and he sits beside us. He confirms that his son does beat Sayura and has beaten him as well. He says he doesn't know what to do. The violent behaviour began back in December. Before that, the boy wasn't that way. He is 23. Sayura is 25. He doesn't know why the boy hits them. There is never any provocation. He just gets angry and goes after them. I say it must be hard for him to watch how his son has changed.

He cries.

I ask if he has contacted a doctor.

Of course.

The young fellow was taken to a psychiatric hospital but conditions there were so terrible that they brought him home after two days. He doesn't go after him so much, but it's Sayura that is the target. Usually every day she gets a blow. We talk longer and then we walk back toward the house. I say that I'll talk to the doctors about getting a psychiatrist to prescribe a psychotropic medication that he can take at home. I will do my best. Then the mother appears. She starts getting almost hysterical. Screaming that her son is ruining their lives, that Sayura is sick and needs help but is too stressed to go for drugs, that there is no money. I calm her down.

This is my chance to see what kind of lucidity the brother has. He has been now publicly exposed. I go to him and put my arm on his shoulder. He looks at his mother with defiance as though it is she who is amiss, that everything she said is an emotional exaggeration. He and I talk. He listens and speaks. His attention goes from me and then back towards his mother. I sense that he and I have some connection. I ask him to work on his anger, that I will get medication for him. He doesn't answer.

Then the mother starts again. She will go to Kazakhstan to work and make money. There is none here and neither her husband or son are earning any. Her husband is standing by himself over by a shed. He seems smaller, lonelier when she says these words. The mother says the problem is that if she leaves then Sayura is doomed. There is no money for her to get to and from the hospital for drugs anyway. She wants her to go stay in the new negative ward at the hospital, where patients who aren't infectious can reside, but there is no money for her food. She says that they tried that before but Sayura became too ashamed to always be accepting food from other patients so she returned home.

I say that today we will take her for her drugs and give her taxi money to come home and that she should make arrangements to go into the negative ward for the next day. I will provide money for her food. We leave through the high green. The breeze is blowing, sun nice. An idyllic setting indeed.

⌀ On the way back to Nukus, I get a call from Kairat. He needs me to come see a patient at TB1 before I go home for the day. I don't want to and ask Aynur: "Tell him, I will see the patient tomorrow."

Aynur tells him. She listens. Then she turns to me: "He says that if you don't come he will have to stay there overnight with the patient because she is out of control."

We drive to TB1. The patient's name is Malicka. She is a nurse about 42. Her daughter is with her. Malicka is agitated. She lies on her bed still and staring, face a grey colour, eyes wide, breathing roughly. Then she lurches up and sits. She starts rubbing her arms. Then she throws herself toward the floor and lies down there. Then she is up and standing. Then down again on the floor. Her daughter is just short of panic. "Mom! Mom!" She moves with her mother trying to hold her from hurting herself, keep her calm.

I ask how long this has been going on. It started earlier today.

Malicka has bruises now on her face and arms from the thrashing about. She has some quiet spells when she sleeps, but then shortly after awakening it's the agitation again. The doctors don't know what to do. She has previously been put on a psychotropic drug and on sedatives. I wonder if there is any conflict with those and the toxic MDR-TB drugs. I stroke the woman's hair, speak to her gently, quietly that she needs to breathe, relax herself. I don't know what else to do. I say I will come again in the morning. I tell Kairat to go home, that it is beyond us. I phone Firoza, the expat doctor, ask about drug conflict. She doesn't know. I go see Zakir and ask. He doesn't know.

Yes, it feels good to be home.

July 22

Before I go to TB2 I stop in to see how Malicka fared last night. Her daughter says it was okay, the nurse gave her another sedative and she settled down and slept. But the daughter is agitated and speaking loudly and rapidly. This is her mom and she is freaked now at the continuation of such bizarre behaviour. Bad enough to have MDR and now this.

Malicka is lying on the floor as we talk, moaning and squirming. I help her up to the bed. I rub her back. She is wild-eyed and jabbering. I whisper for her to relax. I start massaging one of her arms. And I begin talking to her about how her mind is not working right. But the daughter is too loud. I ask her to be quiet. She stops, and I resume talking to Malicka who, though wild eyed, is listening. I can feel her body listening. Then the daughter starts jabbering loudly again. This time Malicka tells her to shut up. I massage her other arm. Fingers, wrist, forearm, upper arm, shoulder.

Malicka points to her head, places my hand there. I massage her head. The daughter says her mom has bumped her head sometimes in her thrashing stages. Says it quietly this time. I rub Malicka's head. She closes her eyes, lies there on the bed, calm. I stay a half hour and leave.

Out at TB2, Deena reads me some of her poems. The words come out so delicately, as though a pattern of crocheted lace that Deena throws into the air to hover, lighter than that air. Her dimples inflect at the end of stanzas. Her brown eyes look up into mine to see if I understand through Aynur's translation. I need no translation. The sound of her voice is the sound of aliveness.

Slohan is happy too. In this sunny weather she looks happier and healthier than I've ever seen her. She is helping the nurse with giving meds to patients, walks around now with an aura of leadership. I ask if she has a boyfriend now because she seems so much lighter. She smiles widely. "No. But there is a man who likes me. I have known him for a while and we talk on the phone."

☙ I phone Guldana at the end of the day. I want to see her. The phone immediately goes to the recording that says there is no one available at this number.

☙

July 23

Malicka died last night.

I ask our doctor, Firoza, if anyone knows the actual cause of death. Malicka hadn't looked that sick, was not so thin. It was her agitation that must have over-taxed her. I want to know if anyone ever checks to see if it can be heart attack or an adverse psychotropic drug reaction. Firoza says that, whenever a TB patient dies, the cause of death is always written as being from TB.

I am glad Kairat made me see her. I will remember her. She was more than just the patient thrashing about out of control. Even when it was happening. She was still Malicka.

☙

July 24

Penetrating means I have to peer past whatever a patient tells me and see the truth. Kizlargul, whom I have known for six months, one of my first three friends in TB2, has stopped her drugs and left the hospital after having been readmitted.

We go out to the home where she is staying. It is a long drive. Kilometres away from Nukus. The last stretch follows along the wide canal. The channel, they call it. The road dips and rises in its hard-pounded earth complexion. We are driving with Naeel. I joke that we should stop to go swimming in the canal and see if National Security comes after us. That maybe it was Naeel they were following when they zipped onto us out in the desert. He laughs that there might already be bodies weighted down in the water.

We come to a stop by a house far along the isolated road. I know now why it was problematic for Kizlargul to come for her drugs when she was going to OPD. At least an hour to get there from here, not counting the 20-minute walk from the house back to the paved road where the marshrutka comes. A man standing by the road confirms this is the house where Kizlargul lives. He is her father-in-law. We walk together down a hard path 100 metres to the simple square house. It is mid-morning and the air is not yet so hot. The man calls into a makeshift tent in the shade beside the building. Kizlargul crawls out.

She is surprised to see us. Nazigul, her polyclinic counsellor, has brought us and we all sit together on a bench. Kizlargul's little daughter also emerges from the tent and goes into the house. I ask Kizlargul why she has stopped taking the drugs.

She just looks coldly ahead and says she could not tolerate the drug regimen anymore. I ask why now? Why after all these months? Continuing to look straight ahead, she repeats what she already said.

I begin my usual spiel about the disease becoming stronger, she is a warrior, her daughter needs her. She says nothing, stays silent. I ask her to return to the hospital. I will give her money if she is in need. "You know I will help," I say. She stays silent. "Will you come back to TB2? The analysis may even be a mistake. You can't let it discourage you. This happens. It's normal. It just means you keep fighting. You can do it."

"No, I won't go back to the hospital."

"But why? Why quit now?"

"I cannot tolerate the drugs."

I know her and vice versa. I have never actually counselled her much, but I know her. I don't believe her. "There is something else. There must be something else."

Silence, head shakes no.

"There is something you aren't saying."

"No."

We sit in silence, the four of us. I look át Nazigul and Aynur wondering if they have any ideas. No.

So, I go back to insisting that something else was inside and stopping her. She keeps insisting nothing else. I sense anger inside holding her back. "You're angry," I say. No response. "You're angry. What is your anger?"

"No, I'm not angry."

Ahh.

I know she is. Then a faint coal starts to glow inside me. I ask why she is out here at her father-in-law's house so far from town. Silence.

"Why don't you stay at your mother's house?"

Silence.

I repeat the question.

She replies without emotion: "My sister stays with my mother."

Here the mother bond is everything. Everything. "But why don't you stay there also? Is your mother too poor?"

"No, she has money from when my father died."

"Then, I don't understand. Why don't you live there also?"

Silent. Staring at the ground.

I wait. Wait. Wait. "Tell me the reason that you don't live with your mother?"

Finally ...

"When I got sick I asked my mother for money so I could get an operation on my lungs. She wouldn't give it to me."

"Ahh, I see. That must have hurt." She cries a bit. I put my arm on her shoulder. "Does your mother know how serious the disease is?"

"Yes, my other sister died from it."

I wait. I want to understand. "Did you make it clear to your mother that the operation could spare you two years of treatment if it worked?" She nods, yes.

"Did you explain that you could die if you didn't get the disease stopped?"

"Yes."

I wait a bit. "What did your mother say to that?"

Silence. Then: "She said, 'Oh well, just another dead daughter.'" Kizlargul places her hands over her face and breaks down in sobs.

The ice of those words hits me and I immediately grab her and hold her. She wails deeply. All I can say is: "Fuck, fuck, fuck." Aynur translates accordingly with the same emotion and low volume. Kizlargul cries and cries. She has become a child, a daughter who has always known this awful truth. A knife so deep in the heart.

I don't want to ever let go of her.

Slowly, it is time to let her sit alone. We talk about the poison. About her mother's inability to love. I ask her what she would do if her own young daughter got seriously hurt and was in danger. What she would do if she was way out here all alone and it was night and no marshrutkas. She answers that she would carry her daughter and go as far as she had to go. I say: "Yes, that's you Kizlargul. That's what a mother does. Your mother is broken. It is not about you. It is her brokenness."

We walk to the back of the house together, just the two of us. We go over to a pile of dried mud bricks. I pick one up and place it in her hands. It is heavy. I motion for her to toss it away. She does. Then I pick up another brick and give it to her. She throws it away. I repeat this ten more times. Each time she takes the load and throws it aside. She smiles. We nod. She gets it.

She agrees to return to hospital and the drugs. I give her money for a taxi. I say I will be there for her. I hug her good-bye and we leave. Her father-in-law is out on the road by our car with Naeel. He says we should go back for a piece of bread; he is sorry not to have offered us some. We politely say it's okay. He shakes our hand, thanks us for coming, asks if Kizlargul will go back to the hospital. We say we think so.

And so it goes.

❧

July 25

The taxis speed like angry, wild bugs as they race on the asphalt, outmanoeuvring marshrutkas; the freedom of the lanes is what they have. Cigarettes dangling, hands on the wheel, foot on the pedal, the posture of momentary freedom. The cops wear innocuous green uniforms with green cop hats shaped like French cop hats. They stand at roadsides everywhere, intersections, straightaways, around corners, out on the highway between towns. With their red plastic batons they wave over drivers whenever they please. Collect their small tax and wave the drivers back on the road. The greeting handshake, an indelible sign of the civility, normalcy of declaring without words— *hello, it's your turn, I am the collector and you are the payer.* 5000 sum later and all is well. The offenses? Stopping too close to the intersection when being waved over. Going 58 kph and not 55 kph. Being too far out or too far in. One cop pulled us over and Jenya got out with his papers. He came back smiling and with all his cash still. What was the problem? He wanted to know why we were all wearing our seatbelts? He hadn't noticed the foreigner. I imagine what it must be like to train to be a policeman, whether the biggest anticipation is to be able to wear the crisp green uniform, to carry the gun, to have family feel an in, or to be able to collect the personal tithes as wanted.

Today is July hot. We have stopped for a traffic light. Off to the side of this wide six-lane street that centres the city is a small swimming hole. The irrigation ditch for the roadside trees flows through a culvert and pools in the mud for a pond just large enough for ten kids to enjoy. And they do. At least that many are jumping in and out, splashing the brown water over their brown slightness, their naked hot day bodies. Bare asses glisten, hair soaked, laughing eyes and yelling. Jumping, dunking, pushing about. Six, seven, ten years old all boys and all naked, the free angles of nowness. And one little girl. With underwear. Not completely signed into the culture just yet. Still signed into heat and coolness, to laughing water. Playing like the others except for the panties. No one yet telling her not to.

❧

July 28

Guldana must be dead, I think. No one at the hospital has heard of her and I can't get through on the phone. I don't know where to look. I want to mourn, but I can't. I have been in Kyrgyzstan. I have cried for Oleg. I don't know how to cry for Guldana. I am glad that I cried for her months ago when I held her in ICU and she was breathing so poorly and I went out to the chalet. Murat was there and I collapsed in his arms and wept because I thought she was dying then. She didn't. She rebounded. Maybe not this time. But who knows.

☙ Young Altingul is now at OPD. Smear negative but too early to know of culture. She comes to OPD with her little boom box blaring, sunglasses, short skirt and swagger. 15 years old now and filled with life. Let it be. Let it be.

☙ Islam has been sent to TB3. They think there is no hope with the drugs. This time I can agree. He will wait there until the beat ends. I will bring him montey dumplings.

☙ Before I go out to TB2, Kizlargul phones me wondering if I am ever going to come out. It is nice to say: "Actually I'm almost on my way." I apologize for having been so busy. "I have been thinking about you." Does that mean anything? To say I have been thinking about you? When the politicians say that their hearts and prayers are with someone who has suffered a tragedy, I know they are lying. Does Kizlargul believe me? If she does what value does it have?

When I get there, I hug her and kiss her on the head. She looks happy. Resigned now to being there, keeping with the drugs. I reflect on the early days when I would come to the hospital. One afternoon I was walking with a group of women outside the gates. A marshrutka drove up and passed us going toward the gates. Kizlargul recognized her husband in the vehicle. She had been expecting him. So she turned back from us and walked to meet him. All the other women stopped and watched. I asked why we didn't keep going on our own stroll. One laughed and said: "We want to see how her husband greets her. If they hug or kiss." Then everyone tittered. They didn't, just greeted and walked together back into the hospital grounds. The women were disappointed.

Gulnas was in that group, one of my first three friends. Gulnas has learned some English but was transferred back to the first ward, the more infectious one. I don't trust the analyses that the patients get. But they have the force of law and the patients believe fully. So, after some weeks, Gulnas got disheartened and left to go to Tashkent. She wants to get a lung operation there, believing the capital will have the surgeons who can fix her. Before she went, I gave her money for her phone and asked that she stay in touch. That was a month ago. Kizlargul says that Gulnas phoned her. She is doing okay but lost my phone number, has passed on her greeting to me.

July 29

Erkin, I love you. I am in Chimbay to see you. I go to see the others also—to give Sayura some food money, stop in to see her brother, and see some others to make laughter about sore asses from injections. But my heart looks for Erkin.

She is sad. She is ready to tell me about her mother's death. We sit on a bench under a tree in the back area of the main hospital. Me, Aynur, and Erkin. Far enough from eyes and ears to be together. Her mom had been sick in the hospital. They were told it was going badly. She was sent home to die. The prognosis was that she might have a month to live. Erkin was her main caregiver at home. She fed her, gave her a daily injection, massaged her. The hours were long and Erkin had hardly any sleep. One day before the end, Erkin had slept and refused to get up when her mother called for help. After regaining her strength she went back to care for her mom.

She apologized profusely, felt much guilt, but her mother said it was okay. Erkin crawled into bed with her. A few hours later her mother died. Erkin knew she had died but didn't call anyone. She just lay beside her for two hours and then arose to notify the rest of the family.

All the while she recounts this, Erkin cries. It is the first time she has told anyone of the events. Her smiling, assured 26-year-old face is not here today.

At the funeral gathering, Erkin was charged with doing all the preparations, calling the mullah, preparing the food, serving, cleaning, attending. She is angry that it was all put on her shoulders but feels guilty for being angry. She thinks she failed her mother right at the pinnacle of her need and that her anger is a failure of daughterhood.

I hold her, stroke her hair. Pretty odd. Old foreigner holding young Karakalpak on a bench outside an outback hospital. Aynur makes everything safe and legitimate. Her soft words give mine safe texture. I say that Erkin was blessed to be with her mother at the moment of death, how we are all human and how it is our moments of weakness that defines our humanness and gives it truth and value. An unflawed human who does not err has less valour, less offering than the flawed human who gives and loves despite the flaw. If there were those who had no flaws, it would be easy to behave accordingly.

☞ Achmed phones to say his daughter has been successfully admitted to the teacher's college. No bribe necessary.

☞

July 30

Late last night, I heard something fluttering its wings against the glass of my bedroom window For quite awhile I ignored the noise thinking it something out on the street or that it was someone else upstairs, but it persisted. Finally, I went over to see as I thought it might be a bird. It was a huge dragonfly. I tried to shoo it off but instead it flew inside against the window's large floor length curtain. I corralled it and it climbed on my finger and stayed there. After exchanging greetings and words I put him/her out the window. But he flew right back to perch on the metal lattice outside the window. So, I wondered if it was a beauty spirit visiting or a spirit of someone who died. It was abnormally large and really intent. Once it was dark, I guess he left. Or she left.

☞ Out at TB3, Islam mostly lies on his cot in that foetal type position with an oxygen mask on constantly in order to breathe. He is just bones. He pulls into a hunched position sitting on the bed in order to spit out the sputum that comes every so often up from his lungs. His 21-year-old female cousin spends each day in vigil and to help him eat the little he does, wash a bit, go to the toilet. I bring him melon, but now he eats very little. I give money so he can give it to his relatives. He talks still but spends almost all of his hours lying on the bed, breathing his short sometimes raspy breaths, and waiting. Waiting. I ask him what he thinks about. He says: "Nothing, I just wait."

The good thing is that he is weak and when you are weak you sleep more. The nurse is good, caring. She gives him injections of something which seems to help. He has black hair that is now almost half an inch out. When I come to be with him, I talk about dying, about filling his mind with love. That if he becomes afraid or thinks he is about to die, to just let himself fall inwards, fall, fall, fall. Let go. Let thoughts of love and joy fill his mind and let go. And if he becomes afraid I tell him he can ask the nurse or his cousin to call me any time of day or night. I sleep with my phone by my bed.

Of course, I don't know what I am talking about. And I don't know if it helps or is appreciated. No one has died and come back to tell us how it is best done. But since I sit with him and stroke his back and head when it doesn't irritate him, I just decide I should say something.

His cousin says that Islam would like to go home, to die in his own room. But the oxygen machine belongs to the hospital and he can't live without it. I talk to the nurse and say I will guarantee the machine, put up money to ensure its safe return. She is about to go to the chief doctor when I speak to Islam about it. He is hunched like a crow on a wire on the side of his bed, staring out and breathing the short breaths into the mask. He says that there are small children at home so he will stay in the hospital.

∽

July 31

Saturday, Islam's cousin has phoned me to see if I am coming out. The electricity has stopped hours before. When I arrive, Islam is crouched on his bed, eyes in half anguish, half panic. He keeps flicking at the on/off switch on the oxygen machine, keeps scanning out to the hall-way to see if the ultra-violet light for infection control has come on again. Then he utters a plaintive call: "Please ... please, get the power back on. I can't breathe!"

I sit beside him and put my hand on his back. He motions for all of us to get out of the room. "I can't breathe when you are in here." The others leave, but I won't go. I don't want to run with his anxiety. We wait together. I have Deelya come back in to speak a few senten-ces for me. I talk about letting himself relax. Let his lungs do the work they can. Let it be that the machine doesn't work. Between breaths just relax. Slow down the breaths. He tries. Easier said than done. It helps for five minutes and then he goes back to flicking at the on/off switch. Better idea.

An hour later the electricity comes back on. The city cuts electri-city for different areas every so often to conserve it or save money or just bother the population, show its power. Who knows?

Each day when I leave Islam, I take my mask off and kiss him on the head. Deelya sees this for the first time and chides me and asks why I take that risk. I don't answer.

August 2

Kurbangul is out of ICU and enjoying being on the first ward. She's in a room by herself and cannot walk yet, but she gets herself out into the foyer to recline on the padded bench and watch TV with the others or just be with them to talk. She feels okay but is still bored. The past weekend she was taken home to visit her daughter. I tell her I will bring her the small portable TETRIS game she asked me for when she was still in ICU. Deena, Slohan, and Gulsara, who has re-converted from negative culture to infectious and has been returned to TB2, are company for her.

I can't go to see patients as often now because I have to go to Takhtakupir once a week to help Kuanish up there until the new counsellors are finally all hired and then I'll have to train them for two weeks. Plus, now it's more incumbent on me to supervise and try to support the counsellors in Nukus and Chimbay with their patients. Then there are the MSF meetings. They get annoyed when I don't show up for a scheduled meeting. They surmise I am considering patients and counsellors more important than the communication structure for the team. They are right.

☞

August 4

Each day either I or Aziz goes out to TB3 to sit with Islam for a half hour. He talks a little with Aziz, not so much with me. We are worried about his cousin. She sleeps there, wears a mask usually but surely it won't protect her. She has weight which is good, I think. At least if she gets sick there will be some to lose. But she is very stressed. I will talk with her tomorrow.

☞

August 5

Marcell has arrived. He is an Austrian filmmaker sent here by MSF to create a motivational movie to be used with the patients. MSF has asked me to shepherd him around, link him with the right personalities to make a good film. I tell him about Daniyar and Gulishan our counsellor who is a cured meningitis patient and now has a son. I also mention Nadiya, an elegant woman in Chimbay who writes poems about her life and who is single parenting her three children after her husband committed suicide a year ago. He is excited to meet with them, but today I keep him with me on my visits to patients in the hospitals and polyclinics. If he's going to make a film, I want him to start from the inside.

At TB3, he comes with me as I take Islam's cousin out of his room and through the leafy sanatorium grounds to the banks of the canal. We sit there in the shade. Murat has told me last night that she confided in him that she took an overdose of pills two days back. Not that many, but she did it because of feeling overwhelmed with Islam's condition and being there all day every day.

I don't mention the suicide issue but ask about how she came to be Islam's caretaker now. She tells me how she has always been close to Islam since both were kids and how he requested that she be the one to attend to him in these last times. She was happy to be asked, wanted to be there for him. But it is proving too much. She needs a break. I ask if she has told their aunt about her struggle and she says yes. Her aunt simply says that someone has to do it and that she needs to tough it out.

This makes me angry. I phone Aziz and we agree he will go to the aunt's and demand that someone spell her off every couple of days. I tell her to go home after we finish talking. I say that if she doesn't that it won't be long before she falls apart and her mind breaks down.

She answers that she knows that because it already has. She tells me about the pills. I put my arm around her while she cries. After a few minutes, I point to the water flowing by in the canal. Far over to the other side are some kids swimming. They are too far away for us to tell how old they are but we can faintly hear their hollering. The light reflects quite beautifully off the flowing brown water. In the middle of the canal some kind of bird swoops down to dip its beak for a quick drink. We talk about beauty. About peace. I ask her to come out to sit by the canal every day when Islam is asleep. To come and sit and give away sadness, worry, the burden.

Back in Islam's room, Marcell talks about other dying people he has seen in MSF African projects. Their hands and feet always look alive. That's how he connects to the living person not the dying one … by looking at their hands, holding their hands.

We also visit Natasha and Massor. Both are feeling depressed at Islam's situation. They mention the sadness of someone so young now so helplessly on his way to the end of life.

But there is another boy here—Azimat. Previously, I have only been courteous and greeted him because I hold off from taking on any more relationships with patients. Today, that changes.

He has seen me coming here regularly—for Oleg and now for

Islam, me bringing them food. Today, he confronts me, calls me over as I am leaving with Marcell. He is 20 and big-eyed. I feel guilty for not knowing him, not giving him attention, how that must feel to him. He is partially deaf, a kid alone and no parents, I know that from the nurse. She also wonders why he gets no attention from me.

"Hey, Mister Calvin, I want to talk to you for a few minutes." He stands at the top of the steps that lead into the ward entrance. I go over to him and look upwards because the steps make him half a metre taller than me. He tells me in a loud, earnest voice about having no parents, being alone with this terrible disease and being hungry. "I have no money. I want you to give me some money so I can buy food to eat."

He was begging but not begging. Asserting actually. He wanted his share. He had seen what I can do to help when I want to. He wants me to want to now. Some kind of help. Come on. He knows I can give something.

I laugh and reply that I could give him 5000 sum but he must do something for me. "What?" he asks. I bend forward and point to my balding head. I say I will give him the money but he has to exert his spiritual powers to make some of my hair grow back.

Azimat bends down to look more closely at my head. I expect him to laugh but he is serious. He gets a perplexed look on his face, straightens back up and shakes his head: "I can't do that."

I insist he must try or I won't give him the 5000 sum.

He bends for another look, touches my scalp gently, the hair thin on the top. Then he smiles. "It is such a big job. If I do it, I will need 500 U.S. dollars not 5000 sum." Everyone laughs.

I give him the 5000.

☙

August 9

In Chimbay, Erkin is recovering from the flu. She came down with it soon after our last visit when she told me about her mother. Today, she wants to quit the drugs. She sees no future for herself. No college, no parents, too many others in the house, over a year left of treatment, no job, what's the point? I suggest that she has been sick and feels such despondency now because she opened up what she had kept hidden. That speaking of her mother's death had triggered all of these negative feelings, her body's downswing.

I ask her to write about her mother again like she did before, to let herself feel all the sadness directly, all the missing of her mother, the aloneness. I ask her not to avoid it but to invite it. That when she doesn't, it just finds other ways to come out and those ways weaken her. I ask if she has gone to visit her mother's grave? That if she goes there it will help her to cry.

"I have never gone to her grave. I didn't go even for the funeral ceremony." She looks away from me.

"Why is that?" I ask.

Silence. Then a whisper: "Because if I go to the cemetery and see her grave, then it will mean she is really dead."

☞

August 14

We are at Daniyar's cousin's house in Hodjeli. It is evening. Marcell and Deelya and I have come to interview Daniyar in this house which also doubles as a small recording studio. His cousin is a pop singer. Daniyar comes here several days a week to practise. He has been working on a song with a young woman he knows. She has financed the recording. Marcell is getting some footage, interviewing a bit. Pretty cool. Daniyar has MDR-TB. It wants to kill him. It's a terrible lung scourge. But he takes his drugs in the morning every day and then often comes here to sing. Lung disease? Daniyar begins singing into the microphone. His eyes into the lyrics. Marcell films.

Then just as we are finishing, I get a call from Islam's cousin out at TB3. Islam is suffering. He wants me to bring him an inhaler like the kind asthmatics use. I say I will bring it in the morning. She tells Islam. He answers that it will be too late in the morning. He needs it now. But I am out in Hodjeli. By the time I get back into town it will be too late to get an inhaler. If I do, it will be later still to get it to him out at TB3. We sent the MSF car back after we got here so it will take a while to get another. I am uneasy. This is the first time Islam has called at night. First time he has asked for help other than for me to bring him montey or melon. Now, I tell him no. What use am I?

Okay, I'll phone you back. I phone Murat at home, his work day long past. "Brother, I have a favour to ask."

Murat will take Islam the inhaler.

We end up waiting 40 minutes for the car to get to us. The story of the microphone and the inhaler.

☙

August 16

I am half way through training the Takhtakupir counsellors. Eight new ones. Eager to learn and delightfully open attitudes. I take two with me each day and rotate the others through a day with a different Nukus counsellor to shadow their work. I make a point of having everyone meet Islam if possible as he wastes toward death out in TB3. He is amazing. His body disappears but his spirit continues. I want them to see MDR-TB at its worst.

Today I have two with me in TB1. We are in the negative ward seeing Muktadas. She's 31 and thin. Not thin as in sick thin, but thin as naturally thin. She has come into the negative ward because she is in volatile emotional straits. She has had a couple of seizures, according to her brother, and she is also, apparently, suicidal. I knew her at TB2. On our first picnic out at TB2, her sister had been admitted a week prior. She was basically bed ridden, but I didn't want her to miss the picnic so I bundled her in a warm jacket, put her on a kitchen chair and carried her out to watch the fire and hear the singing. Muktadas stood beside her during the picnic. They drank juice and ate the wieners and baked potatoes. When it was all over, I was going to carry her back in the same way I brought her out. But Muktadas told me that she would walk her sister back in. As I attended to other clean-up chores, I watched the two of them slowly step their way along the trail and back across the pavement in front of the first ward. Mukta-das told me later that was the first time her sister had walked in months. She was very happy. A week later she awoke in the morning to find that her sister had died in the night. She had been in the same room that wheelchair-bound Venyera had died in a month before.

Muktadas is wild-eyed as I enter. There is only one other woman in this room for eight. She is diagonally across from her. Muktadas' speech is frantic, as she laments that she is not sleeping. I hug her and try to calm her, reach into the part that has made it this far into treat-ment and out of the infectious stage. I joke. She doesn't laugh. She is not fully here. I rub her shoulder. Her mouth moves with repeated lip-licking motions. I wonder if the psychotropic drug she has been put on is the correct one. She says that she has felt odd since they started her on them. She says: "Why do I feel like crying all the time?"

I answer that it's just stress. I say: "It's okay to cry. You can cry now if you want." She begins bawling.

Immediately, the other woman says: "I want to cry also." And she starts wailing. Good thing I have the two learning counsellors. We split up. I put them with this new woman and I take Muktadas to another room, an empty one.

We get there and Muktadas asks the next question: "Why do I want to kill myself?" I talk her through that one, and then go to switch places with the two Takhta counsellors.

The new woman is calmer now. She tells me that her husband killed himself 15 days ago while she was in the negative ward. She has been distraught since. There was no warning. He hung himself, but left a note, saying he was sorry. She has a 13-year-old daughter and three-year-old son. I talk with her about how difficult it is to process and heal from a loved one's suicide and give her two exercises to do. I ask if she feels like giving up also, if Muktadas' suicidal thinking influences her at all. She says no, that she could never leave her chil-dren parentless no matter how desperate she felt, but that the pain is so hard to take.

I ask how things are with her in-laws. She says they are good, that there is support and acceptance for her. It is better than in her parents' home because in that home her sister-in-law is hateful towards her. She will continue to live in her husband's parents' home when she leaves the negative ward. They live in Karauziak, 30 minutes this side of Takhtakupir. I mention that maybe one of the two new counsellors that she just met will be assigned to the clinic where she will be taking her drugs.

I leave the two patients more settled down, and go to find Zakir. I want him to get a hold of Dr. Sveta the psychiatrist in order to sort out Muktadas' medication and the supposed seizures. Zakir says he doesn't think Muktadas is suicidal.

☙

August 17

Marcell from Austria is a kindred spirit. He understands what is real here. Not an outside guy, he wanted the inside from the start. He especially connected with Deena, came back with tears after meeting her out at TB2. He was taken by her eyes, how they look into you with such innocence, vulnerability.

He wanted to capture the heart of what happens here. It was really going well and he had lots of footage, close to finishing. I use past tense because today he got arrested. National Security. To do any filming or tech production in Uzbekistan, one needs copious applications and official sanction. They are very suspicious. Well, we got it all done properly, but Marcell did not stay at the hotel he was registered at. Instead he stayed at an MSF guest house as is our practise. National Security arrested him after 12 days here, took his cameras, and film and he is being sent to Tashkent and then deportation. No amount of explaining deters them.

Counsellor Gulishan has been summoned in for questioning by National Security. Same with Daniyar. The agents saw them both on the film footage, and now they want explanations.

☙

August 18

The questioning yesterday did not add up to anything and now Daniyar is doing a one-hour seminar with the eight new Takhtakupir counsellors. Imagine that, a patient teaching counsellors what is needed from a counsellor. Revolutionary.

He begins by apologizing for being, perhaps, younger than some of their children. He means no disrespect. His dark hair, dark shining eyes catch their attention. This is the first time they have met him. We are outside in the patio area of the psychosocial building, in the shade, chairs in a circle waiting to discover what this 20-year-old can give. He says he will ask some hard questions and he hopes they won't take offense. He is holding a small cue card discreetly in his hand, glances at it. I wonder where he has learned this.

"I want to start by asking you what you think counselling is? Because, you know, we don't need information about the disease. We all have it. We are living experts on the disease. So, what do you think counselling is?" One by one, he asks them to speak. And they do. Immediately, Daniyar is taken seriously.

He goes on to ask why they want this job? He wonders if it is mainly for the money.

Then, what can they bring to the job?

He then tells a bit of his own story. And finally he finishes with them in pairs plotting out the steps they will take to build relationships with their patients. At the end, they ask him if he will sing a song.

And with no accompanying music, the boy tilts his head and croons an enchanting lullaby that needs no translation to touch the heart.

☙

August 19

Phone call from Marcell in Tashkent. After Stefan and he met with National Security headquarters there, they gave him everything back and said he wouldn't be deported after all. They apologized and declared that the Nukus police had made an error. His plane is scheduled to leave tomorrow, but he is free to come back whenever he wants. No problem. Sorry for the mix-up. He can go home with his film and cameras intact, though they will provide a police escort to the airport.

I am especially glad now. One, the film will happen. And two, Marcell will come back again in six weeks or so to finish the film properly. Marcell is the right guy for this film. But we shall see if they let him back in or it was all a calculated ruse to get rid of him. The film should be really good and will help patients. We hope that we can get some footage of Daniyar in concert when Marcell comes back.

☙

August 20

I am in trouble. Today was the last day of the training for the Takhtakupir counsellors. I scheduled the afternoon for all of us, Nukus counsellors included, to go to the canal for a swim. Twenty-eight of us so we needed two Landcruisers, but after they got here the Landcruisers went back to the office. I wanted the week to end this way for several reasons. Fun, of course, but more importantly I want this final training activity to be a statement about gender equality, an experience of both genders behaving naturally equal. At least in this one small way today. That is, I want both genders swimming in this August heat.

When I arrive a bit later in a car, everyone is already there. All the women are standing in their clothes on the shore. All but two of the men are in swim shorts having fun in the water. I yell that the requirement was that everyone had to swim. Some of the women start to make excuses. I take off my shoes and run as fast as I can into the canal, fully clothed. I swim far out and yell back that if they are afraid to be equal in water when it is hot and secluded, then they will always be afraid of bigger things. The water feels lovely.

The two men take off their pants and go into the canal in their underwear. All but three of the women leave to put on their swim gear. And, thus we are all together. Later we eat watermelon. Then I get in trouble.

It is time for the Takhta counsellors to go home. If they don't leave now, when they reach Takhtakupir, there won't be local marshrutkas running to get them out to their homes. I had told logistics that we needed the Landcruisers. I phone Ajinias. He is the Karakalpak in charge of the vehicles. He tells me that the Landcruiser is being washed. I get angry and start to yell on the phone. "I'm not very fucking happy about this, Ajinias!!!" Then I abruptly hang up on him. There have been other times when I was angry at Ajinias for his arrogance and lack of cooperation but I never said anything. This time maybe I have over-reacted, but I am embarrassed that there is no vehicle, and I really am angry.

I get a phone call. It is Yuri phoning from Tashkent. He's the MSF head of logistics there—Ajinias' boss. "Ahhh, Calvin, tell me did you yell at Ajinias and swear?"

I tell Yuri what I think of Ajinias. I refuse to apologize. I say I'll go back to Canada before I apologize. I hang up.

I get another phone call. It's from the Project Coordinator, my boss Sonya. "Calvin, is it true that you yelled at Ajinias? That you swore?"

I tell Sonya why I am angry. She says I have to apologize, that I don't have the right to yell at National Staff. I say I won't, that I'll go back to Canada first. I hang up.

I get another phone call. It's from Yuri again. I tell him I will apologize. But I say I will also tell Ajinias about all the other incidents where I should have told him the truth.

All the counsellors have heard my animated phone calls. Some are glad to see me pissed off, but all are a bit nervous. Here it is best not to show these kind of feelings.

✑

August 21

Daniyar has phoned. He is in dire straits and needs my help with a problem. It's about the girl he has been recording with. She's in love with him and wants to have a relationship. He has talked to me about this earlier. He loves another girl, one who was supportive of him when he was first in hospital and whom he credits for pulling him through the first months of wanting to quit. But this girl has financed the DVD disc they are recording. She has become increasingly insistent. Before, she spoke about marriage and Daniyar gently said no. Then she upped the ante and began talking of suicide if he would not reciprocate. That was when he first called me: "What do I do? What do I do?"

We got through that okay I thought, but now there is a new snag. He is really stressed. She has paid about 200,000 sum for the recording. Now she wants money from him to cover that. He is frantic and wants to know if I can lend him the money. He just wants to excise this predicament. That's too much for me, but I tell him I will get him 100,000. He is profusely grateful. I say I will meet him in an hour. It is 8 o'clock at night. He tells me we can meet outside the Hodjeli train station.

I arrive in the dark. There is a slight drizzle. I get out of the MSF car. A slender man in a black pea coat approaches. We hug. I discreetly place the thick wad of 100 thousand sum notes in his hand. It is like we are in a movie. He says thanks and returns to the shadows. I get into the car and drive back to Vostachnaya. MSF in all its emergency faces? But, after all, he is Daniyar.

August 23

Finally I managed to bring a psychiatrist to meet Sayura's brother. I want her to prescribe a psychotropic medication for him that will stop him from beating up his sister. There are only three alternatives. Let him stay as he is. Have him taken to the psychiatric hospital for treatment which will just see him run away again. Or get the shrink to do something. I don't know if any medication can solve the problem, but I know it is what I can hope for.

He is here in an empty lot with some others selling bundles of long grass feed they have tied up into sheaves. Like the others, he has brought his load on a cart pulled by a donkey. I get out of the car and jump the ditch to get to where he is standing. Other sellers stare. I shake his hand and we touch our heads together. He smiles. On the one hand he is getting puzzled attention and possible gossip judgement from those watching. On the other, he is singled out as having a close connection to a foreigner. Not many foreigners here in Chimbay. The psychiatrist takes the long way around and also shakes his hand. She says she knows him, that the medication will be easy to provide. She says she will bring it to his house.

I decide I need some grass feed. How much is a bundle? 200 sum. Hmmm? 10 cents. Okay, I'll take five. Most of what he has left. He is happy. We carry it over to Jenya's car. It gets squished into the trunk. The trunk yells at Jenya: "Hey, what the hell is this? I've never had this kind of stuff before?" Jenya pretends he doesn't hear the trunk complaining but I think he does. He's always in touch with his car.

☞

August 24

Islam's truth.

Not the religion but the person. The human being named Islam. Though the actual word in Arabic means submission and, right now at least, that applies to him. He is lying flat, stretched out on his cot in TB3. He is literally a skeleton with skin stretched over it. His legs, showing the indentations where his patella moves from femur to tibia and fibula. His tendons pushing outward to declare that they exist. Islam's skin is so smooth, a light brownish, the kind of beautiful texture and colour that the dreaming girls of America yearn for.

He bends forward to grab for the empty clear, plastic bottle at his bedside. Lifting his oxygen mask he spits into the narrow neck of the bottle. Sputum. A term unknown to most of the world. Sputum ... as common as helplessness for every TB patient, it comes from the ravaged hollows in the lungs. These movements over and over again every day for the past year have become automatic. He is on automatic now.

Islam is dying. Obviously. We all know it. His eyes are still bright, but despairingly bright. Only the number of days left is unknown. What is it like to wait for the end like this? A beautiful boy, waiting to end. Like waiting for the train to arrive so you can board. Not one iota of Islam's mind has slipped. He has been wasting and waiting like this for a month.

Is this any different than any other terminal disease? I don't know every other disease but I know this one. Blood coughing, retching, gasping can take you any time. Islam is on the long, slow, starvation slide. His metronome heart, metronome lungs still pumping still bringing in oxygen. Refusing to say I'm dead, it's over. It is not his conscious will. He is a spectator at his own farewell. He speaks little other than to ask for help when he needs it. His skimpy underwear around his genitals the only attire for a month in this hot Karakalpak August.

Now he is making it through these moments before death. Moments because it is only a day or two or several more. If we could know for sure all the mystery would go. We'd be able to grasp for control, say our good-byes, dream the dreams we'd planned before. This Islam also means submission. Submit to not knowing, submit to waiting, submit to the guarantee that there are but moments left. Let go and accept. Islam, the boy, has done that.

He wants to go home to die. He wants to be in his own room again. The room with only the single cot and the guitar propped against the wall. The guitar that knew his long, dexterous fingers. The home where his mother died of MDR-TB, the same disease that's taking him. Only three years before she left him, the eldest son of three, to be the head of the home.

He wants to go home where his relatives can come and be with him. Where he can smell the life he has known, hear the sounds he has memorized since he was born. And his family want him home so they can minister to him while he dies. But Islam chooses not to go home. He chooses to stay in the hospital. This hospital where he hears the commotion of others, their petty arguments, their chuckles, their coughing or farting, their footsteps in the hallway, their snoring at night. They who have flesh still, can walk out into the treed lanes of this former Soviet sanatorium, can sit and visit with friends or strangers, can collect pensions or look out their windows at tomorrow. He chooses to stay and submit.

He chooses because at home there are small children and, if he returns even for the few hours or days he has left, he knows the air will become infected and that those children will become infected. He knows that his family is poor, that there are no bread winners, that the nutrition and living conditions are the swamp for MDR-TB to flourish in. He does not want those children infected nor anyone else who comes to visit. Islam chooses this even though he will never know, will never face any recriminations should others fall victim.

Every so often his breathing takes on more urgency, a rasping, a hesitation. It's easy to look at him with sorrow. With head shaking. With fear. It's easy to want to leave the scene, his sputum bottle, the larger sputum vessel open on the floor, the sharpness of his bones. His pelvis, especially, curves exactly how the anatomy books show it, exactly how the lab skeletons reveal. The skin follows obediently right to the smoothness of the bone. It's easy to want to run away. The room smells. There are marks on Islam's body where he hasn't been washed. His short black hair no longer shines. Rough on his head, it too awaits death. He lies with eyes closed almost all the time. These are the most beautiful eyes in the world. I say the most beautiful because, when he was less sick, it was as easy to see his soul, as easy to see into his heart, as it is to look up at the moon on a clear night. The most beautiful eyes in the world in that none are more beautiful. A mix of greenish blue and brown but mostly deep and bright. No culture in those eyes. No age, no past or future just all now. They are him but more than him. They are neither constrained nor defined by personality or time or situation. They are Islam forever.

It is common to overstate or sentimentalize the dead and dying. MDR-TB sucks all that away. MDR-TB holds our faces to the certainty of our limitation, of our temporariness, of our need to submit. Islam's eyes need no exaggeration. And now as they are hidden in waiting, it is not being able to see them ever again that is the sadness. But more so, those eyes are precisely why it is also easy to be with him every day and to wait with him for his death. They give the choice of seeing truth. The truth that, while his body still breathes, he is still alive. His life still has purpose just as all lives must have purpose. To be born is to have purpose. And as he breathes again and again and again on his bed, each breath is purpose. So he lives. So he is alive. And being with him during this time is being with someone alive. And touching his hair, placing a hand on his head, stroking his face or feet or long fingers is touching Islam and it is easy.

☙

August 26

I am in Bukhara, one of the big stops on the ancient Silk Road, 12 hours from Nukus. We have come on a bus to meet with the MSF team from Tashkent to debate the current state of MSF in Uzbekistan and make plans for the coming year. Bukhara is an easy town. Much more to it than Nukus. There is a big fort, there are big mosques and there are fancy hotels with flags of other countries waving in the wind to attract tour groups. There is a narrow canal flowing through the centre of town and connecting a large square pond within the city's main square. All around the pond are restaurants and tapshens, the raised seating/lounging platforms on which people can drink or take meals. Music blares from the other side of the pond, a kind of Karaoke performance. Everyone everywhere is happy. Some MSF people are drinking beer and eating shaslik on one tapshen. They ask if I'd like to join then. I nod no thanks. Aziz and Kairat have come with me for these two days of meetings and they are sitting at another table with other Karakalpak staff. I sit with them a while but soon move on. This is a night to wander freely.

☙

August 27

Stefan, the Head of Mission, takes me aside at lunch time. He wants to talk about my outburst at Ajinias. We sit together and he says: "So, what happened?" I tell him my exact words. It's the first time someone has actually asked what I said. Then, I say: "Is that really so terrible?" He shakes his head dismissively and says it isn't. He assumed it was more than that. But he says that I need to take a week holiday when I return from Bukhara.

At three o'clock, I get a text message from Murat. Islam died a couple of hours earlier. "Sorry, man," he texts. I return to the meeting. Aziz goes to his room to cry.

I text Aynur and Deelya, ask them to go to Islam's home and talk to his cousin, see how she is doing. Her family never did spell her off to give her some respite. She was there every day until today. I am glad for her that Islam died. I cannot cry. I would like to.

The Sand We Hold

September 6

I had my holiday, just as my MSF superiors insisted. They thought I would go somewhere. I told them I'd stay right at Vostachnaya, just relax and veg out, read, do nothing. They were surprised. I outsmarted them. I could still sneak about a little and see patients on the sly after work hours. I didn't need a holiday. They cannot understand that, while it is true that I give a lot each day to patients, I get back more than I give. Each time I hold a patient I get easily as much as the patient does. A cycling of energy. MSF comes from a medical perspective or an administrative perspective, cut off by that distance. I am older than them. I come from the inside. But on my holiday, I did relax and read a thick book about Post War Europe.

 Gulsara has been sent home. Sort of. The TB2 doctor has talked to her about stopping the drugs. One of my Room 10 friends, I have stayed connected to her and now I am at her house and I say that they do not know. I say that she can choose what she wants. This is her life and it is she who can decide which direction she wants. The side effects will stop if she quits the drugs, but her chances to survive then become small. I say that I will support her either way, but that it must be her decision, not the doctors. She is happy to be home for now, but she says she will return to hospital.

I phone Aziz, ask him to contact Dr. Arzigul at TB2 to make sure they take her back. Arzigul is okay.

⌁ At TB3 in palliative, Azimat, the almost deaf boy, is happy to see me. Islam's death is already in the past. With MDR-TB, deaths become the past very quickly. Like being swept along in a raging river, your compatriot succumbs, you scream or wince with the shock and loss, and then the current takes back your attention. Azimat is sad. Sadder than I've seen him. He speaks of how desperate he is for something to do. The boredom has compounded the aloneness, the pressure on his lungs, the prognosis winked at him by Islam's death. He wishes for a job. An activity of some kind. He says there used to be a stationary bicycle out at TB2. If it's still there, can I bring it for him? I suggest getting him a real one. He shakes his head no, that he might fall off and get hurt, that he has become too weak. A stationary one would be safe and bring back some of his strength maybe.

I don't think I can get him one. What else would be a help? What would be the best thing you could have here? Azimat laughs and says: "A computer. I would really like to learn how to use a computer."

A boy wanting a future.

A boy seeing what other boys in other lands see.

⌁ Grapes are everywhere now. Purple, green, full globes of sweetness. They drop like creations of succulence, an absolute anomaly in this desert. Amu Darya gives the grapes. The yards, the gardens are flooded. The vines, the size of my thigh sometimes, are unwound from the winter protection of soil mounding and strung back up trellises or to overhangs. We have a wall of grapes in the back of Vostachnaya, in the back of the main MSF office, in the Takhtakupir office. They blaze richness at us every day for a month. I've learned to eat the seeds. At home I'd spend the energy on each grape to spit out the tiny seeds, ensuring I'd only swallow the flesh. I started that way here in Nukus, but now I've given up. I eat the whole grape. I chew the seeds. I take what is. I'm sure the chewed seeds provide good fibre for the bowels.

Melons are ripe also. Huge piles of them alongside the road. Various sweet ones and watermelons. Outside an apartment block there were two large heaps of big watermelons. One heap had a sign saying 200 sum, the other a sign saying 300 sum. Hmmm, 10 cents a kilo or

15 cents a kilo. What's the difference, I said to the young boys attending the piles. "These ones," the 10-year-old replied, pointing to the cheaper ones, "I can't guarantee. The other ones I can."

I decided to splurge.

Outside Vostachnaya in the morning, I will hear a melon seller approaching with his push-cart. "Watermelon! Watermelon!" A load of 30 large watermelons on a wooden cart. This scene probably hasn't changed in 100 years. Same tone and volume, time of day. Same handling and tapping to determine ripeness. Same rusty scale to weigh the fruit. Same interaction of money and change. Pushing the cart along the bumpy road.

Only now, the new wonder about what the Aral's breath has blown into these juicy gifts.

☙

September 8

Erkin has gone to her mother's grave for the first time. She knows she is alone now. I think I see peace in her. She asks if I can bring her books to read. We focus always on keeping our patients adherent. But what does that mean? Erkin will be cured. Then what? She was not able to go to college when she was ready because there was no father to provide. Then the other illnesses came. Now she's 26 and a woman in Karakalpakstan. What is her future? At best a menial job that will pay a pittance. No, at best a good husband who can earn a living. A family of her own that she will raise with dignity and depth like her. But all a crapshoot. How to find a good husband? A husband who will see her for who she is and not as his servant.

☙ This afternoon I do a training with the Nukus counsellors. At one point, I hold up a handful of fine sand. I pass it to the counsellor next to me and ask her to hold it for about 30 seconds, look at it, study it and then pass it on. As the sand moves from counsellor to counsellor, some of the grains slip through their fingers to the ground. When it has gone through all 16 of us, the handful is very small. I say this is the way it is with our patients. We hold them, give them our energy and attention. Give them what we have and then let them go. We have no control but what we do. No control but what we give. Their lives are like the sand. Nothing can hold them intact. The sand falls, moves with the breeze. Life dissipates at its own rate. But while we hold that sand, we indeed do hold it.

And we too are simply sand. I tell myself this every day.

September 10

Azimat is sadder. He asks again for some kind of respite. Anything. I lie and say I bought him a soccer ball but forgot to bring it. He says that he doesn't want one. I insist he can kick it against the wall of TB3. All kids like soccer, don't they? Azimat says he doesn't want a soccer ball. He'd rather have a radio. I assent and say I will bring one out on Saturday. He smiles and thanks me. Finally, he has gotten through to me.

I get a phone call from Kizlargul. She will be discharged soon from TB2 and will go to Polyclinic 5 to take her drugs rather than OPD. This is better for her, less of a journey each day. She says she will take her kids to school first and then come for drugs. She will wait at her other sister's and pick the kids up in the afternoon and then go home. She says she is ready now to make it. She will live for her kids' sake.

At TB2, Slohan is still happily volunteering with the nurses to help give out pills and get patients to their drugs. She has had a visit from the fellow who has an interest in her.

Deena is a bit down. She has had a cold, and she is discouraged because she has been here for over four months and her condition has not improved much. The first time she was on treatment she was much improved and out of the hospital before three months had passed. She worries that the drugs aren't working. I smile and remind her how sick and fevered she was when I first met her. Now for months she has been stable. I say: "Look at you. You don't accurately see yourself. You look beautiful in that red bandana. You are doing just fine. Don't let the cold get you down. We all get colds. You are just on a slower, more gradual rate of recovery."

I give her an inflight magazine that I have kept from my Kyrgyzstan flight. I ask her if she has ever flown in a plane. "I have never been out of Nukus."

"Well, in that case you will have to fly to Tashkent when you are cured. Marcell and I will buy you a return ticket. You know how much Marcell likes you. That is a promise."

Deena smiles the shy/sly smile that she has. She looks down and says: "But, I don't know anybody in Tashkent."

"Okay, we'll buy you a hotel room for three days also. Tashkent is a nice city. You might work there one day."

"I do have family in Kazakhstan. In Al-Maty."

"Okay then. It's a deal. We will buy you a ticket to Al-Maty. I'm serious. We will arrange for the money to get here for when you are ready to go." Deena smiles broadly. I can see she is thinking that it's a nice dream but the proof will be in the money appearing. Then she shows me one of her poems.

⟋ Gulsara is back at hospital and is also feeling down. Her mother has gone on cotton campaign and so there is no one at home to bring her food. I assure her that I can get food to her. She speaks of how her husband divorced her when she got sick and how she was pushed/convinced to have an abortion once she was diagnosed. She looks miserable.

I take a hard line and tell her to stop feeling sorry for herself. I say: "Yes right now you are alone. Your mom is away and your sister-in-law and brother are not helping. Slohan has the same problem though she doesn't even have a mother anymore. Stop feeling sorry for yourself. Yes, everything you feel sad about is true, it all happened. So cry, but cry because you are sad and scared. Cry fully. Let it really flow not stay with depression or downness. Get it out of your system and then get on with being cured. Get outside and walk. Go look at the beauty there. You see Kurbangul lying on the bench in the foyer.

She would love to be going outside just to watch life flowing by. So, get out there. If you don't look for beauty you won't see it. If you don't look at what you want for yourself, your body won't go in that direction. Tell your lungs to start working. Tell your body to accept the drugs every day and to use them to get rid of the bacilli."

She laughs at me. A good laugh.

September 11

I give Azimat the radio. He is very happy. He puts in the earphone and cranks up the volume. He is no longer alone. I kiss him on the head.

September 13

Out in Takhtakupir, big Kuanish has received a phone call from a 21-year-old patient. He had been struggling to take his daily regimen of the toxic drugs. He was thinking of dying, wondering if he should just speed up the disease.

So, we pay him a visit. After bumping along roads in the middle of nowhere, we come to a large green area of splendid corn. Our vehicle parked, we open the rough wooden pole gate and walk through a small potato field and some corn to get to the patient's mud house. He is happy to see us. All around the house are small plots of either vegetables or corn. Above, the sky is bright blue. Three shining black turkeys strut across the yard and into the corn. Silence. Idyllic and still. The boy grins at us, and we sit to talk.

This boy has dimples when he smiles. His eyes squeeze to a squint. His round face and close cropped curly hair, a smooth brown, are the epitome of universal youth. Of course, he doesn't want to die. Right now he is strong, muscular. But in just three weeks if the disease awakens, he can begin the decimation that will not stop. He knows that. But what to do?

We try to reach into him, to grab a hold of his young spirit and breathe our own life into it, make the coals glow and flicker into flame again. He opens up and agrees to keep going. At least for a while longer. He promises to call out for help if he needs it. Before we leave, he and I walk together into the high green of the corn field, away from the yard. We stand there in silence just looking into each other's eyes. Being part of the vibrant corn. Part of the green. Breathing. Smiling. Being alive. The message without words is to indeed, keep living.

He goes with us back to our vehicle. I mention how beautiful it is here, how I would like to live where he does, the good energy I can feel. He laughs and says why? He points to the ground where we stand and all around the green plots of his home. "Look at the soil here. It's all contaminated with salt." I can see the faint white caking now that he has drawn my attention to it. "And there are wolves out here. They come to our place and kill the cows sometimes. Desert wolves. They kill the cow and only eat its liver. Sometimes the lungs too. The wolf leaves all the rest."

As we drive away I look back to see the young fellow waving until we are out of sight.

☞

September 17

Azimat has died.

This afternoon, we went out to TB3 and they told us he died yesterday morning. Three days ago, his loneliness had persisted and his aunt came to get him, taking him to her home. There he died. Twenty years old. Big eyes. Open face. Staring out at a life that didn't seem to want him.

I'm glad that I didn't know him better than I did, glad I didn't spend more time with him. I obviously feel guilty for thinking this. But it's easier for me this way. Instead of a stake in the heart, it's a space that I should have, could have, filled better but didn't. Hurts less. But it hurts. Such a sweet boy. Such a sweet boy.

༄ Curmudgeon Natasha is not dying. Though her two daughters don't want her and her bluntness, her demands to be accepted the way she is. When we meet, I always hug her. The second time I did this way back, I asked if she was okay with me doing it. It was easy to recognize that most stayed back from her. She laughed and said: "Don't worry, you'd know if I wasn't."

I took photos of her in the spring while she stood wrapped in a warm jacket under the new, white blossoms of an apple tree. More photos later in the summer sitting cross-legged on the tapshen right outside the entrance door to her ward. She was relaxed in the shade and fanning herself like an aristocratic Korean from another time. Natasha has a hundred proverbs tucked away inside her memory pockets always on the ready to cast away someone's ignorance. She could as easily tell you to fuck off or ask you to pass a cookie.

Today though, she is suffering. Her face is drawn. This is the death ward. Those who come here, come to die. Oleg. Islam. Azimat. Others I didn't meet. Soon, she says, Assan, the one they call Mike Tyson because of his chiselled, dark face will go too. They fade to non-existence while she and Massor try to believe they are living for their own futures. Natasha always speaks encouragment to a patient when they first arrive. She tells them they don't have to die, that she too was sent here to die, but if they react with negativity or resistance she stays away from them. "Fuck them, if they want to die," she retorts. But I know that she speaks so harshly only in order to create a barrier. Today she is hurting. Islam and Azimat were young, their innocence and beauty too easy to notice.

Massor too was hurting. My sad Leonard Cohen. After he found out Azimat had died, he went to the bazaar and came back drunk. He got to the ward after dark and was noisy. The nurses were upset because he was laughing and carousing a bit. Natasha has always had a bittersweet relationship with Massor. On the one hand, he is like her, a survivor. But he has his own ways and is hard of hearing. His independence and self-assuredness bug her. She needs something to bug her. She too has talked of how boring it is to be out in TB3 with nothing but a television. So, when Massor came home drunk once again, it was the last straw for Natasha. Last night she went after him with a knife. Luckily the nurses intervened. This morning, they suggested that Massor leave TB3 for a few days to let everything cool down.

Natasha tells us how angry she was. "If he bothers me like that again, comes home and makes all that racket, the drunken idiot, it will be the last of him. I don't care." And she makes a cutting motion across her throat with the side of her hand.

⁊ We think of babies as human, of course, but not like the rest of us. We think that what happens to them or what they are surrounded with, if it doesn't kill or physically injure them, will be forgotten, magically absorbed into the ether of our wishful thinking. Thus, babies endure all sorts of terrible experiences but we adults behave as though there are no consequences. We do that because we can. And we do it because we know that, if it is never mentioned, the grown baby will never mention it.

All cultures think of babies more or less in this same way. Parents and adults tend to be universal in their parentness/adultness. And cultures tend to consider their cultureness as somehow not to be questioned or reflected on. I've talked to my counsellors and patients about the difference between culture that exists to support and re-inforce the well-being of the community and habits or practises stemming from the power and control needs of those in charge. Such is the plight of wives in Karakalpakstan.

But there is another practise here that I'm not so sure about. If I could, I'd do a survey of some babies, tabulate their views. In my first visits to the bazaar, I noticed stacks of cradles for sale. They looked similar, some more ornate than others, all about the same size. Nicely worked wooden rockers. They all had a round hole cut in the bottom and beside the cradles there was always a container of wooden spigot-type things. I asked Aziz what those were for. And he pointed to one kind and said that it was to put on the baby boy's penis for him to urinate. The other was to fit into the baby girl's vagina so she could urinate. I was quite flabbergasted and couldn't figure out how on earth they could work. But I forgot about it.

It wasn't until months later when I was walking with Juma, our MSF Tajik doctor who lives in the UK, that I learned the whole story.

Soon after they are born, babies are tied tightly into their cradles and have the appropriate devices strapped to their genitals. Thus, snugly strapped in and with the correct wrappings, they defecate through the hole and urinate through the wooden spigots. Moms don't have to bother. Juma said that they are kept in the cradle that way for basically 24 hours of the day, emerging only for feedings. Even when ready to take a bottle, they perhaps need not be released. The babies will live that way for a year. When they cry, the cradle is rocked until they stop.

In Juma's animated and enthusiastic words: "Yes, it's great. They're no work that way, no bother. And it does no harm. That's how it was for me when I was a baby, and it didn't cause any problems."

I have no idea whether or not Juma's depiction is fully accurate, how long each day a baby spends in the cradle, or for how many months. I do know that there are lots and lots of the same cradles for sale in every town's bazaar, and with each comes the gender-based spigot.

I also know that among adults, in Karakalpak and Uzbek society, there is very cursory touching and hugs are almost non-existent. I was told that even the familiar handshake with heads touching each other side to side is a recent import from Kazakhstan. According to Aynur: "The young men started doing that here, only a few years ago. Before that no one did it."

And I know that every time I hold someone, let our bodies breathe together for an extended time, the reaction is one of great satisfaction. One could conclude that they are starved for some kind of physical contact. But until we discover how to poll the babies, it only remains a possible theory.

☙

September 26

Sevinch: Love in the Uzbek language. *Kurbangul:* The flower offering that is a sacrifice to God. When someone takes the long journey of moments to the end of TB, it must be an offering. The long moments of several months or years. The lungs go at their own rate. God's rate.

I am not speaking of any religion's God. But the real God. The one we speak of, the one who must exist because we give it a name. I say "it" because the idea of a being is not compulsory in order to speak of God. God is the short utterance, the sound, the "something" we have no choice but uttering in order to accurately voice what we know. God is the sound for the way it is, the way life unfolds, for what happens—all in the realm of what we cannot explain or understand with any human thought or idea. For what we can recognize. When Kurbangul was dying I was watching God's rate transpire.

She was dying long before I met her, of course, just as we all are dying long before we know it, at least on a conscious level. Humans fixate on controlling and framing everything in such a way as to declare: "I have the answer." We have such a need to believe that everything is about us and that if we can't have it, own it, explain it, test it, then it is somehow non-existent and dismissible. So, we create religious fantasies or marriages to science and the scientific method. It always has to be about us.

We see death, we watch it happen, we bury the body, but what really occurs is beyond us, try as we do to reduce it to biology and medicine. The idea of someone disappearing is incomprehensible. Just as the idea of someone appearing is incomprehensible. Can be witnessed, of course. But beyond reason. The words, the cell division, the stopping of the heart and cessation of bodily functions just don't do it to tell it as it really is. To me, birth and death are not so clear. The "not so clear" is God. And it will always be beyond us.

When I first saw Kurbangul, she was being helped down the hallway of TB1's regular TB ward to meet me in a small appointment room. I was to tell her that she had MDR-TB. Kurbangul does not hear easily, so my translator had to raise her voice to be heard. Thus went our interview in which we had to yell in order to tell her that her frail life had just changed for the worse.

At that time she was already very thin. One made the quick assumption that she wouldn't live long. When she arrived in TB2, the main MDR-TB hospital, I was there to meet her. I had to tell the doctors that the new arrival, whom they had not been notified about, would need a wheelchair. She was immediately relegated to the three-room

ICU ward. There, Kurbangul was to spend most of the next five months. Stuck in a narrow cot. Staring at walls or out the one window that faced an outside wall. In this hospital, you are on your own with whatever your assets or deficits are. No one to bring good food in for you? Too Bad. No one to visit you? Too bad. No one to take you to the shower? Too bad. And no one takes the patients out in wheelchairs.

I liked to race with her in the wheelchair. I wanted her to feel the air flowing against her face, feel some slight exhilaration. I felt small beside her, undeveloped, much more limited in my own capacity to be present and appreciate. She pointed at the tiny apricot blossoms just emerging, said she had never seen them starting before. I brought her one and she smelled it, cradled it in her fingers. After a while, we sat by the irrigation pipes which were spraying water out into the garden. Little rainbows gathered behind the spray. We watched together.

From that first day when Kurbangul entered TB2, as soon as I came into her room she would reach out her long, thin arms and pull me in to her. We would embrace for long moments. Face to face. Her arms wrapped around me and my chest against hers. This is death culture. This is human culture. No gender. No age. No language.

Before she got sick, she worked in a store that sold bridal dresses. One day she must have worn one of them herself, all satiny white and flowing as though the woman in it was the definition of specialness. Maybe she rode in a long, black stretch limousine that slowly made its way to the war memorial park so popular for wedding photos. Wound down the leafy boulevards of Nukus, water channelling alongside the road to soak into the roots of all those trees planted to deny the desert. And finally came to the large restaurant where all the wedding guests possible to invite had gathered at their tables to await the grand entry of the nuptial party. Kurbangul would have weathered her way through the formal rituals of that day and then the inevitable grand loss of her virginity in that night. She would have believed her day had come.

Then, when the TB got her and she was discarded by her husband, and again later after her TB became MDR, she might have known that another day was going to come. Was on the way. Just not sure when. I never spoke to her about any of this.

And after they sent her home from TB2 and I went to see her, I didn't ask about that or anything else in her life. For Kurbangul and me it was always about the embrace. The doctors at TB2 could see that by six months there she was not getting better, was growing thinner, still could not walk. Then she started balking at taking the drugs each day. The doctors decided it was time to lose the risk she posed to them. The doctors who assemble each week to discuss their numbers did not want a corpse in their hospital because corpses cause them problems. The bosses want to know why the corpse became a corpse and who was to blame. The doctors want to avoid blame at all costs. So they haggle with the family to take the soon-to-be corpses out of their hospital. Out and away from hope.

I went immediately to her parents' home when I was told by other patients that she had been sent from the hospital. When I got there, she was lying on a mat on the floor at the head of a large living room. She stretched out those long thin arms to pull me in. We hugged and I kissed her on the cheek through my mask as I usually do. Then I sat and we looked at each other and smiled.

As soon as there was a stillness I asked if she knew why the doctors had sent her home. She nodded, said: "Ahwah." The one word I know best in Karakalpak after "thank you" is "yes". I waited and asked what she understood that decision to mean. Her words came first and in the nanosecond following their utterance came the wail of horror. "They think I'm finished." I bent to her and held her as she cried: "I don't want to die." Pleading, begging without words, but just as surely stating that the life in her was still full. Not me. Not now. No. No. No. Then her audible words: "I don't want my daughter to have no mother." And long hard sobs in my arms. And I'm holding tight. Tight.

She breathed, relaxed and slumped back to her bedding. She looked at me. I looked back and said: "I don't want you to die either." I could have broken down as well, but I wouldn't let it happen. This was not my death. I had no right to add death to her own. So, we talked.

I talked about dying. About taking the drugs, about eating more, about being alive until the moment we do finish. About how her eyes saw so fully.

Then the next day and the next and for three more days I came to sit with her the 30 to 40 minutes of our communion. Sometimes with no translator, sometimes with. Each day she got weaker but never stopped being Kurbangul. Most days her daughter was there in the room, sometimes with another child of similar age. She would watch us. Close cropped black hair, big eyes, not knowing what to think of these visitors in the strange masks. This man who looked like none she had ever seen before in her few years. She was nervous of me. Shy. Backed away. One day she was half asleep when I arrived. Lying a few feet from her mother on the carpet, eyes ready to close but on seeing me willing herself to stay awake. Kurbangul's mother said she was watching to make sure we would not take Kurbangul back to the hospital. Away from her yet again.

After five days of not harming her mother, the little girl came closer to me and tugged at my hand. Before leaving, I swung her around and then up in the air. She giggled. I tossed her up and down.

Each day when I came in, Kurbangul and I held out our arms to each other. I massaged her feet. Leathery, small, almost fleshless. I massaged her hands and long fingers. Soft, losing tone and colour, preparing to die. Kurbangul was so thin. Only her eyes were not thin. On one of those days she held her bone arm between her fingers, then her bone leg and grimaced. She was saying that she could not believe that it was her, that her body had become just bones. She was witnessing her own disappearance. And her eyes did not hide from what she could see.

On Saturday, I got there late. It was already dark. When I came in there was another car outside and some men were sitting on a bench. I did not know them. They nodded at the foreigner going inside. I knew the end must be at hand. Inside, her mother, a portly matron, was at her feet and with tears in her eyes. Three older women sat to the side. I came right to Kurbangul and bent to hug her. For the first time since I had met her at the beginning of the hospital stay, she did not raise her arms. Instead she pushed me away after I had put my cheek to hers. Her eyes were half closed. Her breathing in short, painful puffs. Body moving with each laboured pump of her lungs. I took her hand but she pulled it away. Put it back on her legs bent up toward her stomach in their usual position. I had no translator but her language was clear. This was her time. There was no longer room for anyone or anything else. Just the next breath.

Her mother queried every so often, asking if she could do this or that. Kurbangul ever so slightly shook her head, never taking her gaze away from its half-closed inward focus. Her mother took her hand. Kurbangul pulled away. Her mother touched her leg. Kurbangul pulled away. Ever so slightly. Just enough energy to mean good-bye, I'm leaving soon, let me be. The universality of gesture.

I sat right at her side and watched her as she watched life. There was nothing to say, nothing to do other than be beside her. Every so often, her body would convulse just a bit. No energy even for that. I thought death might take her any instant, but each time her breathing resumed. Short puffs. Rasp. Rasp. Rasp. Eyes not looking anymore. Except inside. Going back to when she was a foetus maybe. Waiting. Witnessing her own finish.

I left before an hour was up. I knew there were only minutes more, maybe hours. With death, the end point comes only when it does. On the way back in the car, my driver drove in silence as I held my head and cried quietly. I knew the muffled sounds of the foreign man beside him were discomforting. He'd rather not be there. But I was happy to cry despite the restraint. Happy to cry.

Today, I had to attend a wedding party. After two hours of eating and talk and toasts, I left to go to Kurbangul's home. When I got there, the doors of the home compound were opened wide, the sign of a death. Kurbangul's sister met me at the house door. Sarbinaz was the sister who had also been at TB2, had arrived there after Kurbangul, and left months before Kurbangul had been sent out. Sarbinaz looked into my eyes. We had known each other at TB2. I had told her to go home from there when she had converted to non-infectiousness. She had remained an extra two weeks so she could be with Kurbangul, visit her sister in the ICU and give her daily hope, daily togetherness. I told her to go home, that her own health would be compromised by staying around all the infectiousness. She finally left.

Sarbinaz embraced me. How the tyranny of culture recedes when death invades our palisades. She embraced me and wailed that her sister was dead.

After the sobbing subsided she asked if I wanted to go to Kurbangul's body. In the darkened room, Kurbangul was bundled in loose cloth, lying straight, face covered, and with the cool sand around her to forestall deterioration. I knelt beside her and spoke. Finally, there was no need for translation or loud volume. I had my last conversation and said good-bye.

Later, outside while having tea and visiting with her other sisters, they told me how her daughter, the little three-year-old who had wanted her mother to never go back to the hospital again, to never be away for so long, those six months seeming like forever, had lain with her mother in the last minutes. The little girl with the big eyes had been beside her. And then had stayed close and holding after Kurbangul had stopped breathing, stayed beside the one with whom she had begun her own journey those short years before when she was on the inside, the inside of intimacy, secure and warm and connected to the only person in her life forever. She stayed with her mother as she lay there in death and held on.

They said that she let go and moved away only when someone came and placed their fingers on her mother's eyelids to close them.

That was when Sevinch got up and walked alone into another room.

September 29

Today is a training session in Takhtakupir. The trip there is on a main asphalted road with lots of bumps but Air Jenya can cruise at 100 to 120, 140 when needed. We also go off to villages on bumpier roads. All over the countryside is desert brush. It's in flower now. Not really flower but an array of muted colour, pastels of purple, yellow, grey-white, as the foliage turns from the autumn. Some higher brush has large clumps of puff ball type seeding. A bit like a land strewn with cotton candy. Really very beautiful. It pulls you in. I could walk there for hours, especially now in this temperate weather. Fall is like in Canada but maybe less cold. I wore a sweater today.

And alongside the road and out into it, sometimes every few kilometres, are goat herds. Long-haired goats and their shepherds. Sometimes a small herd of cows. We slow when going by. The shepherds walking along behind with their sticks, the relationship all understood with little activity of actual shepherding. And then donkey carts. Laden with grass or hay or something else, sticks maybe. And this morning, three camels in a row, all good looking, being led down the side of the road. There is no franticness. No obvious poverty that disturbs. No crowdedness.

Despite the wolves, I think it really is idyllic here.

∂ Poor Aynur. She never knows what will come out of my mouth, what crazy exercise or outlandish statement. Today, it was about getting these new counsellors to think and be outside the box. To reach patients, we all have to tap into greater creativity and resourcefulness. The usual thinking won't be enough. I asked them to go out of the room and shake hands with any seven others in the office complex. Since they were all new to the others, they didn't want to. They were afraid of being judged. But they did it. They returned smiling. One of the office women came into our room to shake my hand and Aynur's; she too smiling. Then I put wide transparent tape over each of their mouths and spoke about not having a voice, how voice meant sound and behaviour, and choices, and being one's true self. In one's life, it may not always be possible to speak freely but it is possible to speak to oneself, to think one's own thoughts, and to know that it is only another's power which prevents voice. That the restriction on our voice ought never be one which comes from us as a habituated response. I asked if it was time to pull the tape off.

I held up a broken chair back in front of my face. It was like I was peering through bars. "We are all living in cages. We weren't born in cages. But experience and fear puts us in one. All of us. The real world is where we belong. See my hands holding on to the bars? We can let go. We don't need to live in a cage."

Next I asked them to follow me and copy what I did, not to follow because I was anything special but because it was the only way to demonstrate the next exercise. I leapt up and hustled out of the room, out of the building, down out of the courtyard and onto the street. My hands in the air, I zig-zagged down the street, skipping, swaying, and waving with the occasional whoop. They all followed suit. We chased a turkey on the road. We arrived at a clump of trees as the street forked into two. I had each stand touching a tree. We all looked at each other there in the middle of life. Everyone was smiling and light. I asked them to look around at each other, make eye contact. I said not another human in all of Uzbekistan had ever done this before. They agreed. I said: "See, no one even noticed us." One counsellor laughed and said that she had seen a couple of older people watching but they had quickly gone inside their homes. Then we walked back to the office. Aynur shaking her head.

✐ Last night I had a great experience. Stefan was here from Tashkent, and I had finished a two-hour marathon meeting with him and his boss from Berlin. Taxing but okay. I left the office to go meet a friend at a restaurant. It was dark. I walked the 18-minute route. Soon after leaving the office, I phoned Murat who had called earlier. He was phoning to talk about having finally been able to cry the night before, and telling me of his wife's reaction. I was in an animated conversation for some time.

Down the dark road I walked and then turned the corner at TB1 as I have so many times in the past. I have only used a cell phone since I came to Nukus, always having disdained the need for constant accessibility. Here I have had to change. I was walking alongside the road and fully engaged in my talking. It was a nice night, quiet, mild in temperature.

I was enjoying the conversation. After a while I came to a small mound of earth in my path and walked up its slope. And then down. Wham! Straight into a four-foot deep ditch almost three feet wide. My phone flew out of my hand. My pack flew off and I slammed my thigh against the ditch walls, hit my head a bit, smashed my other shin. I automatically started yelling. "Oh no! Oh No! Ahhhhhh!" It hurt, and I was sure I must be in sewage.

But then I realized I was dry. I was sore and dazed but dry. Breathing a sigh of relief, I climbed out. Then I realized I had lost my phone.

I started scanning for it. All dark. Shit. What do I do? Then I think, ah, Murat. "Hey, Murat! Murat! Yell. I've fallen in a big hole and lost my phone. Yell!" I hear his voice squeaking far off somewhere in the dark. I start feeling around in the dirt. "Keep yelling." I realize it's in the ditch somewhere. I climb back down. I'm listening and feeling. But then it goes silent. "Murat! Murat! Keep yelling!" Nothing. Then the phone rings and of course it lights also. Ahhhh, it's Murat at the other end of the ditch.

So, all's well that ends well. I grab my pack and brush it off, brush off the dirt in my hair, massage my bruised and bloody shin, sore hip, laugh and go forward. I truly am a cell phone owner now and have taken my place alongside Mr. Bean and his ilk.

☙

October 4

Another patient died this past week. A woman who gave me and Kairat and Aynur a vivid taste of gentle love, of the fragile vulnerability and preciousness of the togetherness of us small humans. She lasted two months or so and lived in her bed in TB1 with her teen daughter beside her. The healthy with the sick together in the air of death. Her name was Ayjan.

She had been a patient many months before I arrived in Nukus. And after being discharged from hospital no longer infectious, had gone home to Chimbay where she took her drugs every day. But she began to miss occasionally and finally defaulted. Kairat had been her counsellor and had tried everything to get her to resume treatment. Then, over two months ago, I was called out to see her at her home.

When Kairat and I arrived, Ayjan was lying on a cot against the outside wall of her home. She was weak and scared. When she saw us arrive, her eyes became animated and she sat up. Kairat wanted me to meet her because she had sent word to the Chimbay TB doctor that she wanted to get back into MDR treatment. The doctor called Kairat to interview her to see if he thought that this time she would stick with the full two years of treatment.

Within a very few minutes it became clear that her physical condition was not good. In my mind, I thought she had waited too long. As we spoke with her, it was obvious that she would die without the drugs and that she fully knew that and was prepared to do the treatment properly this time. Kairat and I looked at each other, and I promised to call the doctor and advocate for her re-admission. At that, Ayjan began crying and grasping my arm, thanking me profusely.

Then she looked directly at Kairat and spoke: "Kairat, I'm so ashamed. Before when you tried so hard to keep me taking the drugs, I ignored you. When I saw the MSF car coming I was angry and sometimes I ran off and hid. I know now I was wrong. Today, when I saw your car drive up, I was overjoyed. I thought that God was having mercy on me. I have been praying that you would come and give me a second chance. I hope you will forgive me." As she said these last words she was weeping and looking into Kairat's eyes.

His face reddened, and I could tell that suave Kairat had melted. He could have cried as well, but he just said softly: "It's okay. We are here now. That shows you how we feel."

That exchange outside a rustic mud brick home in Chimbay spelled out exactly that humanity is the basis of all effective medical care. Each of us bound together in simple vulnerability. One hand held out to another and the two touching.

Then, after Ayjan was admitted to TB1, I would always stop in to see her each week if only for five minutes. We would hug briefly. She would thank me several times again for saving her life and giving her hope. Sometimes she would have swelling in her feet, other times pain in her abdomen, but basically she held her own. Always with her daughter beside her.

After a few weeks, she weakened and was put on an oxygen mask. It seemed she would die in a day or two. But she didn't. She continued living. Until two days ago.

With each patient who dies, I have started a practise of putting their photo on the wall in the front office of our psychosocial building. For the health system, it means another number in the computer which is relegated to the archive file. To the hospital, it's out of sight out of mind as quickly as possible. But I want the counsellors to keep the faces of those we touched and who touched us. I want the team to see them each day and remember them. It seems the least we can do, though I know it makes them uncomfortable, and when I leave at the end of December they will likely take all the photos down.

My regret is that we didn't take photos of all the patients, and once they are in weakened condition I feel awkward about taking their picture. We never got one of Ayjan. She was 48.

And it was from visiting Ayjan each week that I inadvertently was delivered another lesson. In the same room was another woman, about thirty and also in bad condition. I never saw her leave her bed though she was not as weak as Ayjan. There was always a man in the room caring for her. A big fellow in a light blue surgical mask. For a few weeks I would only say hello and greet the sick woman with a handshake. Then, one day, I asked the fellow if he was her brother. He replied that he was her husband.

Our eyes met. I shook his hand and said how proud I was of his attention to his wife. In this land of wife servitude and ease in finding replacements for defective models was a man standing tall in love. Each day, accepting the risk of his own infection to cook for his wife, to help her wash, to comfort her, to keep her company, to be there for her.

That's what we all miss sometimes. We become critics and cynics or titles or just walkers by. We miss how precious the chance to live is for those who ease toward death, breathing raspy or in puffs, breathing against hope but breathing, holding the chance like dust slipping through their fingers. But their fingers can feel that dust. Know the glitter. And we miss the quiet acts of decency and love, the acts that show us what it means to live up to love in every sense of the word.

☞

October 8

In Karauziak, the town before Takhtakupir, I enjoy a nice walk among the drying autumn foliage on some arid trails outside of town. I have been chasing Rustum. He's 23 and madder than hell. For the past few weeks he has refused to come for drugs. He has threatened his regular counsellor and told her to stop bothering him. Kuanish has gone to see him but to no avail. Now, it is my turn.

We arrived outside his apartment block and by chance met his father as soon as we got out of the car. His father was very concerned about his son. Not only has he been refusing his drugs, he has become hostile and aggressive. Outbursts occur in which he breaks tea pots and kicks at the wall. He is newly married also and fights with his wife. Everyone is worried about him. The father wants our help. I didn't know who Rustum is, but I told the father that we were there to help and would go inside to see his son. He replied that it was best if he went in to ask first in order to save any more damage from happening.

A few minutes later, he returned and said that Rustum immediately got angry and refused to talk to us. We were discussing together our next plan of action when Kuanish spotted Rustum sneaking across the building courtyard and out of sight past another building. We quickly moved down another route to try to intercept him.

We saw him. Walking fast and looking over his shoulder in agitation.

I then recognized him from TB2. I just hadn't known his name. I have talked to him before, greeted him, met with him again when he was in the negative ward at TB1. He's a sharp guy, really bright looking. I had seen his mood radically different from TB2 when he was at the negative ward. Now it's shifted again. At TB2 he was always smiling, always on his cell phone, a bit of a ladies man.

"Hey, Rustum! Salaam alaikum!" I yelled and hurried towards him.

He looked back and stopped. It was almost like his body made him do it. We came up to him, and I greeted him with the familiar handshake and head bump. I only got to say that I was happy to see him and worried about him before he started yelling. He was totally agitated. Eyes livid. "If she comes here again," he pointed at Sultana, his counsellor, "I'll kill her. Or I'll kill myself. You come around here while there are guests and embarrass me like this. Leave me alone!" He turned and hurried away, half running.

We followed. "Wait, Rustum! Wait! I only want to talk."

He yelled fuck off and began to trot towards the field and its paths. I told the others to stay behind and off I went trotting after him, every so often yelling, "Rustum!" hoping that he would stop when he saw it was just me. But Rustum kept running, stopping, looking back, seeing me still on his trail, and then trotting off again. After 15 minutes, I have lost him.

But it is nice out here. Peaceful. The bushes and their pastels and some with big fluffy seed pods all quite beautiful.

Unfortunately, I am also lost because I haven't kept track of the directions and several paths and intersections we have moved along.

And this is another good reason to have a cell phone on this job.

☙

October 12

Today is a young patient's 18th birthday. She has invited six other patients and me, Aynur, Deelya and Bibigul to a party at her house. We have become part of her life. I queried beforehand to be sure it would be okay that we would be wearing our masks. Pretty odd. Four ducks acting afraid of infection in someone's house with these young people and the girl's family members all present without masks. But she said it would be fine.

With our masks on we obviously cannot eat the food or drink anything while we sit around the long, low table heaped with birthday succulence. The other patients know us, so only the setting and context is strange for them. The birthday girl is a beauty, her long black hair, tan complexion, moist eyes, dimples cast her as every photographer's favourite, and she loves being photographed. We take several inside and out, joke about getting older, about getting married, about the boys who are there. It's a beautiful time actually. And I would guess maybe the first birthday party of patients and counsellors. In the past she had been angry with her friend who is here because she sensed that the girl coveted her boyfriend. Deelya had to do some mediation work and all is good. A lethal disease has no dominion over teenage priorities.

☙

Aziz has phoned. One of his patients from TB2 left the hospital several days ago. Aziz went to his house for the second time to get him to return, but the man yelled at him and told him to get out. I tell Aziz that I will go see him. His name is Kalibek.

"Kalibek! Kalibek!" Aynur hollers through a crack she has opened in the front door of the house. No answer. There is a natural gas smell around the door from the small pipe which runs over the top of the door frame. There is plastic bagging wrapped around it, but obviously it isn't sufficient.

We walk in, despite no answer. "Salaam alaikum!" I want him to hear the foreigner's voice. If he has been in TB2 he must know me even if I don't know him by name. Still no answer. This is a typical not-so-affluent-not-so-poor Karakalpak home. Meagre furniture. No chairs. Some carpets. Everyone prefers to sit on the floor. To the sides are mats rolled up for sleeping on or for visitors. We look tentatively about and make our way through the empty house in all its spareness to a bedroom. There is a tall man asleep and covered by blankets, face only partially visible.

"Salaam alaikum, Kalibek." No response. I bend forward and try to shake his hand. He pulls it away, keeping his eyes closed.

"We've come to see why you left the hospital."

"Go away. I won't talk."

"Well, you don't have to talk, but we won't leave just yet." I continue on about treatment, about how hard the drugs are, how everyone goes through stages, how we will help, how he is a warrior. On and on. Throughout, he says nothing, never answering a question. Never looking at me. He is long in the covers. I can see his hips. He reminds me a bit of Islam, though taller.

Finally, I ask if I can bring him some food.

No answer.

I go closer and say: "Well, I'm going to bring you some anyway, so you might as well tell me what you will prefer."

Silence.

"I'll bring some sausage." Silence. "I'll bring some peanuts." Silence. "I'll bring some cheese." His hand emerges and shakes a no.

Is he saying not cheese or saying get out?

I continue: "I'll bring some milk." Silence. "I'll bring some eggs." The hand comes up again. Ahhh. "I'll bring some bread." No hand.

"Okay, I'll come back at the end of the afternoon with some food. But no cheese and no eggs."

I bend forward and place my head against his. I hold it there for quite some time. He doesn't move but his hand moves up to rest against my head.

We leave. I think this will be a long shot, but who knows?

In the afternoon, just before quitting time, I come back with the food. When we knock, he tells us to come in. We enter. He is sitting at the low table in the living room up by the television. He is drinking tea, and a large tabby cat is lying next to him. He strokes the cat.

This time he talks. He tells us how his lower legs and feet are swollen. That's why he stopped the drugs and left the hospital. He won't return. His mother has gone to Kazakhstan for a couple of months, and he lives with his father. We talk. His cat's name is Sebastian, and he's had him since he was a kitten.

I tell him I'll visit tomorrow. I still think it will be a long shot, but now he's talking.

⁊ Guldana died on July 19. I feel empty when Murat tells me. Of course, I knew it had to be. We agree to find out where she has been buried and visit her grave. How can I grieve now for someone who died months back? I am guilty for not pressing for information more often after I returned from Kyrgyzstan. I am guilty for just assuming after all I could get was an instant recording when I tried to phone her, assuming and resigning myself. I should have found out and gone to her grave then. But this is the way it is.

⁊

October 20

It is the 7th anniversary of the opening of TB2 as an MDR-TB hospital. We are celebrating and Marcell is back in Nukus to film it. Daniyar is doing the concert. We are all gathered outside, doctors, nurses, visitors, MSF people and patients. It is a warm, sunny October day. *We Are The World* could be written here because, in all of our competing smallnesses and anonymities, we really are the world, unknown vibrancies each pulsing along our own trajectories, each with a story and a destiny that will remain off the notice board of the life outside this never known land. And yet we hold the reins of an epidemic as potentially powerful as any in our human history. So, we are the sweepers and we are the drivers. And today amidst our world of silence and non-existence we revel in music, in dance, and in recognition of each other.

Daniyar points up towards the far end of TB2. "That's where I spent five months, wondering whether I would live or die. I lived. And now I am here singing to you."

Marcell pans the crowd with his camera. Daniyar is singing about his long dead mother and the tears have begun. As before, the Chief Doctor daubs at her eyes. A patient in a wheelchair, an old woman with a bandana, weeps. Daniyar goes to her as he sings and takes her hand.

Then it's on to another song. The beat has picked up and many dance. I have paid the taxi fares to get two car loads of women from TB1 here. This will be the last concert of the season and I want them to be able to dance before winter. Counsellors dance. Other visitors too. We are all together today. An old woman leaves her spot on the concrete bench. Walking with the aid of a cane, she approaches the dancers and joins in.

As the concert progresses—half of which consists of recorded dance tunes—Daniyar announces a dance competition. He declares that it will be between this hot-dog patient who had been strutting his cool moves for a half hour already, a guy in his early 20s. And who? Aynur laughs and says: "You, Calvin." Me?

So there we go. The hot-dog, a fellow named Rollan, is serious. An expression of earnestness out to defeat the foreigner despite our centuries of age difference. These damn Karakalpaks seem never to be able to distinguish foreigners' ages and what kind of deference that should evoke. He's flying at it. So, I decide to do it as seriously as I can.

Soon, the tempo picks up, and Rollan doffs his shirt and shoes to the music as he dances. I choose to keep my shirt on. Too white, too thin, too much hair. But we both fling ourselves into it. Finally, thank god, the song ends just before my complexion goes to blue from oxygen deprivation. Everyone is asked to clap for who they thought was the winner. He ekes out the decision. Later he comes over to me and asks where his chocolate is for winning the competition.

Today, everyone is happy. Deena dances with Marcell. Gulsara jokes with Aziz. Later, Manas gives an aikido demonstration. Many photos are taken.

Like the ghosts of those gone and those still to go from this wind of disease, the vibrant flow of magical music has wisped away, away from all else on the planet. But for these moments, here in the middle of desert, everyone danced. With their feet or with their hearts, everyone danced. Maybe the ghosts as well.

σ

October 22

I am with Daniyar today. I have him with me to help with three trouble spots. First, we go to a village a half hour out of town and a half a century away. Bumping along a road out into the desert, we come to the clutter of buildings in the middle of nowhere. There is no water here evidently. Twice a week, a big truck brings out a delivery. We are hoping to convince a patient to return to the hospital. He left after several months. He is about 50 and almost deaf.

I ask him why he chose to move out here after living in town. "Don't ask, me that," he says. "I was a fool."

But despite the fact he knows Daniyar and me and despite all of our urgings, he has no intention of returning to hospital or treatment. He leaves us to return to the board game he has been playing with neighbours.

Next, we return to town and go to Kalibek's house. I want him to meet Daniyar. Maybe a young man can convince a young man to live.

Kalibek tells us he used to drive big trucks. He would haul things across the region, sometimes making trips into Kazakhstan. Once, he and his cab mate both fell asleep at the wheel and the truck went off the road and tipped over. His boss was angry, and they had to help him do all the repairs. Kalibek laughs as he recounts in detail waking up as he was turning sideways in the truck and that it was a good thing it couldn't go very fast.

But he is not swayed by Daniyar's urgings, as eloquent as they are. Kalibek points at his feet and says they still hurt too much even to walk about for very long. The drugs, he says, will only make them worse.

Finally, it's out to TB2 and a visit with Deena and Gulsara. Deena just needs a hug and a reminder of her Deena-ness. She is a winner, a dimpled sprite of sly-humoured honesty and warmth.

Gulsara is struggling because Doctor Ayeesha has met with her and announced that she should stop treatment. "Go home. Have a rest"—the euphemisms for "it's hopeless". I have never understood how Gulsara left the hospital in the month or so after I arrived, went home no longer infectious and then steadily declined until now she is showing no progress, despite taking her drugs regularly.

As before, I tell her the choice is hers, not the doctor's. That if she wants to stay on the drugs and fight then I will intervene with Ayeesha. Daniyar looks into her eyes and smiles. It is akin to attention from a Hollywood heart-throb. Gulsara was in Room 10 way back. She knew Daniyar.

Gulsara says she will fight. I notice that her fingernails are painted a faint shade of blue, almost white. On each nail there is a pattern of six tiny red dots. Her fingers are a girl's fingers, a girl who sees herself as alive, worthy of decorating her fingernails. I tell her this and ask if I can take a picture of her hands. I will bring her this picture to remind her of who she really is.

October 25

Today, Kalibek turns away in his bed and barks at me to get out and leave him alone, not come back. It has been about two weeks since he left the hospital and stopped his drugs. I had no relationship with him at the hospital, vaguely recognized him. I have been to his house now eight times. Sometimes twice a day—in the morning to see if he will talk and then later at quitting time if he didn't. The point has been to gentle him into a connection. I thought it was working, but now he has snapped away.

I respond that I won't leave. I'll go away and come back in late afternoon. He says he'll run away. I say before I leave I want to see his eyes. He turns further away and pulls a towel over his head. I bend forward and stroke his head and say good-bye.

At 6:30 I return. I knock on his door and pull it open a bit. "Salaam alaikum," I say. "Come in," he replies. He is holding his cat and watching TV. He looks at me and we talk. He swims in aloneness and a sense of resigned given-upness. He misses his mom who has gone to Kazakhstan for three months for work. After 10 minutes I leave and tell him I'll come again tomorrow.

⟋

October 26

Kalibek says even his father is afraid when he gets angry. "When I hear something I don't like, I just seal up like a stone and no one can make me speak. It isn't you. It's just how I am."

He sips his tea as he speaks, this tall angular man/boy. He has a nice face. Finishing the tea, I see there is a whole dried apricot in the cup. He pours in more tea, looks at me and smiles. I sit with my mask on as he speaks. The gas leak outside still has not been fixed.

The days are getting shorter.

⟋

November 1

At Kalibek's home this morning, his whole family, except for his mother, is there. There because they have learned that he is sick and that I come every day to talk to him. They want to know what his prognosis is, but Kalibek has gone into another room and refuses to join us. I assert that I won't speak unless he is present. We sit and wait, but he refuses to budge. Finally, I ask for us to leave the big room and go into the small room where Kalibek sits crouched in a corner, his eyes peering away from the open space and locked onto the corner higher up on a wall where there can be no eye contact.

Now though, I know that Kalibek will hear everything we say. That way he can construe no misconceptions or conspiracies. I want to keep the tenuous bond that we have, but I don't want to miss this chance to bring his family on board. It is a risk, but I didn't plan it.

So, I tell them. I explain how he needs to go back to the hospital, how the drugs are terrible but they work, that they are the best drugs in the world and the only way that we know how to cure MDR-TB. I praise Kalibek, say he is a fine young man and that he needs their understanding and support. All nod, all look deeply concerned. His grandfather takes the lead. He begins an exhortation, half plea, half order that his beloved grandson must resume treatment. Everyone agrees.

Kalibek simply stares toward the wall and says not a whisper. The grandfather and his aunts take turns questioning him, asking if he is ready to go back to the hospital. He says nothing.

I leave, giving them my phone number and repeating that I am there to help if they see a role for me. Kalibek, I tell that I will return the next day.

Aynur asks me why we keep going to see him when it seems so hopeless. These days I spend more time training the counsellors in both Nukus and Takhtakupir, time going from hospital to polyclinics checking on how everything is going. I'm not doing much counselling. I don't feel as deeply connected to patients' lives as I used to when I had my own case load in TB1 and TB2. I troubleshoot now or see my old patients just to maintain the relationship. So, with some like Kalibek, I want to persist. I want to not give up before they do.

And Kalibek? Kalibek's just a boy.

☙

November 2

I'm at Kalibek's house again. He looks disgusted. He scowls at us and starts in at what took place yesterday with his relatives. He is furious that I spoke about him and his condition in front of all those people. And he is furious at them because he doesn't see them as sincere. When he was out at TB2 for two months not one came to visit him. "Where were they then?" he shouts. "They all say those caring words now, but they are just words." He dismisses Aynur and me. "Go away. I'm not afraid to die."

I say that he is carrying lots of aloneness, lots of hurt inside. That he needs to cry. He says that he has cried.

Nefertiti

November 3

Sad day. Gulsara is going home. The doctors have announced there is no use continuing the drugs. I am ready to fight them, but Gulsara says it's okay. She is ready to leave. There is a resignation in her now, not a defeat, but an acceptance. I tell her that we have lied to the patients when we always tell them that the drugs are the only way to be cured. I tell her that statistics show that some with MDR get cured on their own. I say that she can live, that when she goes home I will visit her, bring food. She must eat and build herself up. Set goals.

I would rather have gone to the doctors and railed at them to keep her on treatment, do whatever I had to do to keep her here, but this is her life, not mine. I know that the hospital doctors' persistent attitudes have finally broken her tenuous will, her capacity to believe. But she has decided now. She is ready, I can see that. And I don't know what is best.

November 4

I have brought Gulsara some coloured pencil crayons. I want her to do artwork. She is set up in a room by herself at her parents' home. Her home. She is lying on mats on the floor. Her hair is swathed in her usual bandana but I can see some discolouring in the hair that shows above her forehead. She takes off the bandana and laughs. Some of her hair is rusty orange, the rest dark. A dye job done wrong. That's why she always wears the bandana, she says.

This is the home she was born in. I imagine her like the other two children in the home, waddling around as an infant. Waddling through time to this moment when the foreign friend sits beside her as she lies waiting for the unknown.

She is eating just one cup of solid food a day but drinking two litres of milk. I urge her to increase the food intake. And I want her to draw the tree she spoke of a few weeks before. She had a dream in which there was a beautiful tall, green tree. On its higher branches were different coloured beautiful fruits. In the dream she saw herself climbing the tree and reaching for the fruit. It had been a happy dream, vivid and meaningful. She understood it to be about being cured and the future.

⁊

November 5

Kalibek has stopped talking again. The past two days he has refused to look at me or speak. While I was visiting today, he got up, put on his long, blue cotton housecoat and walked outside. He walked down past his house to the end of the street and sat in the sun. I followed him, still trying to talk, and trying to get eye contact. He stared over my head into the sky. I tell him that I won't come again but he can phone me if he changes his mind about going to the hospital or taking home-based treatment.

⁊ When I visit Gulsara, she is happy. She has made several pictures with the pencil crayons. One is of a tree. And she has been eating more. I give her the large bottle of camel milk that I have brought. It is supposed to be high in nutrition and some believe it helps against TB.

⁊

November 7

On this Sunday walk to the bazaar, I have come upon two old women doing some sort of ritual on the wide sidewalk area. This is an unusual sight in Nukus which has the cut of a trimmed modernity. But I think this is who the people really are, legs straddling the centuries, older age sometimes still retaining the deeper crevices that came before. Before all of us. In a sense, they are only the land itself. The saying dust to dust, ashes to ashes, is far more suggestive than the simple chronological finishing of a life. I guess all of us are the land. So it is that these two old women bundle themselves in the weakened sunlight of today, November 7. All the November 7ths are speaking today. The ones in this top half of the planet where November means something. The sun so welcomed, a blue sky appreciated.

One of the women sits on the dusty concrete farther back. Her face wrapped to protect it. Eyes merely squints of colour. I would come closer to see her better but I already see her better and if I came close she would change. Her age would disappear and she would be now. As is, she is forever. She sits with her knees pulled up. A bundle of wrappings. Round face, wrinkles, flat nose. She could be a leper if there was less nose. She is filled. Filled with stories and lives. Hers and all those she ever knew. All those who ever saw her, heard her voice or she theirs. Right at this time she has a story.

When did she arrive at that spot? What drew her to sit there? Where did she come from? When will she leave? What is she doing sitting there? Squatting there among mounds of cloth or belongings or items. I can't see clearly what is what. I could go closer but then she would disappear. Is she happy? Is she hungry?

The other woman is old also. She walks farther away. She walks round and round a tree. A tree painted white at the base as all the trees here are, a tree of thickness with a canopy spread above still green before winter. At chest high, a white cloth is wound around the trunk of the tree. The old woman walks around the tree, her fingers caressing the cloth as she walks. She might be a mourner talking to dead children. She might be a witch. She might be a spell caster. Or just a prayer. A prayer trudging the trudge of plaintiveness or the trudge of piety. The trudge of acknowledgement. The trudge of thanks or regret. Or just the trudge of the time to do the trudge. Maybe just a trudge. Caressing the cloth.

How long has she been at it? When did she start? Was it this decade? Will it continue for minutes or hours? Has it ever stopped? Maybe she is muttering as she walks. Her head faces the tree and the cloth. I cannot see her eyes. Maybe she is crying. Maybe she is in a trance. I would come closer but she would disappear. Like her friend she is telling me a story. I don't want the story to end. It's a story without words or sound or memory. A story of time.

And there are other characters. Some 10 or 15 metres away closer to the street are two others. These two are standing closer together than the two old women. One is a young man, a youth really, maybe 20. The other is a girl, a bit taller, her black hair draping over her shoulders. Both are dressed in black. The girl has fishnet stockings, the lattice pattern climbing her calf just above the tall black boots, climbing her thigh to beneath her short skirt. She wears glasses. Both these two are focussed and attentive. They grip their cell phones and gaze into them. They are texting. I can tell they have seen the two old women not so far away. But they are absorbed in their phones. They walk in tiny circles or back and forth, weaving a sluggish dance. Every so often one looks over to the other and back to the phone. They are modern. Modern. Their knees are in the middle of their legs. Somehow they have gotten lost.

I'd like to walk over to them and ask if they have ever had an idea. I'd like to ask them to stand together, heads touching and their cell phones held up to each side, and smile so I could take their photo but I don't want them to disappear more than they already have.

☞

November 8

Tonight I go out to see Gulsara. She is weaker now and breathing with difficulty lying in her bed. We talk a bit and then she breaks and grabs for my hand and cries, says: "I'm scared."

I hold her hand. After a bit she gathers in. Then later I look in her eyes and all I can see is life. I glare at her with energy and grit, urging at her to fight. To tell her lungs to work. To go forward.

I will see her again tomorrow and the next. She will either go up or go down fast. Twenty-five, only 25. Life here is as soft and light as the wind on the face.

I still don't know what I am here or why. I don't know what it has all been about. Maybe I am merely what the wind has blown.

Aziz has gone to Uganda for a week of post-conflict training. Here is a slow, continuous conflict.

I feel alone. I am. We all are. Gulsara grabs for my hand and says: "I waited for you to come since morning."

She is alone, though her mother and father are in the house with her. Her father takes my hand and holds it firm and won't let go as I am leaving. I can smell alcohol on his breath. He looks about 60. He says: "Why is she having trouble breathing?" I say: "Because she is really sick." Last time I came he asked if she would get well.

There are no answers here. I went to Nitbek's house an hour before Gulsara to talk with him about how the doctors have also taken him off the drugs because "they aren't working." He pled for another four months to see. In spite of being made sick by the drugs, he pled for another four months. They said no. The expat doctor and the other local working for us. Said no.

I looked him in the eyes and told him to live. He is 87 kg. He is coughing. His wife asked, when he was out of the room, if he was infecting them.

And another who is losing, and another, and another ... But there are many who are winning. And the doctors and nurses ask me: "What are the counsellors doing?" What they mean is that we aren't doing anything. That I am deficient and the counsellors are deficient. I know why they are saying that. No one likes to face truth.

☙

November 10

Gulsara is Gulsara again. She has more vitality. Eyes bright again. She actually looks like the bust of Nefertiti the Egyptian. Nefertiti one of the oldest queens we know so well. Her face an ivory, staring invitation to timelessness. Today she is in this room.

Gulsara looks at me, her dark eyes wide and peering into mine. The intimacy is deep and total. There is no such thing as time. I could lie down beside her and sleep. I never want to look away, never want to move. I can just stay forever, locked together. I have to tell her I love her. I don't know what else I can say to come close to the intimacy. It doesn't really come close. She looks down, her eyes shy. This time of reclining flat on her pillow, her ivory stillness. Her face smooth and flowing with perfect texture, perfect tightness. High forehead, dark large eyes. "You are so beautiful today, absolutely beautiful. You look like a queen."

She raises herself up and yells loudly through the window: "Mom! Mom! I want some tea!" Her mother comes in from outside. Sticks her weary, weathered face in the doorway to this waiting room, this Gulsara room. "Black or green?"

"Black!" Gulsara barks. The queen barked. A voice as strong as the need for tea. She is breathing raspy now. Says the sputum comes so often, sits in her throat, trying to drown her. She coughs and coughs trying to get it up and out. The doctors told her weeks before that one lung is gone. I say she has to heal the other one. I say she has to fight. She can't eat much. Her sleep is spoiled by the coughing. She is angry at me because I told her she could live. Angry at me that she might die.

I never want to say "will die." She is alive. To declare any certainty is to follow the lead of the doctors who sent her home to "take a rest." No more drugs. They weren't working. Gulsara's thinness scared them. They don't like no answers so they write their own. Treatment failure. A euphemism as detached and fearful of truth as body count, collateral damage, friendly fire. All lies saved for war to produce desired numbness.

Gulsara imagines green trees. She looks at their branches and sees birds at rest. Today she is ready to drink tea. And give me yet another audience with living antiquity.

∽

November 12

Gulsara has been sent out to TB3. Natasha tells me that she has been sent there to die. I say not this time. Natasha looks at me with raised eyebrows: "I've seen this kind before. Look at her. She is on her way out." I reply that she has only come for some treatment, that she will leave in a couple of days. Natasha says she'll believe it when she sees it.

Samuel has arranged for Gulsara to come here because she has some kind of bowel blockage. She didn't want to tell me but told Murat and he told me and I told Samuel and he told the community TB doctor and she got hold of a proctologist. And now Gulsara is here waiting for an assessment and hopefully a remedy. For the past several days she has not been able to defecate and has surges of pain that come into her bottom all day long.

∽

November 15

Aynur and I are waiting in the office of the president of the Agricultural College in Chimbay. One of our patients is an instructor there but has not been able to perform his teaching duties for many months, and now they are going to fire him. He has asked through a counsellor if

I can help. It worked for Achmed's daughter at the teacher's college, so we will try the trick again.

The president enters with another man. "This is our lawyer," he declares and wants him at this meeting. The lawyer looks like a lawyer.

I go into my spiel. Our patient needs your help. He is a warrior. Blah, blah, blah.

The president looks at me and waves his finger. "I know this. He is sick. I know. But we have given him time off for six months already. We are a college. He has a job to do. If he can't do it then it is time to replace him. We cannot wait forever."

It seems bleak, and I don't even think I know the patient. But I ask again for some kind of help.

The lawyer pipes up. "There is no legal obligation for us to do anything. There is a contract. We are sorry but we have a school to run."

I sit silent for a few minutes. It works for Kalibek.

Then the president speaks. "Okay, we can't just keep paying him when he does not work. But maybe we can arrange for him to do part-time work. I will call him in and see what times might work for him. We will try to arrange something."

❧

November 17

Today was an odd day. At 10 in the morning I walked to the House Of Happiness. In Uzbekistan, this is what the official marriage registration building is called. I was going to attend the marriage of two friends. It takes about seven minutes to get there from our MSF psychosocial building. Go out the door, walk to the left about 20 metres to the street and then right another 30 metres, then right again down a narrow street to a pathway between storage containers. Wind through them, ignoring the layers of garbage on the vacant lot over to the left, go through an apartment building parking lot, onto a lane and then left on the frontage road for the buildings which line the central artery that cuts Nukus north to south. Another 30 metres to the left and skip up the stairs into the doorway of the Nukus House Of Happiness.

The couple sat on chairs in the chief's office while she read out some documents. Ten minutes later, they were married. Of course, the process had begun a month earlier. Medical checks, x-rays, psychiatric interviews, forms to fill out, and fees to pay accompanied by all the usual line-ups. My friends were elated that it was over. The marriage chief wondered why the man had no ring, why his shoes were scuffed. His new wife blushed.

We agreed to meet later in the evening after work for a private celebration. This was a most unusual marriage for this culture, completely at odds with the norms of various practises. If the man doesn't kidnap the woman and take her off to his parents' home, then he has to come up with a dowry. Thousands of sum for his bride's parents up front, followed by more money and material gifts to the parents, grandparents, uncles and aunts. The wedding itself means a limo, a hall, food, music. My friends chose scuffed shoes and love.

A half hour later, back in the office, our receptionist came in to announce that a phone call had come from the main Nukus office of MSF. A death had occurred that morning. Abu, our I.T. guy, the fellow who takes care of all the computer needs, had felt sick and was driven to the hospital by a young Karakalpak colleague. In the hospital parking lot he had passed out. The young colleague flew into action. A stretcher was brought out. Abu vomited. The medics fumbled about. The young colleague yelled at them to get more help. Abu regained consciousness. Then while in the hospital, he lapsed back into unconsciousness and died. Just like that. A seven-minute trip to hospital. A few more minutes there and it was all over.

Abu was only in his late thirties. He had grey hair and an appealing smile that despite the caution in his face gave him a boyish aura. Of the fix-it guys, he was the most held back, the most defined by a sense of privacy yet without hardness or assertiveness. The kind of guy you might want to know better, that if you did get inside you might like him, might enjoy playing tennis with. But the kind of guy who you weren't going to get inside because he wasn't going to open that door even though something in his eyes said maybe he was a bit lonely for closer company. Abu was thin and smart, a Tatar who the other tech guys came to for training.

He had felt sick for some days. Others had gone to a conference in Tashkent but he stayed behind. Before they left, he had said good-bye, said maybe they wouldn't see him again. He came to work today and never went home.

☞

November 19

Dr. Samuel has asked me to visit with Lala who is in the negative ward at TB1. This is where non-infectious patients go after they have been ambulatory and need attention for other illness or because they can't manage to go to the polyclinic each day for their drugs. There's the one at TB1 and the one in Chimbay.

She is stressed and has a fear of the drugs. When I see her, I re-member her right away from TB2. Before I can start my visit, the crazy doctor in charge of the negative ward comes in and yells at Lala, threatening to kick her out because she is not taking the drugs. Lala just looks at the floor and nods in obeisance while the doctor rants. I wait her out also. Then when she's gone, Lala and I talk.

She has been regurgitating the sad feelings over an abortion she had in 2007. She lives in Karauziak. She has husband problems. He hits her, berates her. She frets that she should be doing better house-work. At home, after taking the drugs, she would try to walk off the side effects but end up vomiting one to two hours later. She worries that she can't be cured. She has an eight-year-old daughter.

I try to separate the seriousness of her problems. Screw the worry about no cure and doing better housework. Start thinking about how to defend herself from her husband. We'll work on that. But about the abortion she can take some practical steps. I want her to make some drawings of the baby she could have had. This connection to a life lost needs to be grieved. Now, when she needs to live, it has brought up her guilt over having cut life away from within her.

And with the drugs, I suggest giving each one names. Take away their power. Name them. Talk to them as she holds them in her hand. These orange pills are Calvin. Okay, I'm going to swallow you Calvin.

These longer white ones are Fatima. Hello Fatima, guess what. You're going down the hatch too. We all laugh. From behind Lala I see Aynur raise her eyebrows and shake her head as she translates.

Then a phone call from Murat. Good news. Gulsara is home again. An impacted bowel was the problem and all is free and loose now. Her pain has gone.

☞

November 26

Marcell, back in Austria, has sent the unedited version of the film. Everyone is really excited to see it. I heard that the doctors thought it was too much about patients and counselling with not enough medical information. That's who they are. I don't think they understand what it's like to be on the drugs. No amount of information will help the patients, certainly won't inspire them. I hope to watch it tomorrow. Someone will lend me me a USB stick so I can bring it to my office and watch in privacy.

Deena has been sick a couple of weeks. Another cold. She got discouraged. So, we have tried to breathe into her — Deelya, me, Murat. I invoke Marcell's spirit for her also. All of us need what can be given by those who can and want to give it.

Intimacy. A facet is having the connection with another that allows the spirit to be breathed in. When I saw her one day a week ago, she was sad and angry at being so alone. She wouldn't look at me. Would only talk a little. I'd ask for eye contact. She'd look and then look away. I couldn't raise her. I talked, spoke of various things. She listened but would not let her mood lift. Or couldn't. Then before I left, I asked if she wanted me to hold her. She said yes, and then lifted herself off the bed for me to embrace her. I held her and she held me. It was the connection.

Later that day, Deena sent me a text message. First time. Mainly in Karakalpak, which she knows I can't understand. She just wanted to do it anyway.

Then when I saw her today, she was still in bed and still thin. Still a bit weak. But she was radiant. Absolutely beautiful. She had a red cotton bandana on her head. Her dress was a rich, dark purple velvet, and the sweater beneath the dress was bright blue. She was stunning. And I thought of what Marcell had seen in her. I saw it too.

_____

December 1

I go to Gulsara's home on TB Street. Just across from Islam's home. Islam's home where his mother died, his sister died, his younger brother now with the disease, and his other younger brother recovered from the disease. And in this home, Gulsara's brother and sister-in-law with the disease but living on their own now, and Gulsara now on her mat bed, so thin, so thin and home from the hospital a month, MDR-TB failure.

No more drugs. No more side effects. Just fate. She lies on her mat thin but alive. Thin but with bowls of food by her side, a bag of dried berries and a vase of aromatic herbs. Gulsara with the silver polish on her toe nails, the fading red dye from the botched job on her locks.

I go to her home every day—even if only for a few minutes. My gesture to say no to death and yes you can live. I've been told that world stats say 20% live despite going off the drugs. She is thin but can maybe gain weight. Maybe it isn't too late. One lung is gone, the doctors say. Her smile is wide, her eyes large and full. Her skin drawn tight now over her skull, casting a much older look than her 25 years. She won't see visitors, not Daniyar, not her old room 10 mate Gulshat, whose parents and two sisters perished from the disease, nor Slohan. Not Deena or any of her friends at the hospital still. When she can walk again, she says she will see Slohan.

We speak now with gesticulations and monosyllables each might decipher. I have come with no translator because it is late. I have brought the watermelon she asked for. It looks like a round dark green bowling ball, this fruit still ready to eat in December. The cold nights not daunting its summer sales. The ice on the puddles not crisp enough yet to end its reign on the palate. Gulsara phoned to ask for watermelon, not to forget. We bought it from the roadside vendor on the way back from Takhtakupir, where I tried to duel with the shamanist grandfathers of a young girl who stopped her drugs and opted for beatings on the back with a stick to chase away the illness. Where I sang *Old MacDonald Had A Farm* for four patients in a clinic and where I held Sveta the dentist, held her long and close from our times in TB1. And tonight I am with Gulsara again.

Her eyes so wide and dark—and so alive. She is mesmerizingly beautiful. I rub her feet, the bare pale skin of aliveness, touch into the nerve centres, the pleasure centres. I pull at her toes, massaging and kneading and commanding, gently commanding in small whispers that they send strength up through her ankles, calves, thighs into her body to walk again soon, maybe even dance with me before I leave in another month. I want her to live. I ask her to be forgiven for any transgressions that might weight her to death. I speak my mantras of hope, my mantras of belief. Live. Live. Live.

Her beauty tonight is too much for me, and tentatively I ask if I can take her picture. Just of her head. On the pillow. Her smile. Her wide eyes. Just her head, not the thinness. Not the repose on the mat. I have to see if the camera will show what I see or if it's just my need to see her as beautiful.

She nods. I find the camera in my pack, hope the cheap batteries have another shot in them, and then I'm pointing at her. She readies for the click. The button presses. A delay, then the shutter. I fumble to check it. Did it capture her life or her death? What I see or what I only want to see?

I look. It's beautiful. It's her. Gulsara. Alive. I show it to her. She smiles. Yes, that's me, how I see myself.

I think how I want to get the print made. She gestures at the camera and me and back to her. Does she want another picture of me with her? I get her to repeat the hand movements, the pointing at me, the camera and her. Then she repeats how I will leave in a few weeks. All in no language communication, just sounds, words, hand movements, eye movements, head noddings.

Ahhh, I get it finally. She wants me to give her my camera when I leave. Yes, yes, she is alive.

And outside when I leave there is the MSF car. I am surprised it is already here. I have lost track of time, how long I have been inside. I open the door, look over to see who is driving, who has come from the office seven kilometres to pick me up. Why, it's Chang. How can that be? He dropped me off and was to return to the office to end his shift. I phoned the office to have them explain it to him, how I didn't want to keep him after his shift. Chang, of Korean origin, speaks no English. It was settled on the phone. The new shift driver was to return for me.

It was all made clear on the phone before I went into Gulsara's house 40 minutes ago. What's going on? Chang looks over. " I will not ... you ... I will not ... I will not leave you," and he motions to where we are. We drive along the bumpy dirt road back to the highway and the 15-minute drive to town. He points out into the dark: "This is not city."

☞

December 6

Here in middle earth I have 23 days left before my 11 months are finished and I go to Berlin for debriefing. So much of MSF on this project of 13 years is confusing. We put all this time and money into trying to stem the epidemic, but I don't think it is possible. Aynur who is quite wise and very able to think her own thoughts after 10 months on the job sees us as dilettantes.

Of course, MSF has little institutional memory. Expats in and out. The locals patiently enjoying the largesse but knowing their system is older and more enduring, maybe even impervious to change from the outside. That said, patients have received more from us than without us. So, on that basis we have given value. But how many of our castles will melt away with the tide, who can know?

My closeness and familiarity with the patient reality bothers many, I think, but I have had no choice. It is my only way to live in truth, and lived truth is all I have to go by.

I realize now that I've likely done very little to bring about a lasting counselling program. Whoever replaces me will change it in their image. I do think I've spotted the right direction and pointed that way. But MSF is changing it all anyway. We expand and diffuse here so that all becomes diluted but more sustainable. So as to contribute a meagre amount that might remain rather than do a good job that won't stay.

And, now finally, I am tired and need a holiday. But, I can make it the next weeks with no problem. The end of a marathon. I wish I could bring out a dozen others with me though. The way they do it in war zones when they're lucky. This is a war zone, just slow and hidden.

☞

December 7

The electricity is off at Gulsara's home. Rooms darkened. Gulsara's room is bare but has a window. I have brought a very large poster to put on the wall. It is a scene from some place in China, large green trees on jutting mountains, a waterfall, and stream. It teems with brightness. She lies on the opposite side of the room from it.

Her coughing bothers her more now. Keeps her from a peaceful sleep.

The electricity has been cut off because they have gone a few months without paying their bill. They will hotwire from their neighbours in a few hours as night approaches but Gulsara says they can't do that for long. Her father's pension for October and November never arrived.

The bill is $35. I say that I will bring out some money for them to pay it later in the day. "Should I give it to your father?"

Gulsara looks at me, and shakes her head. She pulls at her throat, the sign that he will spend it on drink. I nod. She smiles shyly.

Later, she confides a secret to me. Not really a secret but something she has never revealed to any of us until yesterday when she told Murat. She has a six-year-old son. He lives with her former husband. She shows me his photo. They brought him to visit her a couple days ago. I am surprised. She says that Murat was surprised also. She has put his photo beside the small potted green plants that sit by her bed. She can look at the photo and the plants near her and the large poster now covering the wall.

☙

December 8

This is the third time I have visited Lala in the negative ward. She can take her drugs now but is still agitated during the day and is having a difficult time sleeping at night despite the sleep medicine they give her.

She looks great. I don't understand this gap between her vitality and the anxiety and sleep problems. The stress doesn't fit. When I counsel people, I try to listen to what's inside. Sometimes I hear correctly and other times it's off base but my forthrightness spurs the person to take me in the right direction. I blurt out: "Have you been raped?"

I love Aynur. She always translates whatever I say, no matter how off guard it catches her or odd it seems. One time after talking to a patient about masturbation, I asked her how she had felt about translating such graphic interactions: "Was it odd for you?"

"Yes."

"Odd, okay? Odd, bad?"

"Just odd." Case closed, and she looked out the car window.

This time, Lala answers back without hesitation to my question: "Yes."

Ahhh. Tell me about it.

Before entering college and while she was attending for four years, she had been in a steady relationship. They were very close, and all was going great. Her future with him seemed set. Then one day she was kidnapped by another man. She had only seen him once before.

She was taken to his parents' home. The traditional practices were followed and word was sent to her own parents that their daughter now belonged to someone else if they consented to the arrangement. Lala was in shock. All that night, the man tried to have sex with her. She refused, warded him off. It made him frustrated, and he came up with a conclusion. The only conclusion that made sense to him—she must not be a virgin. That's why she was refusing him. She truthfully denied it, but held fast to her decision not to give in.

In the morning, she planned to leave and run back to her parents. But then, while her "husband" slept and as she walked through the home, she passed the man's mother. The woman was blind but awake and could hear Lala's movements. She asked her where she was going. Lala told her she would return to her own home. The blind woman began weeping quietly. Lala kept going. Outside the home, she could still hear the weeping. She stopped.

She thought of what her own parents' reaction would be. She had stayed overnight. They and the neighbours would see it as being sealed. They would believe her to no longer be a virgin. There would be gossip and shame. Her parents would be angry. And the sadness of the woman inside at losing her "daughter-in-law" played in her ears.

Lala returned to the house. That night she gave in to the man. Now, she has a seven-year-old daughter, an abortion, MDR-TB and a nervous disorder.

I hold her hands after she tells me her story. "It's like you were abducted by aliens. Your life was going along totally within your control. You were happy. Life seemed just as it should be, and then you were completely ripped into another world."

She nods.

"So, I guess we can see why you have trouble sleeping. There has been so much out of your control in your life and now your body just shakes. Your spirit has had enough."

She nods.

I say that she must choose. Does she want her old life back, the one that was stolen from her? She can reject this one and leave her husband and his home. After all, he does beat her. And she is educated, smart. She can do it. Or can she accept her current life? The planet she has been abducted to. What does she want? She can't have both. The shaking will last, the anxiety and stress, until she can let go of the past. But she does not have to accept what isn't in her heart. She can go back to what could have been, maybe not resume with that boyfriend but find another of her own choosing. She is young.

Attractive. Smart. A warrior. She fights MDR, she can choose the life she wants.

We sit together in silence, holding hands. Breathing.

She looks toward me. "I will stay where I am. I have a daughter."

☙

December 11

It is Saturday, and I am at Gulsara's with Andrew. No translator, just the two of us. Andrew's an MSF ex-pat doctor from north-east India near the Burma border. He's come to Nukus to learn more about MDR. After three months he'll be sent elsewhere or stay on our projects. He's agreed to come with me for this visit — see the inside of what having MDR is all about. Later at my office I'll give him a briefing about our psychosocial operations. But this is my real office. Here in Gulsara's home. Here without a translator. I want him to see Gulsara's eyes.

We enter the house as usual: "Salaam alaikum." Mother greets us. We put our masks on and walk through the big open foyer, its concrete flooring, high ceiling more like a large garage for a vehicle than part of the house living area. At the end of the foyer is a raised area with wooden floor but still open to the chilly air. To the side is a cooking stove area and a refrigerator. We take off our shoes and enter into the two actual living rooms. To the left is a bare room with the television. To the right is the doorway to Gulsara's room, rough carpetted and bare also.

I go right to Gulsara as she lies in the usual spot on her sleeping mat. I bend to hug her, touch my head to hers. Andrew shakes her hand. She is happy to see us. I come almost every day. Today, I've brought camel milk and a sweet melon. Maybe I should have brought a blender, start a new craze in Karakalpakstan. A new traditional way to cure yourself from TB. I've also brought a portable DVD player so she can watch the DVD of Daniyar singing "Anajan" about his mother and four other songs that he's recorded.

We spend a half hour of gestures and sounds. We laugh together.

But she shows us the bed sores that are developing too quickly on her hip. She lies almost exclusively on one side, says that any other position makes breathing harder. A soft wool fleece cushions her sores. What a beautiful woman she is.

Andrew is a gentle man. He tries to speak to Gulsara. The friendliness of his face will be enough. I can tell he has been touched by her situation and by her vibrant dignity.

When it is time to leave, I go for the usual hug good-bye. I bend and kneel beside her to hold her. She holds back and tugs at my ear. Then, Andrew surprises me. He too moves close to give her a hug. But, in his eagerness to show that warmth, he has not paid attention. And he kneels on the blanket over her thigh. Gulsara yells in pain. Andrew jumps back and changes position. He hugs her. Gulsara is wincing. And Andrew is stuttering apologies.

⌒

December 15

Sarbinaz, Kurbangul's sister, is in TB2 again. She has been there for over a week. Now she is on suicide watch. She is starting to look like Kurbangul, thin growing into her body. Her empowered persona is gone. No longer a woman in charge, a woman looking out for her sister, she is defeated. I ask her to explain what has driven her so deeply into this state.

She says she has problems with her husband. He was angry that she became infectious again, that the drugs were not working to cure her quickly enough, wasn't at home to do her duties. She tried to explain to him, but he would not be pacified. Then a few days ago, when she phoned him, he asked her why she was still alive. He asked if he should buy the cow in order to have it ready for slaughter once she had died.

That set her off, and in the evening she went up to the second floor and was about to throw herself off the balcony railing when another patient saw her, and rushed over to stop her.

She is still disconsolate. She thinks she should give up and follow

Kurbangul and her other sister. I tell her she is an asshole. I try to shake her, bring her to her senses. I remind her of her sister's teachings — eyes open, appreciate, never give up, live. I talk about how Sevinch is without a mother now and how her own daughter will be like Sevinch if she does not reclaim her sense of self, her tenacity.

It seems to help. Her face relaxes, eyes brighten. A bit. For now.

December 16

These are strange times for me. I am on my way out. But each day, I am fully here. It is the way of MSF. We are pieces in the response. Each piece is replaced at designated times. The response remains. And it is the nature of intimacy with those who struggle each day in the face of adversity to live that day. I have been part of that struggle so it matters not that I will leave soon. While I am here it is just me and them. Me and the counsellors, all part of the vortex.

Then, just like that. I will be a memory for them and they a memory for me.

December 20

"What's different about you, today?" Deelya asks.

"Why?"

"You look different. There is something different about your eyes."

"Ah, yes. My eyes."

On Sunday evening, when I came home the radiator pipes were cold. No one else was home yet and Vostachnaya was chilly and becoming chillier. I knew that the furnace must be out. A few months back, they had relocated the furnace from the kitchen to the outside of the house. Sometimes, the water reservoir goes empty and sometimes it is the flame that is extinguished. On Sunday, it was the flame.

I am a counsellor. My mind is quite dexterous. I understand people. I do not so much understand things. But, in my own home in Canada I have lit pilot lights. So I was not about to phone Iskander the MSF guy who does the fix-its. I found the box of matches that we use for the gas stove burners and went outside to re-light the furnace.

I was not planning to be long so I went out in my t-shirt and in slippers. Outside, there was a smattering of breeze. Enough to make me think how cold I would get if I didn't do the job quickly. I turned the gas off in order to examine the set-up.

I knelt on the cement beside the base of the furnace which is encased in a block kind of compartment. I pulled open the metal door on its hinges, and peered inside. Yup, there was the spigot for the gas. I reached up to turn the gas on again. It began to hiss. Next, I struck the match, and held it inside beneath the spigot. No problem.

But, of course, there was a problem. As soon as my hand with the match got close to the spigot, there was a great burst of flame which shot out toward my hand, my arm, and the rest of me. Frightening for sure but no serious damage. Except for a red, slightly tender hand and wrist, plus roasted arm hair. And roasted eye lashes and brows.

"Yeah, Deelya, I guess I might look a bit different now. Do you want to smell my arm?"

<hr />

December 22

Daniyar has a new dilemma. He wants my opinion. The love of his life has been home a few weeks but is now to return to her work in Kazakhstan. This is the young lady who Daniyar credits with giving him the inspiration and support to persist with the drugs in the first months after he got sick with MDR and wanted to run away. They have been maintaining a strong relationship the past year and have pledged themselves to each other. Now there is a problem.

She must return to work because her family insists on it. But she says that, when she returns, a young man is going to kidnap her. She has been warned by her friends. So, now there is only one way to keep the relationship with Daniyar. He wants to know what I think about him "marrying" her. He understands that he cannot support her yet, that he has another year to go on drugs. He worries mostly about what his uncles will say. That situation is always somewhat strained anyway.

"Calvin, what should I do?"

He is 20. He is in love. He has a life threatening disease. He will lose the love of his life if he doesn't act. What is the answer?

"Calvin, what should I do?"

Lala lost her love when she got kidnapped. I know of MSF National Staff who also lost the ones they loved.

"Daniyar, you have one life. It belongs to you."

☙

December 23

Daniyar's uncle is looking for him. He wants to beat him severely. Daniyar is hiding out at a friend's place for a couple of days.

With his wife.

☙

December 25

Christmas in Urgensh with a friend. The second of three days out of Nukus and in a hotel. Two hours south yet it feels like another world. A bit greener, a bit more worldly, Urgensh is in another province with a slightly different dialect, different customs. The bazaar is filled with long shelves of fruit—bulging pomegranates, clusters of imported grapes, shining apples, nuts, raisins, oranges, bananas. Cold in the wind but under a bright, blue sky.

Alley booths sell shiny decorations and knick-knacks for the holiday season. Uzbeks celebrate New Years more so than Christmas, but Santa Claus is still on posters and signs.

In the evening, we eat tasty, grilled fish, picking out the tiny bones and licking our fingers.

☙

December 27

Kalibek has called me to visit. His mother has returned from Kazakhstan and wants him to resume treatment. Aynur and I sit on the mat in the kitchen room listening to them argue. She wants him to go to TB1. He wants to try the home-based treatment. I stay out of it. After at least 14 visits to this home, I know enough to just wait and see.

"Phone me when you decide which option you want and I will try to arrange it."

These are really my last days, so now I go to each polyclinic to say good-bye to those who know me. I take my successor with me to introduce her. She is a 28-year-old PhD from Mumbai. She worked with MSF there addressing HIV/AIDS and MDR-TB. She wears white, high-heeled calf length boots. When we visit Gulsara, I bend to hug her and Aynur and I sit beside her on the floor. My successor sits on a chair farther away and looks down at us.

She is not like me.

I tell her that it would be great if she taught the counsellors hypnotherapy and yoga therapy, both of which she has trained in.

☙ Daniyar phones me. He says all is better now with his uncles. They are not happy that he has "married" and has brought a new person into the household while he does not work to provide income. He tells me that he understands their hostility but that they have been hostile ever since his grandmother took him in and treated him as her favourite. So, this is nothing knew. He says he and his wife are happy. I tell him to keep taking his drugs.

☙

December 28

Aynur, who walked deeper into intimacy than anyone else in MSF ever will, has finally let me hold her. As we walk across the street to drink tea, I kiss her on the head. She laughs, but looks around to see if anyone is watching.

What does good-bye mean to me now that I have been inside the human heart for all these long months that have become an instant? We are all instants. Each hello is a good-bye on the other side of the page. I have experienced the richness of "now" in these 11 months. It has all been now. All been "here" as in this place at the very moment of thinking or speaking or writing. I wrote about "here" way back and nothing has occurred to alter that understanding. The novelty has never worn off.

Good-bye? It makes no sense. Gulsara will never die. Oleg, Islam, Guldana, Malicka, Kurbangul, Jadra, Orelbay, Venyera, Azimat, Shakargul, Ayjan, Gulnas, Sayura, Saule, Kairat, Aydar, Bapbergin, and those I never learned the names of have not died. They are alive still. MDR-TB took their bodies, their corporeal time on the planet, but it did not take them. They all live in me. I will have them—and their relatives—until I die. Then their relatives and mine will have them inside of the memory of us. And so on and so on. All memories will eventually fade, the recordings of what was will become sand. So then will we all be dead?

No, even then we remain just as the sand remains no matter where it blows or how deep it becomes buried. We remain simply because we were.

Philosophical? Only words? Maybe.

But here I have been living more than words and more than philosophy, more than belief. Here I have been reduced from the beginning to simply being. Each day being with others being. Being with other beings. It's literally how it has transpired and with not a shred of planning on my part.

Nothing could have prepared me for the embrace of Kurbangul's long, thin arms, the short breaths of Islam which seemed to last and last until his brightness ceased, the endlessness of Gulsara's eyes as we looked at each other. Needing always to see hope within the hopelessness.

And within the hopelessness, the impossibility of stopping this epidemic, is a subtler energy. The greater essence which does not cancel nor alter the hopelessness. Which does not alter the sadness or pain of the lived reality of all here who suffer in their myriad of ways. What is that essence? How is it greater?

The subtler energy, the essence, is that each of these humans whom I have seen as warriors is exactly that: a human and a warrior. Each is fully alive. Each is filled with pulse, with character, with vitality and resilience. Each is. And that is ultimately the voice they have. The voice of being who they are, of having made their life journey to where it has come to. We are born with this and most of us spend our waking moments looking away from this, away from who and what we are and focussing on what we want, on doing, on everything outside of our selves. Thus, it's natural that we don't see our selves. Miss seeing who we are.

None of us can neither stop the movement of linear time that takes us to our deaths nor greatly affect the circumstances that will lead to sickness or accident on the way to that death. To be born is to be doomed. One way or the other. So really that doesn't matter. What matters is that we do live and while we live we are who we are. Maybe that's the underlying truth in Viktor Frankl's conclusion about purpose and ability to survive horror? Maybe the underlying truth is that ultimately our purpose is nothing specific or unique in its outer characteristics, but simply that we have been born, we have been given life and the life we live is majestic and beautiful and meaningful simply in itself. And of course it is unique.

Coming here to this foreign land with no language, no experience, no training forced me to rely on paying attention, on seeing what was before me each day and responding. The result of this was that I saw each patient that I met as unique, as special. It was akin to walking into a huge arena and everywhere there were small coloured lights and not one was the same as another, similar perhaps but with different tones, shades, brightness.

Good-bye means I love you. Present tense.

⊘ I have gone to the desert today with Manas to finish our time together. He is my aikido teacher. He has taught me to dive head first onto a mat or grassy ground with my hands behind my back and do a forward roll. It took me at least five classes before I had the guts to try it. Until then I thought the likely outcome would be a broken neck. I'm too old for that, I concluded. I'll do the other rolls. Manas never tried to convince me otherwise. He just taught the class and I watched all the others doing all the exercises. Finally, I tried too.

This afternoon, Manas and I are in the desert for an hour. He is 42. When I first met him, all I saw was his friendliness and the simmering anger inside him. I know now why he was angry. Alcoholic father, mom dead too early, step-mom a witch, beatings, learning disability, victimization when he was in the army. But he kept going. He kept developing his dignity and good heart. He taught himself aikido, and in his classes all are equal, all are treated and behave with respect for each other. No gender or age distinctions. Manas teaches aikido three times a week. After six months, I realized he should be a counsellor. And now he is.

We are in the desert to hold the sand of our two lives, pass it back and forth to each other as the wind blows its December voice, as the sun shines from blue.

And later, I go to Aziz's home. He has bought an apartment in town for him and his wife and now three kids. But there have been complications. The owner is unstable. The deal will fall through so for now he is still in his parents' home, a large house in which his brother and his wife and their child lives, in which his sister and her daughter live and in which his parents live. It is a home with problems. But a home with strength and love.

When I arrive, his five-year-old boy is coming in from the rustic outhouse, the small cubicle of wood and pieces of rusty sheet metal hung together in the back yard. I try to take his picture, to capture the display of independence, but his head is looking down in shyness.

Inside we sit at the long low table and drink green tea, eat sweets, peel oranges. Aziz loves his wife. She doesn't sit with us but brings in plates of food for us to snack on, her gentle grace, warm eyes. Aziz has told me how he has almost fallen apart with a sense of helplessness at the times when the problems in his extended family have weighed him into despair, how his wife has cradled him in her arms in their bed and told him she doesn't understand why he just can't accept everything the way it is. That he is her crazy husband, and rocked him in her love.

This evening is my last with Aziz. We know each other well. He gives himself to his patients. I tell MSF people that he is as good a counsellor as anyone in the world.

The last visit of this night is at Murat's apartment. We eat fried fish. There is no running water these last few days in his sixth-floor flat. In the past, Murat has sat on his balcony deciding whether or not to jump to his death. He carries demons inside him. The demons have become fainter, but he still hears hollow echoes on occasion. Like we all do.

The hurt he has held inside, though, has made him a kinder man. "You know, Calvin, I am a pain in the ass to myself sometimes. There are some patients who are real bastards, I can't stand them, but, shit, you know, when they suffer or meet some sad problem, I immediately want to help them and feel this sorrow for them. All my annoyance changes. I even give them money. It pisses me off. I am too soft. They don't deserve it." And he laughs. He shakes his head, but he also knows that he would not change this instinct of compassion.

Before his son, now two, was born, Murat did not like babies or children much. And for a few months he felt distance and antipathy to his new son, but it has all changed. He smiles broadly at that change, marvels at it. Now, he misses his son if he is away from him for more than a day, revels in holding him, teaching him.

Tonight, after eating fish, Murat pulls out his portable organ. He bought it from a relative and has taught himself to play. I watch his round back outlined by a white vest undershirt as he hunches over the organ on the other side of the room. The melody fills the room, his fingers going from key to key.

Over to the side, his son kicks a rubber ball towards me. Laughs and gallops after it.

December 29

I am in Berlin. There are high banks of snow alongside all the city streets. I had to lug my big suitcase here from airport bus to metro to the street leading to Motel One. The handles were broken when it journeyed to Nukus last January, so I have tied rope around it. My small pack is on my back and a plastic shopping bag is in my other hand. I have bought three blue teapots and seven blue, handleless cups to give as gifts when I get home. I am nervous about breaking them as I stumble about with my rope suitcase.

It is 9 pm and Berlin is filled with people. After getting into my room, I have come out again hoping to buy something to eat. A shopkeeper yells at me to get out because he is closing. I can't read any signs about hours of operation, but I am in a daze anyway. I would like to smash the shopkeeper in the mouth.

What am I doing here?

December 30

Berlin is cold. I have spent the day doing debriefings at the big MSF office. It is the usual formality. How was your experience? Any problems? What did you learn? Will you do another mission?

They all mean well. Three know me because they came to Nukus for short visits at various times. But this is down time here for them, holiday time. They have other things they want to do.

The last debriefing is with a psychologist. She begins by informing me that she is on a contract to provide this service to MSF but that she is not their employee. She wants me to know that anything I say is confidential. She is here to listen. Her eyes are wide and caring. She leans forward in relaxed posture. But she does not speak very good English. She has to ask me several times for correct words to explain what she is trying to say.

I smile and say I am feeling great, that Uzbekistan was a dream. She adds that she understands that I am a colleague, a psychologist like her, that she realizes I know the drill. I like her. So, I tell her how absorbed and thrilled I was to have been blessed in Karakalpakstan by so many.

In the evening, I wander down to the lights of the Brandenburg Gate. There is a huge stage set up for concerts both this night and tomorrow, New Years Eve, when I will be on the plane home. Light is everywhere. There are all these strolling people. Booths sell hot wine and every sort of edible. But it is quite cold. I walk over to look at the Reichstag. There is a line-up to go in and tour. I ask about joining it but overhear the guide telling someone else that reservations for the tours are made days or weeks in advance.

Everywhere there are shops open. Restaurants, hotels, trinkets, fashion designs, bars, lines and lines of places to spend money. And lots of snow. This is not Nukus.

What am I doing here? It's time to go home.

Epilogue

January 11

Hi Calvin,

Are you still alive. One person told me that he cares and when he is back to home will call me thru skype and be in touch. But of course things change very quickly. There this person might have close friends who are very worthy for him so what the fuck does he need to give for a Karakalpak?!! Karakalpaks can't be friend for the whites because they are from high level of society (they believe we are so poor creatures), therefore the main idea is just to establish temporary friendship and afterwards just forget about them. ha ha ha

Now serious thing: I regret to inform you that your friend Gulsara with beautiful eyes died on Monday. So that was the last journey for her.

Today I gathered other patients from polyclinic and we went to her funeral. I am sad about it. And now you will be also. Not much to do or say now.

See you later,

Murat The Great

January 26

Hi Calvin,

I went to TB 2 on wednesday at half past four and I held Deena. i brought a ball to her. When i was walking in TSUM in Tashkent with girls, i saw a ball it's got water in it like an aquarium, you can see inside a green fish, a white little ball and many very little coloured tiny balls and when you strike it to the wall the white ball inside it sparkles with coloured lights, so the ball sparkles at night and it's really beautiful. The ball is made of rubber I think and it's like a water scene inside, I don't know how to explain the colour of this ball because it's glassy, clear, crystalline, limpid, pellucid (i found in the dictionary these words). I really like it myself :)

Slohan is at home now, they said she is failure now. About it only the doctor Arzigul and I know. And Slohan of course.

Deena was crying when Slohan left TB2. She called me and said that Slohan is leaving but she didn't know why. Also yesterday when i went to see her she again asked about Slohan, so I told her that Slohan stopped the treatment by herself several times, maybe that's why she left home now, but you never stopped the treatment you took the drugs for two years, so don't worry about that. She's really smart and she thinks if Slohan is made treatment failure it can be her too.

Bye

Deelya

February 13

Hi Samuel,

Greetings from the snow country of western Canada. How was your holiday home with your family? I'm now visiting my grandson in the north of my province so there is even more snow here than back in my home 400 km to the south. About 1 metre here. I've been gone from Nukus now for 6 weeks but part of my heart is still there. I have heard that the MoH doctors will make Deena a treatment failure. That has really disturbed me. I know they already sent one of the patients that I was close to off to TB3 as a failure and that was sad for me.

In Deena's case it will be a terrible tragedy and a wrongness if they stop her treatment. That's why I am pleading with you to intervene for her.

You were the one who got Deena back into treatment when she got sick for the second time. Now, you will have to save her life again. I saw her the day before she was accepted back in TB2 for the treatment to start again. I thought she could die that very night. But when she got into treatment again, she gained. It saved her. It worked. That it is now taking longer does not mean it isn't working. This is her second bout with MDR. It makes sense that the drugs may take longer.

As long as her clinical condition is not getting worse and as long as she wants to stay on the drugs, we owe it to this young girl who has shown such strength to go thru it once and then choose, beg, to go thru it a second time, that we not be the ones to give up on her. The disease killed her mother. The disease killed her brother. If we let them stop her treatment it will not be the disease that kills her, it will be us.

I know that your responsibilities are now in the new rayons, but you know Deena and you can influence the MoH. You are the only one they will listen to. I am sorry to burden you with this, but here I am helpless to do anything, and Deena has no chance without us. They will say that the drugs are harming her but they won't harm her or shorten her life more than MDR once it takes over again.

Calvin

February 14

Hi Calvin,

Thanks for your email.

I am fine. My holiday was good; I enjoyed the time I had with my family.

Nukus is still cold but we have no snow.

I didn't know about Deena's situation as I am not able to attend the conselium in TB 2 as often as I would like. Preparation for the expansion and other things keep me busy in the office. I promise to talk to TB 2 doctors about her case as soon as possible.

I am currently in the process of putting together information on a couple of patients categorized as "failures" which I will forward to the TB advisor to see if he can suggest a different way of treating patients who take too long time to achieve culture conversion. If he agrees we may prolong treatment for such patients.

I will keep you posted.

Best regards

Samuel

February 26

Hi Calvin,

Probably you already know that Deena died yesterday. It is sad.

I was at the conselium and we agreed that in case the MOH doctors are planning to give defaulter and failure outcomes to any patients they should involve MSF doctors and the psychosocial department. I hope things will change.

Best regards

Samuel

☙

February 26

Marcell,

I got email / read email 30 minutes ago and phoned Deelya. Deena died Wednesday evening. The consillium had refused to let her back on treatment. I dont know if she had gotten the verdict. Deelya had seen her that afternoon at her home before she herself knew the verdict. She said Deena was tired and they talked. Deena was ready to go back to the hospital. Deelya wanted to hold her but Deena was lying down so she stroked her legs, her feet which were swollen, her arms, and held her hand. Deelya is in shock still. Me too. And now you.

I had been writing frantic emails to Samuel and the new Canadian doctor. They are ones who emailed me. Deelya had gotten a phone call the morning after she had seen Deena, and her phone said it was Deena. "Oh, hello Deena!" "No, this is Deena's sister, she died last night just shortly after you left."

Deelya phoned Aziz, Samuel, Murat.

We loved her but it wasn't enough. But it was.

Calvin

Date: Friday 26 Feb 2011 21:40:17 -0800

From: aziz432@yahoo.com
Subject: The one who was always there
To: calvinwhite@hotmail.com
CC: deelya@rambler.ru; murat33@rambler.ru; aynur_agk@mail.ru

Deena, the one who was always there. Any time of the day, smiling, sad, angry, nodding, welcoming, telling the truth, carrying all negatives so that to leave others only positive, tired, writing songs, loving father, living with reality that no one could after a long chronic chemical life. Which proves she was honest, strong and smart. For all the mistakes and misbehaves that happened to her life in this battle, we can't remember her blaming anyone. Acceptance was normal for her, good or bad. She could stand for herself in not accepting unfairness, if she had a power, relative in upper institutions, minister-father, money etc, but she had only counsellors who did their best till the end, but failed. Deena wasn't a failure, 'cause she was open to any treatment, any options to make her alive. Failed those who are blind to see humans struggling, didn't react in time.

Today there is no Deena anymore. who used to send message to call back, send signal, say to bring melon or chicken, not only for herself but to share.

Life with Deena tells us: take care of yourself and take care of others who are in need for that.

The room is cold, no life, but survival. Deena, the one who was always there.

Aziz

Acknowledgements

I want to acknowledge Medécins Sans Frontières. Despite our disagreements, they are an NGO that saves lives and makes a difference. We need them. My life has changed because MSF allowed me to work in Uzbekistan. I will always be grateful.

I will also always be grateful to my former wife, Jacquie Sharpe, for encouraging me to go on the mission.

Michael Mirolla, Connie McParland and Guernica Editions are why this book exists. Thank you so much.

Marcell Nimführ has graciously allowed me to use some of his fine photographs for the book and, particularly, the cover of our beautiful Deena.

Some of the essays in the book have previously been in the *Ottawa Citizen* and the now defunct regional B.C. magazine, *NORTHof50*.

All of the Karakalpak counsellors in Nukus will forever be in my heart. Thanks to Collins Kidake for being my friend in Nukus and to my sensei, Manas Daniyrov, for his help.

Although most of the names used in the text are fictitious, this book was written as a testament to bear witness to the strength and beauty of those we served in the hospitals and clinics in Karakalpakstan. As such, it is in memory of:

Venera
Oleg
Guldana
Islam
Kurbangul
Shahargul
Gulsara
Deena
Sluwhan
Kural
Gulbazar
Azamat
Oralbay
Malika
Nietbek
Roman
Gulnaz
Ayjan
Aybek
Aydar
Kayrat
Sarbinaz
Mukhabat
Jadra
Saule
Sayora
Bakbergen
Munavar
Tokhtagul

About The Author

A former high school teacher and counsellor in Salmon Arm, British Columbia, Calvin White translated his experience developing educational and therapeutic approaches for troubled teenagers into leading a team of local counsellors in Uzbekistan, a remote corner of central Asia. As a mental health specialist for Médecins Sans Frontières, he spent a year creating therapeutic practises aimed at saving the lives of hundreds of patients suffering from multi-drug resistant tuberculosis. During this time, violent communal attacks broke out in neighboring Kyrgyzstan, so he was also sent for a month to help the victims of that crisis. White's writing background includes scores of essays and interviews that have appeared in Canada's major newspapers including the *Toronto Star* and *Globe & Mail*, a book of poetry published by Turnstone Press, and a non-fiction book entitled *The Secret Life Of Teenagers*. As well, he has written curriculum units for college level educational/counselling programs.

RECYCLED
Paper made from
recycled material
FSC® C100212

Printed in December 2014
by Gauvin Press,
Gatineau, Québec